At a Loss for Words

At a Loss for Words

HOW AMERICA IS

FAILING OUR CHILDREN

AND

WHAT WE CAN DO ABOUT IT

Betty Bardige

Foreword by
T. Berry Brazelton, M.D.

 Temple University Press
PHILADELPHIA

Betty Bardige, Ed.D., is a developmental psychologist, educator, and child advocate. As vice-president of the A. L. Mailman Family Foundation and board member or advisor to many educational and philanthropic organizations, she works to shape early childhood policy at local, state, and national levels. She is also the co-author, with her mother, Dr. Marilyn Segal, of *Building Literacy with Love*. Dr. Bardige can be reached at betty@mailman.org.

Temple University Press
1601 North Broad Street
Philadelphia, PA 19122
www.temple.edu/tempress

Copyright © 2005 by Temple University
All rights reserved
Published 2005
Printed in the United States of America

♾ The paper used in this publication meets the requirements of the American National Standard for Information Sciences—Permanence of Paper for Printed Library Materials, ANSI Z39.48-1992

Library of Congress Cataloging-in-Publication Data

Bardige, Betty Lynn Segal.
   At a loss for words : how America is failing our children and what we can do about it / Betty Bardige ; foreword by T. Berry Brazelton.
      p.   cm.
   Includes bibliographical references and index.
   ISBN 1-59213-392-4 (cloth : alk. paper) – ISBN 1-59213-393-2 (pbk. : alk. paper)
      1. Early childhood education—United States.   2. Children—Language.
3. Educational equalization—United States.   4. Language acquisition.
5. Child development.   I. Title.

   LB1139.L3B363   2005
   372.21′0973—dc22

                                                      2004059873

2 4 6 8 9 7 5 3 1

To my mother, my husband, and my children

Contents

Foreword

L anguage is an important and virtually inevitable part of a child's development. Communication with important adults is built in at birth, as a way of being sure to be taken care of. Right after birth, a baby communicates. He is born with six different cries: hunger, pain, boredom, fatigue, discomfort, and a cry that accompanies letting off steam at the end of the day. These cries attempt to draw an important person to him and get that person to meet his needs. They are a baby's first language—a language that his parents will learn from him in his first three weeks of life.

A baby's sucking pattern is also designed to draw out parental responses. From birth, he starts sucking with a typical hungry suck-suck-suck. After a few minutes of initial satiation, he falls into a new pattern: suck-suck-suck-pause, suck-suck-suck-pause. When he pauses, a nurturing parent automatically looks down at him, chucks his chin, and says "Come on" or "Keep eating."

My colleagues and I compared the pauses when a parent said something with those when she didn't. When the mother talked to the baby, her stated goal was to keep him sucking. The pauses where she responded were lengthened by the baby, as if his goal was to heighten communication as a major part of feeding. For him, even as a new baby, feeding was not just for food—but also for communication. This expectation, when it's fulfilled, leads him to feel cared for as well as taken care of. A whole new, exciting world opens up. "I'm important—it's *me* they care about!"

As early as six to eight weeks of age, a baby begins to differentiate mother, father, and a stranger in his behavioral and vocal responses. He not only learns what to expect from each parent, but his behavior in response is geared to draw them to him. With his mother at two months, he squirms slowly, fingers, toes, mouth, eyes going out and coming back smooth, three times a minute. As he smiles and gurgles, she responds with excited smiles and gurgles. She is predictably his! With his father at two months, his every movement is jerky and excited. His face is all "up" as if eliciting the playful poking and joking that new fathers resort to. Play becomes their communication, as early as two months of age. A new father soon knows his role because the baby leads him. He comes in to play and poke!

As the baby begins to smile and to vocalize, he realizes that he gets a joyful response from these important adults. Their responses fuel his attempts to add vocal behavior to the broad expanse of cries as a technique for drawing them to him. Vocal and responsive behavior become richer and richer. The bases for language are laid down in the first months—between child and parent.

As a baby communicates with a parent, as early as three months of age, he learns a rhythmic burst-pause pattern, as if waiting for the adult's response. Parent and child get into a responsive rhythmic dance. He will have learned from his burst-pause sucking pattern that his parent will respond in the pauses—behaviorally and verbally. He has learned that communication is a timed dual operation. Each important adult has a characteristic behavioral and verbal response to which the baby adapts his own unique behavioral response. He is learning to expect and to separate important people from unimportant ones in the first few months. Language and responsive behavior are already linked in his mind as opportunities for learning about his new world. And he is already learning how to elicit these responses from important adults. "I'm learning that *I* can get them to respond to me in my own way. When I use my body to communicate, they can't resist *me*! I'm important."

As the year progresses, exposure to the speech of the important people in his life shows a baby how to learn words! What a feat! His first word is likely to be "dada"—what could be more politically advantageous? The next, delivered with more squirming and eliciting behavior, is often "mama." No mother can resist. These two important adults are at his disposal. More complex speech follows as they lead him on. "Look how they fall for *me*."

These important early steps are laying the groundwork for language as important communication and learning. The baby is doing his part in working toward the goal of learning language. As he and his caretakers communicate with each other, they are learning the steps that lead to his self-esteem and ultimately to his intelligence. With language, he can display and even shape this intelligence, but he also knows how to shape his world with his communication skills. He is on his way. He *knows* he can do it. He begins to believe in himself—and he's ready to shape the world!

It is no wonder that speech is important to us as humans. It is one of the two behaviors that separate us from the great apes—speech and the delicate pincer-grasp of thumb and forefinger. In the human child, communication is linked to verbal and to behavioral responses. Each enriches the other. By one year of age, a baby who tells you what she wants will shape her behavior to express it. Already a parent will have several modes of communication from which to read and interpret her needs and her desires: her face, her body, and her primitive linguistic and behavioral responses.

Then comes real language! It is powerful. Now the baby's language leads in shaping her behavior and vice versa. From the first these modalities of communication are influenced by the environment around the child. When the environment is responsive, the baby's behavior is enriched. When it is sparse, the baby's responsive behavior is severely constricted. Language shapes a child's behavior, her self-esteem and belief in herself, her imagination, and her learning about the world. Although, it is first her way of learning about her caregivers, it quickly becomes the environment's way of fitting her for future learning from the world around her.

A parent who talks to her child right from the first is fitting that baby for a rich future. He will rapidly begin to imitate her—in behavior and in language. Being able to express himself will ensure his future. As this excellent book points out, communication is the hallmark of how well a child will perform in our culture. Our culture demands that children have easily available, rich language and the imagination that it represents. Their capacity to express themselves is our window into their brains. All of our tests of their capacity will be based in their ability to communicate primarily in language. Language is an asset that we require in our society as we assess our children's progress along the way. If they lack this, they are automatically set up for second-class roles. As this book points out, language and the ability to communicate becomes one of the most important ways children slot themselves. And it begins so early. Hence, in the first years, it is critical that we provide verbal enrichment.

This volume leads us to realize that other caregivers may be of vital importance as well. Since two thirds of our small children are in early child care, their experience in child care with communication and language is critical. At home and also in early child care, children are already being set on paths that will determine their future. Children who are taught to "use their words," are already being taught the most important assets in the world we have available for them. Parents, talk to your babies from the first! Caregivers, talk to your babies from the first. And with older ones, "use your language!"

This wonderful volume points out the importance to each child not only of a strong language base, but also of the emotional background that it represents. We know now that both intelligence and resilience are founded in emotional learning. Without the necessary emotional base that comes from a devoted environment, a child's intelligence is not likely to flourish. And in the early years, when the bases for emotional learning are laid down, children whose parents or caregivers are too stressed to talk or to read to them are already at risk for their future. We must be able to back up parents early to feel competent to communicate with their children. We must provide quality child care that values communication and conversation as much as feeding and diapering.

This book emphasizes the importance of the quality of a child's life outside the home. This demands that we provide them with a ratio of 3:1 adults in infancy, adults who are paid, trained, and respected. We are investing in our children's future!

Such adults who have the time and energy to communicate with small children, if they read this book, they will find ideas for reinforcing children's language and satisfying their hunger for words, conversation, and learning.

But our nation has not been responsive to such support systems as child care for working parents. We know now that rich early language experience is important to learning and to the ability to demonstrate this learning. We need to emphasize this as a priority, to provide our children enriching environments in which they can develop their potential for learning. This excellent book provides opportunities and programs for both parents and teachers which will do just that. It is a cookbook of ideas for use for both parents and caregivers of small children. Its dedication to language development is an eye-opener to us all.

We know that the stresses and demands on families and family life are increasing. The number of intact families are decreasing. Poverty and its destructive pressures on the ability to nurture their children are increasing. We know that children's future ability to respond to the demands of our culture is based on the opportunities for communication in the early years. Emotional intelligence is the key. Language is a window into that, and one that is responsive to home and to child care. We must provide stressed families with optimal child care. It will cost, surely. How much? We don't know, but not as much as a battleship or bombs. One study shows that every $1 spent in early childhood saves at least $7 later in the child's life. Prevention and salvaging their future is critical. Our prisons are overloaded, and they cost us an enormous amount per adult child.

From this book, we know what to do. Why don't we do it? Education, such as optimal child care, and Early Head Start programs for all children are proven ways to prevent problems, and to ensure our national future. Why don't we fight for them?

Parents are too stressed today to take up the fight and yet they are our most likely advocates for change. We need for parents to demand what they need—enriched environments for their children that emphasize the communication that is critical to their future. This volume can back us all up to fight for what we and our children need!

T. Berry Brazelton, M.D.

Preface

If parents only knew what they were entitled to in a civilized society, they would demand it.

—David Lawrence, Jr.[1]

anguage is characteristic of human beings, as natural as breathing. Children say their first words around the time of their first birthday, and almost all are speaking fluently by the time they are four. When they are getting what they need, young children are natural chatterboxes and nonstop learners. Their rapidly expanding language connects them to others, helps them control their behavior, and enables them to take in a wealth of information. It thus provides the foundation for literacy, success in school, "emotional intelligence,"[2] and life success.

But too many children are not getting the stimulation and attention they need to develop a strong language foundation. They can't learn without exposure to language, and they can't learn well without lots of opportunity for practice. In too many of the settings where our young children are spending significant portions of their days, multitasking adults have too little time to talk with individual children, listen to what they have to say, and encourage further learning. Too many of our children are not getting the kind and amount of practice they need to learn their language well.

Nationally, approximately one third of the children entering kindergarten are significantly behind their peers in the critical area of language development.[3]

Many parents and citizens are unconcerned, believing that the children are simply lacking formal education, which the schools should, can, and will provide. Research shows otherwise. The children who come to school with half the vocabulary of their more advantaged peers can catch up with intervention, but catching up is a challenge that becomes harder and harder as time goes on.[4] Larger vocabularies enable children to learn faster, to learn to read more easily, and to learn more new words and concepts from what they read.[5] At the same time, children who can "use their words" to develop more positive relationships with peers and adults and are less likely to exhibit behaviors that interfere with their learning, motivation, and overall enjoyment of school.

Recognizing the importance of early learning, many modern societies provide public support—in the form of paid family leave, publicly funded child-care programs, and other assistance to families—to give their children a strong start.[6] Such supports are lacking or insufficient for too many American families.

As parents and grandparents, as citizens and taxpayers, we can demand better.

This book is for all of us who care about the future.

Acknowledgments

This book began because my husband, Art Bardige, grew tired of hearing me tell anyone who would listen about the importance of increasing our public investment in early education. "Stop preaching to the converted," he would say. "Write a book."

I never knew where to begin. Then one evening I came home from a presentation by Dr. Catherine Snow on the importance of oral language and, unable to contain myself, began lecturing him. "Did you know that the achievement gap is really a vocabulary gap that starts when kids are eighteen months old? Remember, how I told you that most child-care programs for infants and toddlers aren't any good, because teachers are so underpaid and undertrained? Our child-care settings are at their worst when we need them to be at their best—during the time when children are learning to talk! We've got to find a way to support them, or our kids are really going to be in trouble. They won't have the language facility that they need to succeed in school."

"That's obvious," he said. "Everyone who has ever known a two-year-old knows that they are bursting into language. Of course they won't learn by sitting in front of a TV or in an overcrowded classroom where the teacher doesn't have time to engage them in conversation. It's like learning to hit a ball. You can't just watch—you have to pick up the bat!"

And so, with Art's steadfast support and constant prodding, I have put the knowledge and passion I have gained through twenty years of work on early childhood issues into a book that I hope will be enjoyed by the not-yet-converted as well as by early childhood experts and the parents, caregivers, and teachers of young children.

As is often the case, the book became a family affair. My son, Arran, gave it its title. His sharp critique of the first chapter in draft form helped me to frame the arguments for a wide audience. My daughter, Kori, a teacher of young children with autism spectrum disorder, fed me resources, references, and anecdotes and invited me to visit her classroom. My son, Brenan, offered support from afar, as he worked to help high school students who had not had the benefit of a strong early language foundation to develop the confidence in their ability to learn what should have been their birthright. My mother, Marilyn Segal—who is also my mentor and frequent collaborator—read every draft with an ear for rhythm and an eye for typos, along with her professional expertise. Her work and that of her colleagues at what is now the Mailman–Segal Institute for Early Childhood Studies at Nova Southeastern University informed my understanding of what quality looks like in a diverse array of early childhood settings and of how it can be achieved and sustained.

I owe special thanks to Luba Lynch, executive director of the A. L. Mailman Family Foundation, of which my mother, siblings, and I have served as a "hands-on" board for more than twenty years. With Luba's guidance, the Foundation has been able to play an inventively catalytic role in the early childhood field, and we have come to know many of the dedicated innovators whose research, projects, and organizations are cited in this book. Luba has provided me with a steady stream of resources, along with encouragement and helpful suggestions.

As the book began to take shape, many people offered encouragement, support, and helpful critiques of early drafts. My friend and colleague, Ronnie Mae Weiss, became my first partner—giving me deadlines, reading drafts with a skeptical eye, and helping me to stay on track. Rick Weissbourd, who believes that there may be nothing more important to children's success than early language development and worries that while we provide many different, often expensive, interventions to help older children who are not doing well, we are doing frighteningly little to influence the everyday interactions between adults and young children, provided encouragement and advice at each step from concept to publication. Louise Derman-Sparks, who had joined Art in urging me to write, provided steady encouragement and insightful corrections.

Susie Cohen, always more than an agent, read multiple drafts with genuine interest and curiosity. Her questions, suggestions, and gently expressed frustration with unnecessary detail helped me to clarify and hone the manuscript. Emily Fenichel, whose knowledge of the infant-family field is both wide and deep, read chapters and key revisions as I produced them, directing me to omitted information and suggesting important directions. Costanza Eggers-Pierola guided me through the complicated issues of second language learning and cultural dissonance, helping me to understand both the power of bilingualism and the challenges faced by immigrant families.

I am deeply indebted to Dr. Edward Zigler, father of Head Start, Early Head Start, and the School of the 21st Century, for his thorough critique, mentorship, and guidance.

I also need to thank Joan Matsalia and Betsy Lipson for their insights into how adults can encourage young children to "use their words" and expand their communication repertoires, Beth Fredericks for helping me turn a summary into a credible call for action, and Joan Lombardi for encouraging my efforts and leading me to a publisher. I am grateful to Dave Lawrence, Jr., who answers every e-mail immediately no matter where he is in the world, Joan Liddicoat and Sue Bredekamp for encouraging words and helpful critiques and corrections, and to Peter Wissoker, whose patient championship, guidance, and support carried this book from manuscript to publication.

I affectionately thank Berry Brazelton, who believes so strongly in the importance and power of parent advocacy that he made room in an impossibly busy schedule to write a foreword to this book.

A final acknowledgment goes to the too often underappreciated and undersupported parents, caregivers, and early childhood teachers who work so hard to provide our children with the strong foundation upon which their success—and the success of our country—will rest.

Part I

Every Child's Birthright

1 Jack and Jill

Jack and Jill
Went up the hill,
Full of hope and laughter.

Jack got to play
And learn all day,
But Jill kept struggling after.

W hy do some students learn easily and joyfully while others in the same classrooms continue to struggle? Why are so many of our children coming to kindergarten so far behind their peers that "All children shall start school ready to learn"[1] is an unrealized national goal rather than a safe assumption? Why is there an "achievement gap" between haves and have-nots, and why is it so difficult to close?

The answers to these questions are complex. Yet it is becoming increasingly clear that much of the explanation lies in what we are doing—and not doing—as parents and teachers, as communities and as a country, to support our youngest children. The more we learn about the astounding capabilities of young children, the rapidity of their learning, and the impact of that learning on their later development, the clearer this becomes.

Before we examine the evidence though, let us look at two real children whose daily experiences and approaches to learning illustrate what research captures on a larger scale.

Jack and Jill[2] are two real children who live in suburban towns in eastern Massachusetts. At the time of this writing, Jack is two-and-a-half and Jill has just turned three. Both children live in two-parent families where both parents work, so both children spend much of their time in a formal childcare setting. Both are oldest children with a younger brother. Both children are healthy, with no biological risk factors, sensory-motor impairments, or diagnosed handicapping conditions. Both come from middle-income, English-speaking families and hear only standard English in their daily lives.

Unfortunately, this is where the similarity ends. Jack's parents have jobs that allow them some flexibility in when and where they work and enough discretionary income to purchase relatively expensive child care. Jack spends three days a week in a family child-care home with an exemplary educational program. The rest of his waking hours are spent with one of his parents or, occasionally, with a grandparent. Jill's parents both work long hours with no flexibility. Jill spends two days a week with her grandparents and three days at the best child-care center her parents can afford. Jill's mother works required overtime nearly every week; Jill and her baby brother spend a lot of time in her office waiting for her to finish.

In their solitary play, interaction with adults and peers, and especially in their use of language, Jack and Jill are as different as night and day. These differences, as we shall see, are priming one child to flourish and the other to struggle when they reach elementary school.

Jack is full of curiosity and constantly on the go. He has only recently learned to talk, but he keeps up a steady stream of conversation. His pronunciation is a bit idiosyncratic—c's become t's and s's are sometimes left out entirely—but his parents, teacher, and playmates understand most of what he says.

Jill is much more "well-behaved." She'll sit quietly for an hour, playing with a toy, or, if no toy is available, fiddling with her fingers or just watching whatever is going on around her. Her speech is quite clear, but she tends to speak only when spoken to.

Spend a little time playing with Jack and with Jill, and you'll see even starker differences. Let's eavesdrop on a typical playtime conversation between Jack and his mother. Notice the range of ways in which Jack uses language, how much he knows, and how his mother extends his vocabulary as she joins him in play.

Jack: Go park now?
Jack's Mother: Yes. We can go to the park. Can you get your jacket on?
Jack: No jacket. Park.
Mother: It's cold outside today, Jack. You have to wear your jacket if you want to go to the park.
Jack: No. No cold. No jacket. Go park now.
Mother (putting on the jacket as Jack squirms): Ooh, where did your hand go? Oh—Here it comes! Hi, Jack's hand! Oh, no—the other one got lost! There it comes! OK—You do the zipper. Then we can go to the park.
(Jack pulls up the zipper and looks to his mother for affirmation.)
Mother: Good job, Jack. You're getting good at zipping up your jacket.

On the way to the park, Jack's mother sings the train song that Jack learned at child care. Jack shouts out his favorite line "Chug, chug, toot, toot, off they go!"

As soon as they reach the park, Jack lets go of his mother's hand, runs for the train, and climbs on.

Jack (concerned): Seat all wet. Rain?

Mother: Yes. It rained last night. The rain made a puddle on the seat.

Jack: 'Tand here. I drive train.

Mother: Where are we going today, Jack?

Jack: Tontord.

Mother: Oh, you want to go to Concord? Should we buy some cookies at the bakery?

Jack (handing his mother an imaginary cookie): Here tootie.

Mother: Thank you, Jack. Umm. This is a delicious chocolate chip cookie.

Jack (driving the train again): Choo, choo. Goo, goo. I drive train.

Mother: Jack, what kind of engine does this train have?

Jack: 'Team engine. See 'moke 'tack?

Mother: Does it have a tender?

Jack (pointing to the small platform behind the engine): Here tender.

Mother: Do we need some more coal for the fire?

Jack (jumping off the train and pulling up pieces of grass): I get toal. Need lotta toal for fire.

Mother: That will make a hot fire.

Jack (throwing "coal" into the "fire"): Fire hot. Train go fast. (He turns the steering wheel rapidly back and forth.) I drive fast. Go Boston.

Mother: We're going to Boston. Should we stop at the zoo?

Jack: See 'raffe.

Mother: OK. Here we are at the zoo. Let's go see the giraffe.

Jack: No. You 'tay on train. Go to Tontord.

Jack's large vocabulary is above average for his age, though not unusually so. Neither is it unusual for children as young as Jack to have a favorite book or a compelling interest, and therefore to know specialized words like "steam engine," "coal," and "tender." Jack's range of language use is also age-appropriate. He uses language to point out interesting things, to express emotions like anger, impatience, and concern, to get others to do what he wants them to, to ask questions, to recall past experiences, to accompany his private play, and to play out an imaginary story. He plays with language, and uses language to play with others. Jack is a good pretender, and he is particularly good at roping in adults and holding their attention. He gets a lot of practice.

Now, eavesdrop as Jill interacts with her mother's coworker, Linda (with whom Jill is very familiar and comfortable), on one of her weekly visits to her mother's office. Notice the range of ways in which Jill uses language, how much she seems to know and understand, and how she responds to Linda's attempts to engage her in conversation.

Linda: Jill, would you like to help me water the plants?
Jill: Water the plants.
Linda: Yes, the plants are thirsty. I need to get them a drink of water. Do you want to come with me?
(Jill looks at her mother for guidance.)
Mother: Go with Linda, Jill. You can help her.
Jill: Help Linda.
Linda: Good. Come with me.
(Jill gets out of the chair and follows Linda.)
Linda: Here. Would you like to carry the cup?
Jill: Cup. (She takes the cup.)
Linda: OK. Here we are at the sink. I'll turn on the water, and you fill up the cup. OK?
Jill: OK. (She watches silently as the water is turned on, without lifting the cup.)
Linda: Put the cup under the faucet.
Jill: Under the faucet.
Linda: Here, like this. OK. That's enough. Now we'll take it to the plants. (They go over to the plants.)
Linda: OK, now let's give the plants a drink.
Jill (unmoving): Give plants drink.
Linda (helping Jill pour): Here, pour it in, like this. Should we get some more?
Jill: More.

Jill's pronunciation is clearer than Jack's, but, compared to his, her language sounds impoverished. It is. She typically repeats words she hears, but rarely initiates conversation. In everyday interactions with adults and peers, she doesn't introduce new ideas, ask questions, or point out details. Neither does she use her language routinely to push others around. Her vocabulary is limited to everyday words, and she seems to lack both imagination and playfulness. Most disturbing, her receptive vocabulary is limited; she doesn't seem to grasp simple directions or understand basic conversation. Jill's spoken, or expressive, vocabulary is below average for her age, though not out of the realm of normal. Her lack of curiosity, her willingness to do as she's told even if that means doing nothing, her difficulties in comprehending basic conversation, and her limited use of language for her own ends are not appropriate for a child her age, although they are all too common. Even in familiar situations where she feels relatively secure, Jill tends to keep quiet. Instead of practicing her communication skills, Jill has learned to shut down.

For Jack, language is a path to learning. Every day he learns new words, new distinctions, and new information. By the time he is three, he will be speaking in complete sentences and peppering the adults in his life with questions. He'll be asking why the things he sees work or happen the way they do, what people are doing and why they are doing it that way, and when an anticipated event will happen. He'll be telling stories of past experiences and playing out real and pretend scenarios with his friends. Long before he gets to kindergarten, he will know the names of numerous animals, vehicles, tools, foods, places, and people—and important facts about each. When he masters reading, we can expect Jack's learning pace to pick up even more.

Jill—though only three—is already being "left behind." If she and Jack continue at their current word-learning paces, Jill will enter kindergarten with less than half the vocabulary that Jack will have. According to Dr. Catherine Snow, who led the National Academy of Sciences team that reviewed the research on reading,[3] first graders who know fewer than five or six thousand words are very likely to have trouble learning to read. Their early difficulties tend to be compounded when they move from simple texts with short, regularly spelled words to more naturally written narratives. When too many of the words are new, it's hard to get the gist of what you are reading.

If Jack and Jill continue to follow the pattern revealed in the research, Jack will be learning new words from context, while Jill will still be struggling to understand the story. By third grade, when both Jill and Jack are likely to be able to read to themselves, Jill will still be reading simple texts, while Jack will be garnering new information and rapidly expanding his vocabulary. His early language advantage will enable him to learn more independently and more quickly, so his learning curve will be steeper. Jack and Jill could receive the same elementary school curriculum—even in the same classrooms—and we would still expect the gap in their educational achievement to widen as they grow, unless Jill receives intensive intervention. When they take standardized tests in the fourth grade, we would not be surprised to see Jack scoring at the sixth-grade level or above, while Jill's scores are likely to be in the second- to third-grade range.

But this doesn't have to be. Jill and Jack are two very different children, but they don't have to go through life with vastly unequal chances at success.

If Jill could receive, every day, the same sustained adult engagement that Jack gets, she would not be at such a loss for words.

To understand what it is that Jill is missing, let's take a closer look at how she and Jack spend their days.

Jack's days usually begin with a bang. Sometime around six, he wakes up, jumps out of bed, charges into his parents' room, and leaps onto their bed. His morning cuddle lasts only a few seconds, then he is ready to pull his parents out of bed and engage them in play. Sometimes, his Mom or Dad gets up with him; usually they buy a few more minutes of rest by reading him a book or two from the stack they keep beside the bed. Jack's favorite is the train book: he loves to label the steam engine, diesel engine, cattle car, and caboose; to find the smoke stacks, cattle guard, and tender; and to shout "All aboard!," blow the train whistle, and remind the conductor to punch the tickets.

Jack's dad usually gets Jack dressed and readies the breakfast, while his mother attends to the baby. This is Dad's special time to be with Jack. Getting dressed involves a lot of jumping, tossing, and tickling, along with a few tummy kisses. But it is also full of opportunities to learn and practice language. Dad lets Jack decide whether he wants to wear jeans or overalls, the red shirt or the one with a train on it. Jack follows his father's directions, helping to put his hands in his sleeves, pull up his socks, and push his feet into his shoes.

At breakfast, Jack and his parents keep up a steady stream of conversation. They talk about what Jack is eating for breakfast, the taste and texture of the food, what the baby is doing, where Jack will be going that day, and some of the things they are going to do. Just as his mother did at the park, Jack's parents keep the conversation going by expanding and elaborating Jack's "sentences." They don't correct his grammar or pronunciation, but, as they repeat what Jack says in their own words, they give him the correct forms. They add only one or two new ideas at a time, making sure that Jack is with them. When they introduce new vocabulary—which they do fairly frequently—its meaning is usually clear from the context or the situation. The discussion stays focused, for the most part, on things that Jack has seen, heard, or done or has learned about from picture books.

Most adults naturally talk in this way to young children—when they can take the time to focus on one child and respond to most of what he says.

With both parents working long hours, Jill's family finds it difficult to take the time for such intense involvement. Mornings tend to be hectic. Jill's dad leaves for work at 6 A.M., and getting Jill and her brother to child care and herself to work on time is always a challenge for Jill's mother. For Jill, getting dressed is a process to be accomplished as quickly as possible, not a game or a chance to learn and practice new words. When Jill doesn't follow a direction promptly, her mother usually jumps in to help rather than waiting for Jill to figure out what to do and how to do it. Likewise, Jill's mother's talk during their morning routine tends to have a practical focus. She uses fewer words than Jack's parents do and is less likely to engage Jill in the conversation. There are more commands, fewer questions, simpler sentences, and far less silliness. As with Jack, the focus is on things that are seen, heard, touched, and directly experienced. But Jill and her mother focus more on the here and now, less on what has happened, will happen, or might happen.

A classic study by Betty Hart and Todd Risley, published in 1995,[4] followed the language experiences and vocabulary sizes of forty-two children in three groups—children whose mothers were on welfare, children from working families with low to moderate incomes, and children from professional families. The researchers found differences in the size of the children's vocabularies that were statistically significant at eighteen months and continued to grow, until by thirty-six months the children from the highest income families had vocabularies twice as large as those from the lowest (see Figure 1.1).

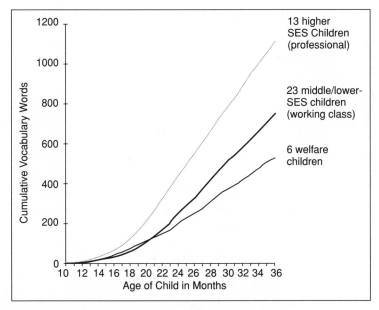

FIGURE 1.1. The Widening Gap in Young Children's Vocabularies.
Note: SES: Socioeconomic Status
Source: Hart, B., and Risley, T. (1995) *Meaningful Differences in the Everyday Experience of Young American Children*. Baltimore, Paul H. Brookes Publishing Company, p. 47.

The differences in the children's vocabularies, manifest so early, persisted through age ten and resulted in differential school performance.

As documented by the researchers, children in the professional group heard substantially more language and more varied language than those in the lower income groups. In fact, the three-year-olds in the professional families used more different words during the taped conversations than did the PARENTS who were on welfare! Also, the professional parents shared more information, asked more questions, issued relatively fewer commands, and were generally more responsive to the child's communications. Both how and how much parents talked to their children were reflected in the children's vocabularies.[5]

As shown in Figure 1.2, the differences in the amount of language input the children received are striking. By age four, the children in professional families would have heard an average of fifty million words, while those in the working class families would have averaged just thirty million. The six children whose families were on welfare were likely to have heard only fifteen million words. It would take a lot of input during the first few years of schooling to close a gap of that magnitude!

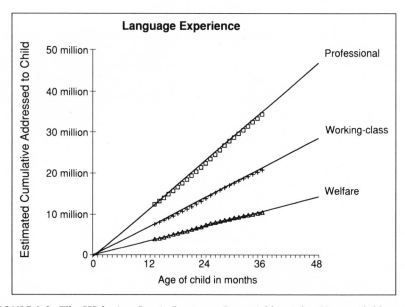

FIGURE 1.2. The Widening Gap in Language Input Addressed to Young Children. *Source*: Hart, B., and Risley, T. (1995) *Meaningful Differences in the Everyday Experience of Young American Children*. Baltimore, MD: Paul H. Brookes Publishing Company, p. 198.

In a subsequent book,[6] Hart and Risley trace what they call the "dance" of communication and explain why these differences occur. They found that in homes across the economic spectrum, parents used roughly the same amount of talk geared to accomplishing the routine tasks of family life, including managing their children's behavior. The differences occurred in the amount of "optional" talk, when parents and children played together or exchanged communication as they engaged in parallel tasks. "As partners in play," the researchers found, "the children tended to be more cooperative, the parents more approving, and both of them less demanding and more likely to comment on the nuances and elaborate what was said."[7] In other words, some families supplemented their routine interactions with their toddlers with freer, more playful conversations, and toddlers in these more talkative families were both hearing and practicing more varied and complex language. The children's increasing knowledge and communicative facility elicited increasingly complex and information-rich language from their conversation partners, and their learning tended to proceed at a rapid pace.

Jack and Jill's language experiences at home fit the pattern that Hart and Risley observed for families spending more and less time in "optional" talk. But both Jack and Jill spend a significant fraction of their waking hours with people other than their parents. The differences in their interactions with their parents might not be so significant if their child-care experiences were comparable.

Both children spend three full days each week in a licensed child-care setting. Jack is in family child care, while Jill goes to a center, but this is not the important difference. The difference that counts is quality. Jack's child-care environment has been rated "excellent" by independent observers and experts in the field.[8] Judged according to similar criteria,[9] Jill's classrooms would be rated "mediocre." The center she attends meets basic health, safety, and program requirements, but its deficiencies in teacher expertise, provision of individual attention, and activities that stimulate language are contributing to Jill's language delay.

A recent large-scale study by the National Institute of Child Health and Development (NICHD)[10] found that children whose mothers were warm and encouraging during structured teaching tasks tended to show more advanced language development. Three-year-olds who had been in high quality child-care settings, with teachers who provided good language stimulation, tended to score higher on tests of receptive (understood) and expressive (spoken) language than those who had received lower quality care. Neither of these findings is surprising. What was significant was their interaction: the researchers found that the quality of children's child-care experiences could mitigate or exacerbate the impact of a less engaging and responsive parenting style. This finding mirrored their results for emotional development. In that realm, the research showed that when children with problematic attachments to their mothers were in high quality child care, their relationships with their mothers improved. Likewise, strong family attachments could protect children in poor quality care, but the children who were insecurely attached to parents *and* receiving poor quality child care were at serious risk for emotional, behavioral, and developmental problems.

In general, children who get a healthy dose of language interaction at home or in child care develop hefty vocabularies and strong functional language; children who do not get enough input or meaningful practice in either situation are likely to be at a loss for words.

TV doesn't count,[11] and neither does overheard conversation. Although children will learn individual words, songs, and stock phrases from TV and videos (particularly the names of TV characters and kid culture slang), the bulk of language learning occurs through conversational give-and-take. When they have interesting things to talk about and interested people to talk to, two- and three-year-olds learn many new words each day and rapidly develop rich vocabularies.

Jack's parents carefully researched his child-care placement, and were lucky enough to find an unusual treasure—an experienced, highly educated provider who is a leader in her field. Her family child-care home had been accredited by the National Association for Family Child Care,[12] a certification of excellence.

Jill's mother also wanted the best for her child. When Jill was a baby, she brought her to work with her, taking time to feed and change her, but otherwise leaving her in a swing or bassinet while she worked. This arrangement worked until Jill was six months old; then Jill's paternal grandparents agreed to take her. That arrangement worked for a year, until Jill's brother came along, and the grandparents declared that they could only take the children two days a week. Jill's mother investigated several centers and family child-care homes, but all were either full or too expensive. Shortly before Jill's second birthday, a slot opened up in a child-care center near Jill's mother's workplace. Jill's mom was thrilled! The center was large, clean, and well equipped. The staff seemed friendly. The two-year-old classroom was filled with active toddlers, and there seemed to be an ample supply of books and toys. What was missing, however, was an ample supply of confident, caring, well-trained adults who could give Jill and the other children individualized attention and stimulate their learning.

A significant body of research links children's language development with the quality of their child-care environments and links the quality of the child-care environment to the teachers' training and education, the staff/child ratio and "class" size, and the level of compensation the staff receives. Let's look more closely at Jack's and Jill's child-care experiences to see how the markers of quality—professional training, low child/staff ratios, and adequate staff compensation—translate into differences in classroom environment and practice that impact children's language development.

Jack's provider, Elaine, has a masters degree in early childhood education and has been running her own family child-care home for ten years. She has taken courses in early childhood language and literacy development and working with children with special needs. Her prices are somewhat higher than the average and she's only open four days a week—8 A.M. to 6 P.M.—in order to allow time for planning, administration, professional development, and leadership activities. With the help of two assistants, she handles a mixed-age group of no more than ten zero- to five-year-olds at a time. She has been caring for Jack since he was three months old.

When Jack and his mother enter the playroom in the morning, Elaine greets them warmly. Stooping down to Jack's level, she talks directly to him about topics that she knows interest him. She helps Jack choose a toy or activity, and then spends a few moments talking to his mother.

Throughout the day, Elaine engages Jack in conversations and sets up opportunities for him to talk with her and with the other children in the program.

The day is about evenly divided among routines, planned activities, and child-initiated play. Planned activities reflect the children's interests and trigger their curiosity. Taking advantage of the mixed-age group, Elaine frequently plans multiday activities in which children work on a project together and older children help the younger ones. She stays with a theme for a week or more so that children and their families can participate in planning activities. For example, this week's theme is "space," a follow-on to explorations of "weather" and of "things that go up in the air." One of the families has contributed a small tent to serve as a spaceship, which Elaine has set up in the living room and stocked with astronaut helmets and flashlights. Other families have brought in picture books to supplement Elaine's already extensive library. As the theme develops, children will talk about what they already know and what they want to learn. They'll pore over picture books and listen to fiction and nonfiction stories, brainstorm ideas of what to add to their spaceship, bring over toys to serve as pretend play props, chronicle their imagined travels in space logs, and make scenery to enhance their journeys. A family supper will give them a chance to observe the night sky together.

During today's "morning activities," Elaine and her staff take up stations in different rooms. One assistant goes to the kitchen, where she helps children paint the stars, moons, and planets that they have made from self-drying clay and will hang on space mobiles. The other takes up a position beside the spaceship, where she can encourage and enrich pretending as pairs of children get their turns to "blast off." The younger ones enjoy pushing buttons, looking out the windows, and pretending they are going for a ride. The older ones practice the "countdown" and blast off on a trip to Pluto. Encouraged by their teachers, they look through the books to find out more about their destination.

Meanwhile, Elaine sits on the floor of the playroom, where she can observe and expand children's interests as they play with the toys and with each other. Let's eavesdrop.

Elaine: What are you making, Kayla?

Kayla (24 months): Pasta.

Elaine: Mmm. That pasta smells good. Is it ready?

Kayla: Ready.

(She brings her pot and spoon over to Daniel, who is playing with some Legos.)

Elaine: Did you want to give Daniel some pasta?

Kayla: Yes.

Elaine: Can you tell him?

Kayla: Mmm.

Elaine: Say, "Here's some pasta for you, Daniel."

Kayla (to Daniel): Here pasta, Daniel.

Daniel (age 4): Thank you, Kayla.

(Kayla goes back to the play kitchen. Daniel takes out the drum and starts to bang loudly.)

Elaine: Daniel, I'm thinking that you should take the drum over to the corner, so you don't hit anyone with the sticks.

Daniel: OK.

Elaine (to Jack, who is wandering): Jack, do you want me to help you build the Lego train?

Jack (age 2½; picks up a toy plane and flies it over his head): Rrrrr, Rrrr.

Elaine: Jack, your plane is going really high. Are you the pilot?

Jack: I pilot. Fly plane. Rrrr.

Elaine: Is it going to land? Maybe it needs the runway.

Jack: Yes. Need runway.

Elaine (laying out two pieces of Lego road for the runway): There you are, pilot.

Jack: Rrrr. R-r-r. Plane landing on runway. People get off. Take off again.

Elaine: Daniel, that's nice music you're making on the drum. I was wondering, if you turned them over, would they make a different sound?

(Daniel turns the drum over and bangs on its metal bottoms.)

Elaine: That sounds like another instrument. Do you know what it is?

Daniel: I don't know.

Elaine: Something big, that's made of metal.

Daniel: Yeah. Those things you crash together. What are they called?

Elaine: Cymbals. Or, it could be a different kind of drum. Have you ever heard someone play a steel drum?

Elaine and her staff take time each day to document what the children are learning. Indeed, it was Elaine who first noticed Jack's interest in trains. Jack had been playing with the toy train one day, and had been uncharacteristically possessive when another child wanted a turn. The next day, he toddled over to the shelf and pulled out the train as soon as he arrived. Elaine noticed that Jack was trying to say "train," and pointed out this new interest to his mother. Over the next few weeks, Elaine introduced Jack to picture books, songs, crafts, and play activities that capitalized on his interest. Jack's parents added a trip to the library to find more train books, rides on a real (subway) train, and visits to the park with the climb-on train. Soon Jack was becoming a train expert—and his train vocabulary was soaring.

While Jack is rapidly learning new words and concepts, Jill is marking time.

Jill and her brother spend two days a week with kindly grandparents, who love and nurture them but see their role as "watching" the children rather than educating them. The TV is on most of the time, and the children rarely go out of the house. Rather, they play with their toys, watch (and occasionally help with) cleaning and cooking chores, watch children's videos or cartoons and a couple of adult shows, eat meals, and take naps. Jill's eighteen-month-old brother is "a handful," and his grandparents spend a fair amount of time stopping him from climbing on the furniture or taking things off the shelves. They are careful to keep both children clean, safe, and comfortable, but they leave the "teaching" to the child-care center.

For the past two years, Jill has spent three days a week at the for-profit child-care center. Such centers range widely in quality, and the one Jill attends would be considered about average by early childhood experts.[13]

The space is clean and safe, the teachers are gentle, there are lots of age-appropriate toys and books for children to use, and the teachers follow a planned program of activities geared to the children's ages.

Still, the environment has often been too noisy for Jill, and rarely provides her with enough meaningful stimulation or opportunities for extended conversation. The toddler program, which includes gym and playground time as well as classroom activities like story reading, block play, puzzles, and teacher-initiated games, would seem at first glance to provide many opportunities for learning. Unfortunately, much of what the children learn are the school's routines—like lining up to go out to the playground, bringing books to the teacher at reading time, and putting the toys away where they belong. The teachers use music—played constantly at high volume—to energize the children, control their behavior, and signal transitions between activities. Teachers literally talk down to the children, issuing orders and suggestions from a distance and rarely getting on the floor, stooping down, or lifting children up so they can converse face to face. Much of the teachers' language consists of gentle commands and requests to remind children of the rules, prevent or resolve conflicts, or direct a group in an activity.

Teachers do find some time to play with individual children, respond to their bids for attention, and comfort them when they show distress. However, these interactions are usually very brief (less than half a minute) and are often nonverbal. It is quite common for a child to go for as long as half an hour without hearing any language addressed directly to her and without making eye contact with an adult.

Last year was especially difficult for Jill. She cried much of the day for the first six months, and the adults in her classroom were unable to comfort her. Still, her parents felt they had no choice but to keep Jill at the center.

Like other children at the center, Jill moved up to the three-year-olds group three months before her third birthday. She seems happier now, but she is still not getting what she needs. With a more academic focus, the program for three-year-olds provides brief lessons in letter naming, counting, calendar reading, recognizing colors and shapes, nutrition, and topics of interest such as space travel and dinosaurs. These are often followed by projects—such as cutting out pictures of vegetables and gluing them onto paper plates—that extend a lesson theme but do not call for much thinking, creativity, or conversation.

The teachers do a good job of keeping the group calm and focused, which is especially important to Jill, who tends to freeze or withdraw when there is too much noise. They use language to prepare children for transitions, to remind children of safety rules, to explain the steps in a process such as an art project or game, to help children notice when others need sympathy or help, and to expand children's understanding of concepts and categories. Still, a trained observer would rate the support for language learning as only fair. There are few open-ended questions and only brief adult–child conversations in which information is exchanged or children's ideas are elaborated.

The classroom is nicely organized into interest centers, with labels, signs, books, and bulletin board displays that help lay the groundwork for literacy. Children can play freely in areas that the teachers declare are "open," but their time is fairly limited. As the teachers set up a new activity or clean up from lunch or from a messy project, children are given time to play and converse with each other. Constraining the time and areas for free play helps keep the classroom in control, but it means, unfortunately, that teachers are only minimally involved in what could be the most linguistically rich parts of children's days. They do not actively facilitate exchanges among children, introduce new elements into their pretend play scenarios, or help a loner like Jill to win acceptance into a group. They miss the opportunities that Jack's teachers seize to accelerate children's learning.

During free play and playground time, Jill gravitates toward the water table or the sandbox, relatively quiet places where she can play without being jostled by more active children. In a well-run classroom or family child care home, these areas can provide extensive opportunities for practicing language. The water table can be a bathtub for baby dolls, a laboratory for exploring soap bubble properties, floating and sinking, or color mixing, or a place for making "rain," water falls, whirlpools, and waves. Likewise, the sandbox allows for pretend play with cooking and restaurant themes, for experimenting with emptying, filling, molding, and sculpting with different consistencies of sand, and for all kinds of individual and cooperative construction of holes, castles, cities, rivers, dams, roads, tunnels, wedding cakes, and even volcanoes.

As children work together, request help or materials, describe their constructions and discoveries, and make plans and predictions, they learn and practice verbs like sift, pour, dump, dig, splatter, splash, sprinkle, drip, dribble, poke, collapse, flow, pat, slosh, and seep and adjectives like damp, soapy, slippery, slick, rough, sticky, full, squishy, muddy, powdery, bubbly, heavy, deep, upside-down, and leaky.

But these possibilities are only realized when adults are intentionally involved in setting up intriguing experiences, introducing words and ideas, asking and answering questions, and creating environments that encourage interaction and conversation. Jill's teachers do not have enough training, experience, or planning time to do these easily and consistently. It is hard for them to attend to individual children while keeping a group of fourteen productively engaged.

Jill's play tends to remain "stuck" at the messing around stage, with little use of language or systematic investigation. She splashes the water and digs in the sand, sometimes washing a doll or making a simple mud pie. But only rarely does a child or adult ask her what she is doing, present her with a challenge, or capitalize on the opportunity to extend her learning.

Like many other for-profit centers, Jill's center has invested in space and equipment. However, the program scrimps on staffing, using teachers and aides who meet minimum training qualifications and asking them to care for as many children as the licensing regulations allow. It pays the low salaries that are typical of the early childhood field, average for child-care workers but not enough to attract and hold educated personnel. The result is a rotating staff who must be quickly trained to work together. In order to make their tasks easier, the center relies on a set and simple curriculum, using activities that are easy to implement and control. The children spend large parts of the day in group activities run by the teacher or her assistant, like listening to stories, singing songs, playing games like Chase and Simon Says, or completing structured art projects.

Jill may hear a lot of language in the course of her day, but she has few opportunities for real communication. She has obviously gotten enough practice to learn to talk, but not enough to develop confidence or proficiency. Her learning is slow because she rarely participates in activities or conversations that engage her curiosity and stretch her knowledge.

A child like Jack, who is good at demanding attention from adults and peers, might be fine in Jill's classroom, even though it would not be ideal. A quiet, compliant child like Jill is easily overlooked.

For Jill, neither her grandparents' home nor the child-care center is of adequate quality. At this critical point in her development, she is missing out on the opportunities to learn and practice language that should be every child's birthright. Without these opportunities for almost constant conversation, Jill cannot build the foundation she needs in order to thrive in a highly literate culture.

In poll after poll, education emerges as the top issue of public concern in the United States today.[14] We invest public and private resources in programs of school reform, initiatives to reduce class size, and state and national efforts to raise standards and increase accountability. We add mentorship programs, tutoring programs, and after-school enrichment programs. We experiment with vouchers and charter schools; we extend the school day and year. Many of these efforts pay off—to some extent.

Children's attendance and spirits improve, a few students make dramatic progress, there is a statistically significant rise in test scores. Yet those in the trenches often feel that they are fighting an uphill battle. Their victories bring children from the valley floor to the hillside, but rarely carry them all to the mountaintop. The playing field is not level, and those who start behind are likely to have a difficult time catching up.

Could it be that the problem lies in "starting behind?" Could it be that all of our efforts in education and youth development would be far more successful if we provided children with a strong beginning? Could something as simple as the way we talk with children when they are two and three years old make a difference in their entire lives? And, if this is the case, should we worry about *all* of our children, not just those who are poor or face obvious challenges?

Most of our children are beginning child care at a very early age, with multiple caregivers and for long hours.[15] Their caregivers, by and large, receive low pay, inadequate training, and little support, yet they are providing the children with a large part of their language experience at a critical time in their development.

Whether they observe in child-care centers, family child-care homes, or the homes of children's relatives, neighbors, or family friends, researchers find that Jill's experiences are far more typical than Jack's. In study after study, the investigators rate fewer than half of the settings for two- and three-year-olds—children in their most formative language development years—as characterized by "positive caregiving" or "developmentally appropriate" care.[16] The *Starting Points* report, published by the Carnegie Corporation in 1994, called this a "Quiet Crisis." Ten years later, this crisis remains insufficiently addressed, as the stakes continue to rise.

The low-income children who show up disproportionately as "low achievers" on mandated academic tests may be like the canaries who were brought into mines as an early warning system—the first to succumb to an insidious danger. Poverty is a risk factor—for all sorts of reasons that will be explained in later chapters. But poverty isn't the only problem—middle-class children like Jill are also at risk. And, of course, being poor doesn't make you a bad parent or a bad language model, though it can make your job more challenging.

Recognizing that language and literacy are more important than ever for success in school and in life, how can we assure that our children will be prepared? How can we provide parents with the supports and information they need to give their children a strong language start? How can we bring child-care programs and settings up to an adequate level of quality, so that children engage in rich and stimulating conversations during their language-learning years? How can we wisely invest public resources to create systems that all of us can count on?

There are about eight million two- and three-year-olds in the United States today,[17] and experts estimate that at least a third of them,[18] like Jill, are not getting the foundation they need. This book explains why—and what parents, politicians, and concerned citizens can do about it.

2 Prime Time for Language Learning

Humans are social animals, and their children come into the world primed to communicate. Language and symbolic thought, the hallmarks of humanity, develop very early. The first five years of life, and especially the years between one and four, are prime time for language learning. The brain is growing and developing rapidly, forming new connections as it learns. These connections, in turn, enable rapid information processing and new learning.[1]

Virtually every child who can physically speak and hear (and many who can't) masters at least one language by age five.[2] Their learning is so rapid that some scientists have postulated a "language instinct" that is hardwired into the brain and activated by hearing, practice, and conversation.[3]

But being able to speak a language fluently is not the whole story. As we saw with Jack and Jill, it is the qualitative differences in the way language is used that matter, and these, like language learning in general, are rooted in early experience.

This chapter zeroes in on the period of dramatic language development that occurs for most children between the ages of one and four. In this short period, children go from grunts and gestures to complex storytelling. This is the time when language learning is easy, when children "burst into language" and parents are constantly surprised by how much their children know. If we want to ensure that all children learn their language well, it makes sense to direct our efforts to the period when they are most eager and able to learn it.

By looking at the developmental milestones that all children traverse and at the experiences that help them attain and build on these milestones, we can gain a deeper understanding of the conditions necessary for healthy development and for optimal language learning. We can see what it is about young children that makes their language learning so rapid and understand what it is that children should be getting during this time of rapid learning. As we examine parenting, caregiving, and teaching practices that enable children to develop robust vocabularies and effective language use, we can begin to see what it would take to give a child like Jill the essential early language and learning foundation that Jack can take for granted.

Children's language development begins very early. During their first month, babies recognize and turn toward the voices of their most frequent caregivers. They make eye contact, watch eyes and mouths, imitate facial expressions, and begin to learn the turn-taking "dance" of communication exchange.

Although babies' first communications may not be intentional, attentive parents and other caregivers are able to interpret their meanings. For example, they can differentiate between the rhythmic, intense cry that means "I'm hungry," the sharp cry that means "I'm in pain," and the whiney cry that means "I'm uncomfortable." Often without realizing what signals they are noticing, they recognize that when a baby hiccups, tenses her body, tightens her lips, screws up her face, stiffens her body, or curls her toes, the baby is saying "I am overstimulated or overwhelmed and I need to be soothed." Most important, they tune in to the baby's rhythm of interaction. They follow the baby's lead as she makes eye contact, engages in back-and-forth play, signals that she needs a break by briefly turning away, and then resumes the play when she is ready.[4]

Before long, babies are tuning in to the rhythms and inflections of language. Adults the world over speak to babies in a language that psychologists refer to as "Parentese."[5] They use low, smooth murmurs for soothing, rising intonation to elicit or direct attention, a rising and falling pattern to indicate approval, and sharp, quick sounds to mean "Stop!" or "Don't!"[6] Indeed, parents of young babies often discover that it doesn't matter what they say, as long as they say it in Parentese. Often, a baby who fusses when his mother talks on the phone or carries on a conversation with another adult will be perfectly content if his mother continues the conversation while looking at him and adopting the high pitch and singsong inflections of Parentese.

Along with its recognizable melodies, Parentese has features that grab the baby's attention and facilitate language learning. Its high pitch and accompanying eye contact mark it as language, and specifically as language directed to the baby. Words are enunciated more clearly than in typical speech, usually with elongated vowels, making it easier to hear where one word ends and a new one begins. Key words, especially nouns and verbs, are often given exaggerated emphasis, making it easier to associate a word with a thing or action. The speaker often repeats the same sentences over and over with slight variations, giving the baby more opportunities to focus on the key words.[7]

By the time they are six months old, most babies have begun to babble, or to play with speech sounds. At first, babies throughout the world babble the same sounds, but gradually, those not used in languages the baby hears drop out. At the same time, the baby begins to imitate the inflections she hears, and her babbling, though still only gibberish, comes to sound more and more like meaningful sentences. She may also learn to follow simple verbal directions, such as "Wave bye-bye," or "Touch Daddy's nose."

During the first year, the baby will learn to communicate through purposeful nonverbal signs. He will lift his arms to signal "pick me up," push away your hands to signal "I don't want that," point with one finger to tell you to look at something, turn or shake his head to tell you he doesn't want what you are offering. As caregivers interpret and respond to a baby's signs, the baby learns the value of conversational exchanges.

The importance of talking with babies before they can talk themselves cannot be overestimated. The more that researchers study infants, the more astounded they are at the extent of their capabilities and at the rapidity of their learning.[8] Babies can remember and reenact complex events before they can speak.[9] When the adults in their lives give them words—for example, by talking about a recent event, babies' eyes light up as they make connections between the words and the experiences. After a few repetitions of a nursery game like "Pop Goes the Weasel," babies learn to anticipate the "pop" and are excited by their own mastery.

Sometime between the beginning of the second year and the middle of the third, language development really heats up. The toddler begins to put words together into short sentences like "More juice," "Baby crying," and "Daddy bye-bye car." This new ability to combine words allows her to say things she has never heard. As she discovers the power of words to communicate, she uses language for many different purposes: to make requests, call out greetings, direct attention to something she finds interesting, ask questions, describe what she sees or hears or what she is doing, entertain herself and others, protest, and invite interaction. To her parents, it seems as if a minor miracle is occurring.

Some children move from single words to conversation in a rapid burst; others gradually increase the length and complexity of their communications.[10] As the child relies increasingly on language to communicate, his vocabulary development skyrockets. According to Stephen Pinkner, author of *The Language Instinct*, "Vocabulary growth jumps to the new-word-every-two-hours minimum rate that the child will maintain through adolescence."[11] (This "jump," of course, is neither as predictable nor as instinctive as Pinkner portrays it. It is dependent upon opportunities to hear new words repeatedly in meaningful contexts and to practice those words in conversation.)

The typical two-year-old says between 50 and 100 words, but the range of "normal" is quite wide. Three-year-olds who are developmentally on target understand about 2,000 words, and use nearly 1,000 different words in their everyday speech![12]

At about the same time she begins putting words together, the toddler starts to pretend. At first, her pretending looks like deferred imitation: she will put a hat on her head or "drink" from an empty cup. In effect, she is labeling the objects with her actions, showing that she knows what they are for. Soon, however, she will use one object to stand for another. She may "drink" from a block and then hold it out to an adult for a refill, perhaps using words like "cup" or "more milk" to make her intention clear. By their third birthdays, most preschoolers are adept pretenders—acting out a variety of scenarios alone, with friends, with adults, and in their play with toys and small objects. Familiar themes like eating, sleeping, cooking, and going places, or favorite stories from books and videos, are reenacted in skeletal form and gradually elaborated into complicated stories that are played out over and over again with endless variations.

In one of his weekly columns, comic writer Dave Barry gave this description of his two-and-a-half-year-old daughter's favorite pretending game:

> Snow White . . . is a game she plays 814,000 times per day, using little figurines to act out the parts. Snow White is played by Snow White. The seven dwarfs are played by six dwarfs (Sleepy is currently missing). The wicked witch is played by a Fisher-Price Little People construction worker, who wears a hard hat, as if to say: "I may be evil incarnate, but, dang it, I am not exempt from OSHA regulations!" The poison apple is played by a plastic apple from Sophie's play kitchen. It's roughly 10 times the size of Snow White's head; even if she didn't eat it, this thing could SCARE her into a coma. The handsome prince is usually played by a handsome prince, although recently he was misplaced, so Snow White was awakened from her coma by a romantic kiss from: a sheep. It's from the Fisher-Price farm set, and as sheep go, it's reasonably handsome.
>
> Over and over, in Sophie's little hands, these figurines act out the story: Snow White is put to sleep by the giant mutant apple; she is awakened by the handsome prince/sheep; everybody dances around happily, including the hard-hat witch.[13]

When child development experts speak of the preschool period as "the magic years"[14] or say that "play is the work of children,"[15] they are talking about this endlessly compelling pretending.

This explosion of language, symbolization, and sharing of meaning doesn't happen all by itself. Children can hear torrents of words from radio, television, or overheard conversation and pick up none of them. For example, many Dutch children avidly watch German TV, but they don't learn to speak German unless it is spoken in their homes or taught in school. Likewise, hearing children whose deaf parents were advised to keep the TV on for them failed to learn spoken language through that medium.[16] On the other hand, young children who can follow the gist of a conversation that they are not supposed to be listening to often surprise or embarrass their parents by repeating adults' words.

Mother (to Father): I want her to eat some vegetables. Don't give her her M-I-L-K yet.
Three-year-old: But I want my M-I-L-K, right now!

For the most part though, language learning proceeds through practice and interaction.

Healthy young children spend a lot of time practicing language. Parents commonly overhear them talking to themselves, for example, saying "hot," "no," or "touch gently" to remind themselves not to grasp a tempting but dangerous object. Young children also talk to their toys, their hands and feet, and to objects that interest or threaten them, as well as to the people in their lives. In addition, they sometimes repeat words, syllables, and sequences just because they like their sounds. For example, I vividly remember my three-year-old daughter, who loved Beatrix Potter's *Tale of the Flopsy Bunnies*,[17] repeating the phrase "handsome muff" over and over to herself because she liked hearing it, though she had only a rudimentary idea of what it meant. Indeed, researchers have found that practicing nursery rhymes, nonsense ditties, rock lyrics, and tongue twisters helps children develop an awareness of sound patterns that serves as a stepping-stone to reading.

But the real progress occurs through communication. It occurs when a baby's big brother hands her a rattle and she smiles and he says (in Parentese) "Oooh. You LIKE the RATTLE" and she smiles again and gurgles. It occurs when a toddler says "Wha's dat?" and a parent supplies the name of the object that the child is pointing to. It occurs when a caregiver says "umm, delicious peas" and a two-year-old uses the new word in a sentence like "More peas" or "All done peas" to indicate his desire. It occurs when a teacher reads a book and a child uses the new vocabulary to name or ask about the pictures. It occurs when a child utters a two-word sentence like "Daddy car" and her grandmother expands the sentence as she checks to see if she interpreted it correctly. "Yes, Daddy got in the car. He's going to work."

The basic rules of grammar are relatively easy to learn, and most children master them in predictable stages. They start out by combining two words—subject–verb, possessor–possessed, or adjective–noun—into "sentences" that reflect the word order of their language. As they elaborate these simple sentences into three-, four-, and five-word utterances, they also begin to add grammatical markers, such as plural and past tense endings. At first, children overgeneralize the rules, applying these endings to irregular verbs and nouns with irregular plurals, as in "We goed to the store" or "The sheeps eated up all the grass." Gradually, they learn the exceptions; by age five their usage conforms to the conventions of their community.

Children who as babies hear more than one language spoken by the people around them will learn the grammar of each language separately, and rarely confuse the rules.[18] For example, they will not omit a tense marker like -s or -ed to indicate past or present in English, or use an adjective ending such as -a or -o in Spanish that does not match the gender of the noun it describes, although people who learn a second language as adults tend to make such mistakes. Deaf children whose hearing parents and caregivers do not use sign language will invent their own gestures and gesture sequences, which follow regular grammar-like rules.[19] Only children with rare disorders, such as a specific language disability or some forms of autism, fail to learn the basic patterns of a language.[20]

Late talkers are not necessarily slow in their language learning.[21] It is quite common for children to have difficulty with articulation, which they either outgrow or overcome with a short course of speech therapy. Once they are able to speak clearly, their language development is likely to be very rapid because they already know the meaning of so many words and phrases. During their period of silence or "mumbling" they have been actively communicating—stringing together grunts and gestures to express their wishes, questions, and ideas and responding to the increasingly complex language that is spoken or read to them.

The differences that matter are vocabulary—the aspect of language that gets measured in IQ assessments and college admission tests—and "expressiveness," the extent to which language is used. Children whose homes or child-care environments are rich in books, interesting things to explore and talk about, and people interested in talking about them develop rich vocabularies and use their words in a variety of complex sentences for a variety of purposes. Children with less responsive people to talk to and less to talk about are likely to recognize fewer words and use words in more limited ways. In one study, a group of children entering kindergarten showed a range in receptive vocabulary (number of words understood) scores from 1 year, 9 months to 10 years, 8 months![22]

The good news is that children who are slow to develop their vocabularies can catch up. Unlike grammar and pronunciation, which are learned most easily in early childhood, vocabulary does not get harder to learn as one gets older. The bad news is that "catching up" gets harder and harder as time goes on. This is because children who develop richer vocabularies by age three or four tend to increase their vocabularies at a faster pace, so the gap widens every year. This widening gap should be no surprise. The more words of a sentence or paragraph one understands, the easier it is to pick up new words from the context. Similarly, having a richer vocabulary enables a child to ask more nuanced questions, make more precise observations, draw on more sources for making analogies, and give and understand more detailed explanations or inferences. Thus learning is accelerated, and with it the potential for mastering new words and asking new questions.[23]

So, what do parents and caregivers need to do to ensure that children learn enough vocabulary in their early years to be prepared to succeed in school? Is ordinary experience enough, or do we need to add special training and supports? The best answer seems to be "both." The experiences children need are ordinary ones, but, through no fault of their own and often despite the best efforts of their families, an increasing percentage of our children do not have sufficient access to these ordinary experiences.

Children need help from adults if they are to learn their language well, and adults can do a better job of helping if they know what works. Reading and talking about books, telling simple stories, singing together, reciting nursery rhymes, playing word games, sharing pretend play with props or puppets, asking and encouraging questions, elaborating children's ideas and sentences, and other forms of effective language "teaching" are such fun for children and adults alike that they are easy to incorporate into everyday routines. They feed the constant flow of engaged conversation—with opportunities to hear and practice language, to note the impact of one's words, and to try again and again to make one's meaning clear—that fuels the child's learning.

Most children who spend their days conversing with attentive, responsive, informative, and playful adults will get what they need through ordinary experience. Unfortunately, for far too many American children, this is not the case. The people with whom they spend large portions of their days lack the unhurried time, the skill at teaching young children in a group, the knowledge of techniques for facilitating language and literacy, or the fluency in the language that they use with the children to provide them with enough language input, practice, and feedback. A society that expects all of its children to achieve high levels of literacy needs to intervene during prime time for language learning. In other words, we need public policies and public investments that support parents and other caregivers who are responsible for young children's early learning.

It is not difficult to provide the additional training and support that adults who spend their days with young children need in order to be successful facilitators of their language learning. But it does take resources. Fortunately, we have a large body of research and practical knowledge that can guide us in deploying those resources effectively.

Let's look more closely at the "ordinary" daily experiences that adults provide for children who are learning their language well.

Infants with "attuned" caregivers have an easy time communicating; their caregivers are adept at reading their signals and respond in ways that are comforting and engaging. These babies spend lots of time enjoying back-and-forth "conversations" with looks, gestures, grunts and squeals, babbles, and eventually words. They happily explore an interesting environment and constantly learn how to make new things happen. As the babies show off their skills and discoveries, their caregivers share their delight. Over time, these babies learn that they can use words to connect with people and to influence their behavior.

Toddlers and preschoolers who are developmentally "on target" are hungry for words. Learning to talk, and to use language to give meaning and form to their perceptions and imaginings, is their paramount developmental task. They are driven to practice at every opportunity. They are constantly asking "What's that?" "Where?" "How?" and "Why?" When their questions are answered and encouraged, when the people around them show genuine interest in what they are thinking and what they have to say, their learning proceeds apace. As one grandmother observed, "I'd forgotten how much energy it takes to spend a day with a three-year-old. My granddaughter wants to know everything! I don't think she stopped asking questions or insisting I pretend with her for more than five minutes, unless her mouth was full. And of course, she expected me to have all the answers!"

If keeping up with one three-year-old can be exhausting, how can a teacher or caregiver keep a whole group of young children engaged? A good child-care program, whether home- or center-based, provides ample opportunities for children to explore topics that interest them in depth. In a home, children can join in as adults shop, cook, garden, do household repairs, run errands, and pursue hobbies. They can help prepare for holidays and celebrate the special rituals that their families cherish, or learn firsthand about cultures that are different from their own. They can take walks through the neighborhood and encounter pets, wildlife, rocks, pine cones, fallen leaves, flowers, construction sites, police officers and fire fighters, older children, babies, shopkeepers, and different kinds of vehicles. They can listen to stories or watch videos and then play out the scenarios or retell favorite parts. And of course, they can use books (including library books) to learn new information, find answers to their questions, encounter new stories, revisit old favorites, and spend special time with people they love. With adults to encourage their explorations and accompany them on their travels, young children gather a wealth of information. As they walk through the world with wide-eyed wonder, their vocabularies, pretend play, and constant conversations reveal their ever-expanding knowledge.

In schools and school-like programs, teachers often introduce topics of conversation through curriculum units on popular subjects like the farm, seasons, dinosaurs, or pets. Using books, pictures, games and puzzles, pretend play materials, artifacts, art materials, and occasional visitors or field trips, teachers provide opportunities for children to explore and talk about topics that interest them. Some take their cues from the children, implementing a "project approach"[24] or "emergent curriculum." Building on an interest expressed through a child's pretend play, art work, storytelling, or question, they might begin by gathering a group of children and brainstorming with them what they know about a topic and what they would like to learn. There is ample time for conversation as children plan, investigate, and share their discoveries. Hands-on learning experiences, books, visitors, and field trips provide answers to children's questions—and spark new ones. Children are encouraged to represent their discoveries in a variety of media: pretend play, drawing and painting, sculpting, dictating stories, singing songs, making books with captioned pictures, and working together to create murals, displays, class journals, thank you letters to class visitors and field trip guides, block constructions, and elaborate settings for games like "house," "store," "astronauts," or "animal hospital."

Another approach is to use a prepared curriculum[25] that is rich in language and builds upon children's daily experiences in their families and communities. Such curricula can be purchased commercially or can be put together by a teacher (or better yet, by a team that includes parents as partners). Units can be organized around favorite books, appealing topics such as babies, space, transportation, the circus, or dinosaurs; seasonal themes like holidays, growing plants, or weather; places such as the city, the beach, or the farm; or concepts such as colors, light and shadow, families, or growth and change. The theme provides the topic for conversations in the various areas of the classroom, on the playground, and during small and large group "lessons" where teachers facilitate discussions, read stories, teach games and songs, and impart information. Children have many opportunities to practice new vocabulary in a variety of settings as they interact with each other and with their teachers and as they bring home their creations, discoveries, and questions.

There is no "best" curriculum or teaching approach, but there are common factors among the early childhood education programs that have proven effective in providing children with a strong foundation for literacy and school success[26]:

- warm, secure, and playful relationships with caring adults who come to know each child well, affirm his emerging strengths, and adapt to his interests and preferred ways of learning
- a planful approach to daily activities, balancing active and quiet, individual and group, and child-initiated and teacher-initiated activities, and addressing all areas of the child's development
- "developmentally appropriate practice," that is, using age-appropriate techniques like pretend play and puppetry that are particularly engaging for young children, presenting concepts that children can grasp because they build on what they already know, and choosing activities and lessons that are challenging but not overly frustrating
- lots of reading—of posters, magazines, signs, labels, captions, software, items such as cereal boxes and tickets used in pretend play, notes, cards, letters, and especially books, both read with children and given to them to "read" themselves

In an extensive observational study of low-income toddlers and preschoolers, Catherine Snow and her colleagues recorded their conversations at home and at their child-care programs.[27] They continued to collect data until the children were in grade school, and analyzed their learning outcomes. Their clearest and most striking finding was that children who as preschoolers engage with adults in more "decontextualized" talk, or conversation that goes beyond the here and now to include references to past, future, and imagined events and to abstract ideas, fare better on reading comprehension tests through the sixth grade. Snow also found, as have other researchers, that a large vocabulary at school entry is a strong indicator of later success.[28]

What would happen, we wonder, if all children could engage in rich, interesting, and increasingly decontextualized talk throughout each day in the years between one and four, their prime time for language learning? Could providing these ordinary experiences to all children ensure that nearly all would enter school primed for success? As we shall see in the next chapter, the answer is "Very likely, yes."

Early language experiences have unique power. After reviewing an extensive body of research, an expert panel convened by the National Academy of Sciences to review the science of early childhood development concluded, "What happens during the first months and years of life matters a lot, not because this period of development provides an indelible blueprint for adult well-being, but because it sets either a sturdy or fragile stage for what follows."[29] In the next chapter, we will examine some of this research to gain a fuller understanding of why early language matters so much.

3 Why Early Language Matters

I f you're a parent or a grandparent, you've probably seen a poster that quotes Robert Fulghum's classic essay, "All I Really Ever Needed to Know I Learned in Kindergarten."

Here, according to Fulghum, are the essential guidelines for a meaningful life, phrased in the simple language in which they are communicated to young children during their first experiences with schooling:

Share everything.

Play fair.

Don't hit people.

Put things back where you found them.

Clean up your own mess.

Say you're sorry when you hurt somebody.

Wash your hands before you eat.

Flush.

Warm cookies and cold milk are good for you.

Live a balanced life—learn some and think some and draw and paint and sing and dance and play and work every day some.

Take a nap every afternoon.

When you go out into the world, watch out for traffic, hold hands, and stick together.

Be aware of wonder . . .[1]

Fulghum's wisdom is shared by elementary school teachers, who recognize that the critical capacities that enable children to succeed in school and in life are social and emotional. Children who are "ready for school" are able to get along with others, to keep their impulses under control, to empathize, help out, and do their part, to take on challenging tasks, persist in the face of frustration, and accept setbacks with good humor, and to approach learning with a sense of wonder. Preschool teachers might also add their signature instruction to Fulghum's list: "Use your words."

Research supports these common sense ideas. In his classic book, *Emotional Intelligence*,[2] Daniel Goleman summarizes a vast body of research on the development of social and emotional competence and its critical contribution to success in all areas of life. He explains how emotional factors can "hijack" judgment and interfere with learning. These truths are encoded in our language, in terms like "paralyzing fear," "blind rage," "overwhelming stress," and "irresistible desire."

Goleman goes on to explain how children can be taught Fulghum's basics: emotional control, empathic understanding, more accurate reading of social cues, strategies for positive conflict resolution and helpful intervention on behalf of others, belief that effort makes a difference, and effective social problem-solving techniques. His examples extend well beyond early childhood as he traces the ongoing growth of these critical capacities.

Early educators and parents who urge children to "use your words" are laying a strong foundation for emotional intelligence. They teach young children to ask for what they want instead of whining, to convince a playmate to share instead of grabbing a toy, to negotiate instead of hitting, to assert their rights in the face of bullying, to talk themselves through challenges and puzzles, and to request help when they need it.

This foundation builds a "sturdy stage" for later development. Children who, as young preschoolers, become skilled at making and keeping friends generally have an easy time with the transition to formal schooling.[3] Those who cannot keep up with the verbal repartee of their peers may be stigmatized or rejected; those who have difficulty controlling their aggression or containing their frustration are likely to experience continuing problems. The words children hear and the words they can say play a surprisingly important role in their emotional and social development, which in turn play often underestimated roles in their ability to learn.

In his book, *The Vulnerable Child*,[4] psychologist Richard Weissbourd tells the stories of children who fail, who get caught in downward spirals of low school achievement, friendlessness, victimization or aggression, and poor emotional health. Some of these children have experienced classic "risk factors"—poverty, divorce, parental depression or substance abuse, or biological vulnerabilities such as chronic illnesses or mild disabilities. Others seem to be in the wrong place at the wrong time. For them, small problems, unaddressed, escalate into difficulties that become stubborn and pervasive. Dr. Weissbourd repeatedly points out that healthy development at one point is not a guarantee of smooth sailing later on. Likewise, many problems can be addressed and transcended; others may be made moot by a change of scene or a new beginning. Yet Weissbourd's stories—drawn from around the country and including children from all walks of life— show us why shaky foundations make children vulnerable. When adversity strikes in any of its myriad forms, children whose foundations for mental health, academic achievement, social participation, or peer acceptance are fragile are likely to get into deeper and deeper trouble.

Psychologists use the concept of "resilience" to describe much, though not all, of what Goleman means by "emotional intelligence" and to denote the opposite of vulnerability. Resilience is the ability to cope with difficulty, rather than being defeated or overwhelmed by it or responding in a way that is destructive or self-destructive. Resilient children "bounce back"; they thrive despite adversity. Many of them are "survivors" who "beat the odds." Resilient children are not necessarily "tough" or "invulnerable." They can be hurt—and may even be hurt very badly—but their scars do not lead to permanent incapacitation or lifelong handicap, unless the trauma is so severe as to overwhelm their resilience.

Resiliency is in part inborn. It helps to have a flexible or easy-going temperament, a sunny disposition, and a strong physical constitution. It also helps to be physically attractive; as children who look appealing are more likely to get help.[5] However, the real keys to resilience are capacities that can be learned and developed, and most of these involve facility with language. Indeed, these capacities rest upon strong early language foundations. It turns out that early communication patterns—including responsiveness, affirmation, encouragement to use words, sharing of information, and engagement in extended conversations—are important for resiliency and emotional intelligence, just as they are for vocabulary development.[6]

So what does the research on resiliency tell us? In a retrospective study of adults who had managed to thrive despite childhoods spent in troubled families,[7] Drs. Steven and Sybil Wolin identified seven "resiliencies," or protective factors. These are:

- *Relationships*: mentors, friends, support networks; the ability to pull others in and keep them connected, to ask for help when needed, and to make others want to help
- *Insight*: the habit of asking tough questions that pierce the denial and confusion in troubled families; the ability to describe what is happening and to analyze why, to recognize patterns and make predictions, and to use language to represent difficulties and challenges as problems that can be solved
- *Independence*: emotional and physical distancing from a troubled family; the use of school as a sanctuary and as an arena for success; the tendency to "master" pain by focusing on one's own accomplishments and positive relationships
- *Initiative*: a push for mastery that combats feelings of helplessness

- *Creativity*: the ability to express feelings and represent experience through the arts, including writing, drama, visual arts, and music
- *Humor*: the ability to laugh at oneself, to appreciate irony, to look on the bright side, and to use levity to make difficult situations easier to bear
- *Morality*: concern for others and a desire to do good

Dr. Linda Gilkerson and her colleagues have studied interactions between children and their parents or other caregivers in minute detail to see just how adults help children to develop resilience. Their findings underscore the key role of early relationships and especially of language.

Dr. Gilkerson presented these findings at a national conference on early childhood mental health by sharing a dramatic case study.[8] "Angie" was a child with multiple risk factors. She was born into poverty in a rough urban neighborhood, the only child of young parents who split up soon after her birth. Her father continued to stalk her mother, and would beat her severely when he could find her. Angie and her mother moved often, but they could never escape for long. Eventually, Angie's mother became despondent and began using drugs. When Angie was ten, her mother killed her father in self-defense. Angie saw the argument and ran inside just in time to avoid seeing the shot.

Knowing only this much of her story, most people would expect Angie to be in serious academic and emotional trouble as an adolescent and young adult. Research backs up these dire predictions. Poverty (especially during the early childhood years, when the brain is most vulnerable to nutritional deficiencies, toxic substances, over- or understimulation, and psychological trauma), being raised by a single parent, maternal depression, parental substance abuse, having a parent who is the victim of violence, witnessing violence, frequent unplanned and disruptive moves, and living in poor neighborhoods with correspondingly poor schools are all proven risk factors. Because risk factors tend to compound each other, having three or more tends to lead to "rotten outcomes," such as emotional and behavior problems, school failure and drop out, substance abuse, delinquency, teen pregnancy, difficulty in obtaining and holding employment, and perpetuation of cycles of victimization and abuse. In one study, children with two risk factors were four times as likely to develop social and academic problems as those with one or none; four risk factors increased the risk tenfold.[9]

Angie defied these odds, and, at age eighteen, entered a four-year college with a full scholarship. She had all of the classic hallmarks of resilience—adult mentors outside of her family (most recently, her French teacher, who drove her to college and helped her register), obvious intelligence and verbal ability, demonstrated independence and initiative in caring for herself and her mother and taking challenging high school courses, concern for others expressed through active volunteer involvement in school-based community service activities, insight into her own strengths and the challenges she faced, and a healthy sense of humor.

But where did these strengths come from? Dr. Gilkerson traced them to Angie's early relationship with her mother. In videotapes from Angie's first year, we see Angie's mother holding her, talking to her, responding to her bids for attention and for brief time-outs from interaction and stimulation, engaging in the "dance" of communication that facilitates "secure attachment" and a sense of "basic trust." In Angie's second and third years, we see her mother encouraging her emerging verbal abilities by listening intently to what she is trying to say, responding to her attempts to communicate by repeating and expanding her language, encouraging her to use words, complying with her requests, soothing her with comforting words and songs, telling and reading her simple stories, encouraging and answering her questions, and sharing information. Later, we see Angie's mother helping her learn to read, teaching her, and helping her with schoolwork.

Dr. Gilkerson points out some of the specifics. Like other parents or caregivers of resilient children, Angie's mother uses language to help make Angie's world more predictable and encourages Angie to do the same. She gives Angie time words, like "soon," "tomorrow," "Friday," and "after lunch," so that Angie can anticipate events. She prepares Angie for transitions and new experiences by telling her what to expect and coaching her on how to behave. She provides explanations that make things that appear scary (like masked trick-or-treaters) less so. She takes advantage of "teachable moments" to encourage her daughter's learning, and also deliberately introduces books, questions, and information to expand Angie's knowledge.

Again, we see the power of language to reduce or prevent fear or stress and to keep potentially destructive behavior in check. Children who master such language at a young age have several advantages:

- They learn constructive ways to calm themselves and reduce their own stress and impulsivity.
- They are seen by teachers and other adults as more mature and competent.
- They are liked by peers, who can trust them not to be overly impulsive or aggressive and who enjoy playing with them because they can use language to keep the play going.

- They approach challenges as problems to be solved, and get lots of practice in effective problem-solving techniques—including the technique of asking for help.
- Their learning and emotional wellness are enhanced, and enhance each other.

Claudia Cooper[10] analyzed the written work and behavior of elementary school students whose language and home and school learning had been followed since they were toddlers. All of the children came from low-income families. Many were thriving, though others were not. Cooper found, not surprisingly, that children whose homes and schools had been more stimulating and supportive were more emotionally resilient. These children were also more expressive in their writing.

Young children's language development—and the security of the relationships that facilitate it—has a strong influence on their emotional development, which in turn influences their adjustment to school, their interest in learning, and therefore their learning and academic achievement. Yet children whose families do an excellent job of supporting their emotional and social development may still be at a loss for words if they enter schools where their language and style of communicating is not fully understood and appreciated, if they haven't learned sufficient vocabulary, or if they are unaccustomed to the type of literary language that they will encounter as early readers.[11] Because in our culture schooling relies on verbal and written communication, language facility has a direct as well as indirect influence on academic outcomes.

Verbal facility and "emotional intelligence" are intertwined, but they are not the same. We all know people who are verbally "smart" and emotionally "out of touch" or socially "clueless," as well as people who struggled with formal education but whose emotional wisdom and ability to bring people together make them leaders in their communities. At the same time, we can see how "using words" contributes to both emotional adjustment and academic achievement in schools with high verbal demands. Early language learning prepares children for the social challenges of school, making it easier for them to concentrate on learning. It also paves the way for learning to read.

Children who read independently on grade level by the end of grade three are likely to complete high school and go on to college. According to a panel of experts convened by the National Academy of Sciences, "A person who is not at least a modestly skilled reader by the end of third grade is quite unlikely to graduate from high school."[12] Children who come in with stronger prereading skills are, not surprisingly, more likely to become proficient readers in the primary grades.[13]

But this is not the whole story. Third grade is used as a marker because this is the first time that a group-administered paper-and-pencil test can be used effectively with nearly all of the children.[14] With younger children, such tests often produce inconsistent results because children who know the answers may not demonstrate their knowledge in the test-taking situation. They may not fully understand the directions, may not realize that they are supposed to do the problems quickly, may have difficulty sitting still or holding the pencil, or may simply decide that the instructions make no sense and it would be better to follow their own logic, as illustrated by the following story:

> A first grader, taking a paper and pencil vocabulary test, was asked to "put an x on the girl's knee." She started to follow the instruction, then changed her mind and carefully drew an x above the girl's ear. "What are you doing?" her teacher asked. "I said to put the x on the girl's knee." "I know," replied the child nonchalantly, "but that would look ugly. I put it in her hair so that it would look like a pretty ribbon."

Third grade is also a watershed. In kindergarten, first, and second grade, most children are learning to decode—to translate printed words into spoken ones. The texts that they can read themselves are often way below their comprehension level. They are filled with short and regularly spelled or common words, as well as pictures, repeated words and phrases, and context clues that make the decoding easier. By the end of third grade, children are expected to read at their comprehension level. At that point, if not sooner, learning to read gives way to reading to learn. Now children with larger vocabularies have an obvious advantage. Knowing more words enables them to read more difficult texts more easily. Not only can they read the words whose meanings they know, these words provide a context for other, unfamiliar words that helps to make their meaning clear. Thus good readers extend their vocabularies and enhance their reading prowess, often without even realizing that they are learning new words.

E.D. Hirsch, Jr., president of the Core Knowledge Foundation, argues that the "reading gap" between children from more and less advantaged backgrounds is better described as a "language gap" or "verbal gap." "Such a shift in terminology might reduce public confusion between 'reading' in the sense of knowing how to decode fluently, and 'reading' in the sense of being able to comprehend a challenging diversity of texts. It is the second, comprehension, deficit, based chiefly on a vocabulary deficit, that constitutes the true verbal gap indicated in the NAEP [National Assessment of Educational Progress] scores."[15]

It is not difficult to teach most children specific prereading skills, such as identifying letters, writing their names, and matching words that begin or end with the same sound. Programs for four-year-olds that explicitly teach these skills often produce dramatic gains in kindergarten and first grade, with graduates scoring above their peers on reading tests given in their classrooms. Yet these gains can be short-lived and may "fade out" by the end of second or third grade.[16]

Although more recent research shows that children's gains as a result of high quality Head Start and other early education and family support programs have long-term persistence,[17] some early studies had found only short-term effects.[18] At least part of the explanation seems to be that some early programs, which reached only four- and five-year-olds in part-day classes, offered too little too late. They imparted specific skills, but they didn't do enough to enhance children's vocabularies and their expressive language use.

The Abecedarian Project, led by Craig Ramey, showed the power of a high quality, comprehensive program that started in the first year of life.[19] Dr. Ramey and his colleagues worked with children of very low-income mothers who had not completed high school, beginning when the children were less than a year old. They provided a high quality early education program for the children, full day, five days a week, year round. In addition, they provided support to the mothers through home visiting. Children in their program and in the control group (children from the same pool who were not lucky enough to be randomly assigned to the program, or "intervention") received nutrition and health care support.

Using state-of-the-art individually administered developmental tests, the researchers tracked children's intellectual performance at regular intervals. Significant differences in average scores between the children receiving the intensive intervention (treatment group) and those who weren't (controls) were apparent by eighteen months and continued throughout the project (see Figure 3.1).

Considering that the children in the study had not been expected to be "ready for school" by age five, the Abecedarian Project's results were remarkable. In this group of children living in poverty, whose mothers lacked a high school education, the average IQ was the same as that for the general population. In addition, although 40 percent of the children in the control group received IQ scores in the "developmentally delayed" or "retarded" range at age four, only 5 percent of the children in the treatment group scored this low.

A follow-up study of the Abecedarian Project participants and controls produced even more remarkable findings.[20] The researchers provided

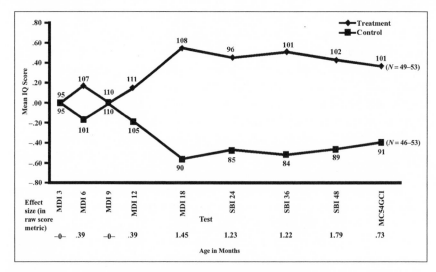

FIGURE 3.1. Abecedarian Project Results: Average Intellectual Performance Scores of Treatment Group and Controls Across the Preschool Years.
Source: Ramey, C. T., Campbell, F. A., Burchinal, M., Skinner, M. L., Gardner, D. M., and Ramey, S. L. (2000) Persistent effects of early childhood education on high-risk children and their mothers, *Applied Developmental Science*, 4(1): 2–14.

enhanced support in grades K-2 to half of each group. This support included continuing consultation for their classroom teachers to help strengthen and individualize the curriculum, support for their parents in helping with schoolwork and educational activities at home, summer programs designed to maintain academic progress, and individually tailored learning activities.

Not surprisingly, students benefited from this support whether or not they had received the early learning program. However, when reading, math, and IQ scores were compared at the end of third grade, the importance of early learning became clear. Children who had received both enriched early education services *and* special support in their first years of elementary school scored the highest, followed by those who had received *only* the enriched early learning program! The children who had received support only in kindergarten, first, and second grade did not do as well as those who had been involved only in the preschool program (see Figure 3.2).

The effect of the early learning program was strongest on reading, because that was where children who had not had the enriched preschool experience were most likely to earn low scores. Over time, the impact of the K-2 support washed out; at age fifteen it had a small effect on reading,

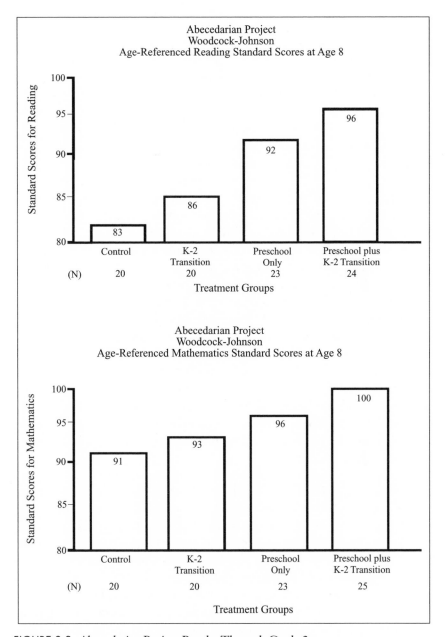

FIGURE 3.2. Abecedarian Project Results Through Grade 2.
Source: Ramey, C. T., Campbell, F. A., Burchinal, M., Skinner, M. L., Gardner, D. M., and Ramey, S. L. (2000) Persistent effects of early childhood education on high-risk children and their mothers, *Applied Developmental Science*, 4(1): 2–14.

none on mathematics, and none on the likelihood of repeating a grade. However, the impact of the enriched preschool program continued to be striking—a ten-point difference in IQ scores, significantly higher reading and mathematics achievement, and significant reduction in the likelihood of being retained in a grade or placed in special education!

For children who are living in poverty and whose parents lack education, there is considerable evidence that high quality early education programs make a difference, especially when they begin before age three and provide intensive services. Hart and Risley's work[21] may explain why.

In 1965, Hart and Risley were working with a half-day preschool program designed to boost the cognitive functioning and school readiness of low-income children. They zeroed in on language, and developed methods of measuring the growth in children's vocabularies, as evidenced in their daily conversations in the classroom and on the playground. This method involved tape-recording the children, transcribing their words, and keeping track of words that were new or were used in new ways.

Using vocabulary growth as an outcome measure, Hart and Risley tracked the impact of various educational strategies. They also compared the children in the preschool, all of whom came from poor families, with counterparts in a university-based preschool, all of whom came from professional families. Their most successful intervention involved a theme-based curriculum centered around field trips. Teachers would use books, puzzles, and other educational materials and lots of formal and informal discussion to prepare children for a trip to the bank or fire station, introducing specialized vocabulary that would be reinforced during the trip and then practiced in pretend play.

The children eagerly lapped up the new words, concepts, and experiences, and used their new vocabulary as they played "bank," "store," "fire station," and "farm" in the house corner and block area and on the playground. Yet, when the researchers looked at the rates at which the children's overall vocabularies were growing, they still fell short of those of the wealthier children in the university-based preschool. The ever-widening gap did not bode well for their educational futures.

Concluding that they were providing too little too late, Hart and Risley decided to look at what children in different income strata were learning in their everyday home interactions in their first three years.

Hart and Risley observed forty-two children and their families for one hour a month for two and a half years, beginning when the children were ten months old. They carefully tracked the children's emerging "in use" vocabularies, as they had in their preschool observations. In addition, they recorded and analyzed everything that was said to the child during their observations.

After years of intensive analysis, Hart and Risley were able to substantiate some remarkable conclusions:

- There were wide differences among the families in the amount of language used, and especially in the amount of language addressed to the child. These differences, which were strongly associated with social class, are reflected in the size and rate of growth of children's vocabularies.
- Children who heard more words developed larger vocabularies by age three.
- The children whose parents were on welfare heard an average of about nine million words spoken to them in ordinary conversation by the time they were three, those from working class families heard about eighteen million, and those from professional families heard nearly thirty-three million! (These estimates were arrived at by multiplying the average number of words the researchers recorded per hour by the number of hours that the typical child would be awake. The hidden assumption, of course, is that children are spending most of their waking hours with their parents, or with people who talk to them about as much as their parents do. That assumption was more likely to be valid in 1982, when Hart and Risley began their work, than it would be today.)
- Not only the number of words addressed to the child, but also key features of parents' communication styles (described in the next two points) contributed to children's vocabularies and IQ scores at age three and to their vocabulary and general language scores in third grade.
- Not surprisingly, children who heard more "yeses" and encouragement—including repetition or expansion of their language, answers to their questions, praise, and approval—and proportionally fewer "no's"—did significantly better.
- Other communication style features that made a difference included *language diversity* (measured by the number of different nouns and descriptive words parents used per hour), *symbolic emphasis* (a measure of information richness and decontextualization derived by counting nouns, modifiers, and past tense verbs and dividing by the number of utterances), *guidance style* (giving children choices, measured by looking at the proportion of questions vs. commands), and *responsiveness* (listening; letting the child take the lead).

The features of parents' communication styles that Hart and Risley identified as making a difference in their children's language development are similar to what experts identify as "good" quality in child care and early education programs (I've italicized key words to highlight the similarities):

For infants and toddlers:

- Staff members *do a lot of talking* to babies and toddlers, engage in verbal play, *name and talk about objects, pictures, and actions*, read books to children and say nursery rhymes, *respond* to children's crying, gestures, sounds, words, and maintain eye contact while talking to the child
- Caregivers are patient with a crying baby or upset toddler.
- Staff are *warm and affectionate*, initiate verbal and physical play, and *show delight in children's activity*.

For preschoolers:

- *Frequent adult–child conversations*
- *Language is used primarily to exchange information* with children and for social interactions.
- Staff *add information* to *expand on children's ideas*.
- Staff *encourage communication* between children.
- Staff use *nonpunitive discipline methods*, model social skills, and help children develop appropriate social behavior. [22]

When centers and family child-care homes fall down on quality, it is most likely to be in those areas of quality that matter most for vocabulary and expressive language development.[23] When too many children are present, it is difficult to find time and quiet space for intimate, responsive adult–child conversations. When teachers are inadequately trained, they are less likely to be responsive to children's early attempts to communicate, to offer children choices and use positive guidance, or to use decontextualized language, expand on children's ideas, and ask open-ended questions that encourage reasoning and explanation. When the classroom or family child-care home lacks an intentional curriculum, whether preplanned or emerging from the children's interests, language used by adults and children alike is likely to be less diverse and less rich in information.

For children growing up in poverty, and for those whose homes do not provide good quality language experience, good quality early care and education programs can make an enormous difference. So can home-visiting programs that teach parents to engage in language-promoting interactions—if they are well designed, sufficiently intensive, and offered during the critical language acquisition years.[24] Several of these programs are described in more detail in Chapter 9. Here, we discuss just one of these programs, the Parent–Child Home Program, because its graduates have been followed for many years in several studies. One of these studies,[25] done in Pittsfield, MA, followed program children and matched controls through high school graduation. Program children were half as likely as their counterparts to drop out of high school. In several shorter duration studies, program children scored at average or above average levels on elementary school reading and math tests, despite their initial disadvantages of poverty and often also of language differences.[26]

The Parent–Child Home Program provides twice weekly home visits, beginning when the child is between eighteen and twenty-four months and continuing for two years. The home visitor, who speaks the family's language and often comes from their neighborhood, brings a book or a toy and shows the parent how to use it to support the child's language learning. The sessions are intended to be fun for all participants. The intervention is simple and relatively inexpensive. It is also extremely well targeted. It provides very frequent services during the critical two years when children are learning language, it engages the parent as a partner, and it develops habits of reading, playing together, and encouraging a child's questions that will continue long after the program ends. No wonder it has such a powerful impact!

What about children who are not growing up in poverty? Do high quality programs make a difference for them?

The Infant Health and Development Program[27] was designed as a replication of the Abecedarian Project, but with babies who were considered at risk because of low birth weight or prematurity or both rather than because of severe social disadvantages. Some of the children in this study were born to undereducated single mothers living in poverty; others had parents who were college graduates. By age three, children in eight sites who had received health, home visiting, and family support services along with very high quality early education, full day/full year, from six weeks through age three, scored on average thirteen points higher on an IQ test than did counterparts with similar backgrounds who only received the health, home visiting, and family support services (see Figure 3.3).

Furthermore, only children of college graduates scored higher than children who had received the enriched early education and whose parents had not completed college. In fact, the children in the early intervention programs whose parents had not completed high school did almost as well as those whose parents had taken some college courses. The scores of the intervention group children whose mothers had not completed high school, like those of the intervention children whose mothers were better educated, were higher on average than those of children in the general population, in spite of the initial biological risk factors that had made them eligible for participation in the study!

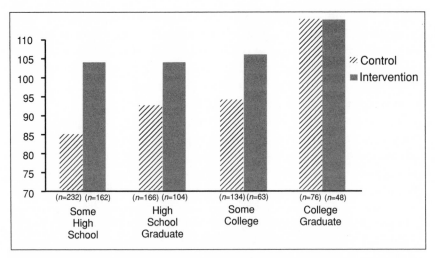

FIGURE 3.3. Infant Health and Development Program (IHDP) Results. Children's IQ at 36 months: Maternal Education × Treatment Group.
Source: Ramey, C. T., Campbell, F. A., and Ramey, S. L. (1999) Early intervention: Successful pathways to improving intellectual development, *Developmental Neuropsychology*, 16(3): 385–392.

The Infant Health and Development Program services ended when the children were three. At that point, the children who had received the enriched early education programs showed higher receptive vocabularies, on average, than their counterparts who had not had this opportunity. When the services ended, however, these two groups of children were likely to have the same chance of getting, or not getting, the opportunities to use their words and gain new ones in frequent, stimulating conversations with the adults charged with their care. In contrast to the Abecedarian Project, which continued to at least age five, the Infant Health and Development Project did not show significant IQ advantages for former participants at age eight. Neither were there clear advantages in reading scores.[28]

Putting all of this research together, we can see that it is essential for children to learn Fulghum's basics and know how to use their words before they get to school. But that is not enough. Children also need to learn a lot of words. And they need a lot of ongoing encouragement to use them in a variety of ways.

When children are given the opportunity, learning and using lots of words is easy, natural, and fun. It is what two- and three- and four-year-olds do. We need to find ways to ensure that all of our children get those opportunities.

The learning opportunities and encouragement of communication must begin early to build a strong foundation; they must also continue. As summarized by Ed Zigler, Matia Finn-Stevenson, and Nancy Hall, authors of *The First Three Years and Beyond*, "Evidence tells us that support and intervention in the early years are critical but that this period is not the only time that helps to define how we will evolve as individuals, nor is it the only period during which course corrections can be made and help given to improve children's lives and optimize their potential."[29] But the course corrections can be costly, both in the resources spent on remedial efforts and in the pain experienced by the child who is academically or socially out of step with his peers and with the expectations of his society.

The 2001 Elementary and Secondary Education Act,[30] championed by both President George W. Bush and Senator Edward Kennedy, set forth a key challenge for the United States: "Close the achievement gap." As our leaders have recognized, we cannot afford to be a society that leaves nearly a third of our children behind because they cannot meet the educational standards we set.

Many experts believe that we can close the gap if—and most likely only if—we start early. How early is early enough is less a matter of scholarly debate than of political will. The scholars are in agreement: for health care and parenting support, birth is too late to start.[31] In the critical realm of language development, we must ensure warm, responsive caregiving in the first year. And we must begin *at least by age two* to assure the rich, engaging conversations that promote the development of robust vocabulary and expressive language.

There may be nothing more important to children's school and work success than early language development, and there is nothing more important to children's early language development than adults who regularly talk with them in enticing, encouraging ways. Yet while we provide many different, often expensive, interventions to help older children who are not doing well, we are doing frighteningly little to influence the everyday interactions between adults and young children that shape development and set the stage for success.[32] Indeed, providing high quality programs for two- and three-year-olds and the adults who interact with them may be the best educational investment we can make.

These high quality programs can take place wherever children are: at school, at home, in community settings such as playgrounds, churches, and libraries, or in a combination of places. They don't have to be formal or esoteric. But they can't be scattershot. Young children are relentless learners by nature. They need lots and lots of learning opportunities, each and every day. They need the critical mass of meaningful conversation that

Hart and Risley, Snow, and other researchers have identified: conversation addressed to the child, sufficiently decontextualized, rich in vocabulary, filled with information and positive affect; encouraging of interaction; responsive to their questions and other communications; and affirming of their efforts, curiosity, and growing selves.

In the next two chapters, we will visit a number of settings where children are routinely engaged in rich and interesting conversation, and see how teachers, caregivers, and well-supported parents help very young children build a "sturdy stage" for later learning.

4 Supporting Early Language at Home

Children who are in group care, whether at a center or in a family child-care home, can learn a lot of language from teachers and peers. What about at home? How can parents who are home with their children provide the communication challenges and rich language support that well-trained teachers infuse into children's days? How can parents who worry that their children are in less than ideal child-care situations make up for what may be missing? Individual parents are asking these questions; increasingly, they are also becoming matters of public concern.

When Cambridge, MA, decided that the city needed to do more for its children, the city's Kids' Council developed an Agenda for Children. Initially there were nine goals, and all were important. But after gathering input from parent groups, providers, civic and religious leaders, and concerned residents, the Kids' Council chose just two for its initial focus: Ensuring that all children and their families could read, and providing safe spaces and nurturing activities during out-of-school time. The city's Family Literacy Collaborative, a consortium of early childhood and adult educators and family support professionals, is working with city employees, health care providers, librarians, and a range of community institutions to weave a web of supports for young children and their families. The Collaborative and its Agenda for Children partners formulated a TALK Campaign, with five essential messages for family literacy.

1. Talk and listen to your child every chance you get.
2. Let your child see you read, write, and do math.
3. Learn with your child.
4. Talk to teachers about your child's background and culture.
5. Expect the best for you and your children.[1]

At public events, well baby visits, and neighborhood "reading parties," parents receive information about community resources and are given books for their children in their own language. They also get bibs, wash cloths, and refrigerator magnets that remind them to talk to their child during feeding and bathing, as well as while they are preparing a meal. Simple posters explain why talking makes a difference:

Because ...
Your voice soothes your baby ...
That is how a baby learns to talk ...
That is how a toddler learns lots of new words ...
That is how a preschool child learns all about the world they live in ...
Talking and listening prepares a child to learn how to read and write ...

Paul Lawrence, a retired Harvard Business School professor who led the private fund-raising piece of Cambridge's public/private partnership, says it even more simply: "From the time they are born until they enter school, children need to be bathed in love and language."

Miami, Florida's "Teach More, Love More"[2] campaign reaches more than 9,000 parents and caregivers with a newsletter published eleven times a year in three languages. Each issue contains tips to promote language and literacy and overall healthy development. Here are some excerpts from the March 2002 issue:

Talking with and listening with your child are crucial ... When you engage "with" a child, you are open to learning from one another, to back and forth dialogue. You genuinely give attention to the child. ... The importance of *playing and exploring* cannot be overstated ... *Reading with your child* helps your child become reading ready. Even before children can say their first words, reading says to them that books are important. "Reading with" means more than reading printed words; it means talking about the pictures ... and expanding on the story.

These messages sound simple, and they are. Any parent can check out library books, tell family stories, make books for their children from magazine pictures, family photos, and children's own art work, and sit with a child and "read" together, taking turns talking about the pictures, saying the words, and making connections between the story and the child's real-world experiences. Any parent can do those things—any parent with time.

How, given today's hectic schedules, can parents find the time? How can they find enough time to "bathe their children in love and language," to ensure that they hear more than fifty million words spoken caringly to them by the time they are five?

Johnson and Johnson Pediatric Institute and ZERO TO THREE: National Center for Infants, Toddlers, and Families and have produced a series of booklets, endorsed by the American Academy of Pediatrics, called *The Magic of Everyday Moments*.[3] Each booklet focuses on a four-month period in a child's life. "The booklets are not intended to be general guides to *everything* that is happening at each specific age." They focus instead on "the special interplay between parent and child that makes everyday moments so meaningful."[4] They show parents how to take advantage of daily routines—like feeding, dressing, bathing, and getting ready for sleep and everyday activities like reading or making dinner or going for a walk to bond with their child and foster her learning. They help parents to see these ordinary rituals through a child's eyes, and provide suggestions for making them meaningful and fun.

Here are a few of the things that parents are encouraged to try when their children are between twelve and fifteen months.

- Read, read, and read some more.
- Label her feelings for her, "You're mad I took the stick away!"
- Narrate what's happening. "We're rolling the ball. You have the ball . . . now I have the ball."
- When she says part of a word, repeat the "true" word for her. When she says, "juju," you say, "You want juice."
- Offer toys that represent objects in his world, such as play food, to help him practice being a "big person."
- Give your child the opportunity to make things happen. Blow bubbles outdoors that he can chase, poke, and pop. Provide simple musical instruments such as a tambourine or maraca.
- Include your child in everyday activities. She will feel proud and competent when she helps you do simple chores like putting the napkins on the table.
- Let her help as you dress her. She can get her arms into sleeves and feet into shoes, and she'll feel so proud of her accomplishments.
- Provide opportunities for him to play with other children. Research shows that toddlers are fascinated by and learn from their peers.
- Establish a regular bedtime routine: bath, book, song, and bed . . . or whatever works for you. The specifics aren't nearly as important as the fact that your toddler will be able to predict what's going to happen when and not have to worry about surprises.
- Mealtime is another good place for routine. "Before you leave the high chair, we have to wipe your hands."
- Encourage make-believe by helping to set the stage and joining her play. "Are you making dinner? Can I try some?"
- Provide lots of good props. A block can become a car; a chair can become a cave. Let her know how much you appreciate her imagination.

Many of the techniques and activities that teachers use in classrooms and family child-care homes adapt easily to hectic home schedules. The following language activities for one- and two-year-olds are adapted from an emergent literacy textbook for early childhood teachers and caregivers.[5]

- *Nature Walk.* New walkers like to go places, but they also like to stop and look at things on the way. When a child stops to look at something, give him words for his discovery. A simple walk around the block can be a chance to visit a favorite tree or building or mailbox, to see green grass and a pretty yellow dandelion, to find a big boulder to climb on or a smooth, brown pebble to bring home, and to discover a wiggly worm or an anthill in a patch of dirt. It's also an opportunity to learn and practice all of those new words.
- *Rain Walk.* Dress your child in raincoat and boots, or grab an umbrella, and head out into the rain. You might catch some rain in a cup, listen to rain sounds on different surfaces, make muddy footprints and watch them wash away, float a stick in a gutter and follow its path downstream, or try to catch raindrops on your tongues. You can look at your reflections in puddles, watch the ripples that the raindrops make, and make more ripples by jumping or tossing a pebble. Go out again after the rain has stopped and then a day later. Are the puddles and streams still there? Where did they go? Talk with your child about her ideas.
- *What's Coming Up.* Use words to prepare toddlers for transitions. "Play time is almost over. Then we have to get you ready for your bath." "Let's get our jackets on so we can go outside." "Some new friends are coming to see us. You can say 'hi' and shake hands, like this."
- *Problem Solving.* Give toddlers simple problems to solve, such as opening a shoebox, fitting lids onto pans, nesting measuring cups or bowls, or getting a clothes pin out of a soda bottle. Use words to cue them when they get stuck. "Let's see what's in the box. Can you take the lid off?" "I think the red one goes next." Encourage them to use words, too, by asking simple questions: "Which one should we try next?" "Which part is stuck?"
- *Which One Do You Want?* Give toddlers choices whenever you can. It helps them feel powerful and in control. It is also a great way to teach new words, especially colors, shapes, and other adjectives. "Should we put your boots on first or your jacket?" "Do you want the red truck or the blue one?"
- *Shopping Cart.* An imaginary shopping trip can be great fun for two-year-olds, who enjoy collecting and transporting lots of stuff. Use a play shopping cart, a small stroller, or a riding toy with a basket, or give him a tote bag to fill. As you go around the house, encourage your child to ask for the things that he wants to "buy." When it's time to clean up,

you can play the game in reverse, with the child acting as a storekeeper who needs to stock the shelves. Encourage the child to name items as you help him put them back where they belong. Use words like "next to," "behind," and "under" as you talk about what goes where.

- *Telephone.* Use toy telephones to encourage toddlers to talk to friends or to you. When you participate, you might ask about events in the immediate past (What did you have for lunch?) or the near future (Are you going over to Michael's house?).

- *Loud and Soft.* Two-year-olds are just learning how to modulate their voices and enjoy experimenting with loud and soft. Play simple games where you give the child a word or phrase to say and have him say it loud, even louder, and really, really loud, as well as soft, softer, and whispering. Often it's easier for two-year-olds to use their "inside voices" after they've had a chance to make some noise and have practiced the difference between loud and soft.

- *Mixing Colors.* Make a paint-set in an egg carton by filling each cup with a mixture of half water and half school glue. Help children add a few drops of food coloring to each cup, in different combinations, until they get colors they like. Using cotton swabs as paintbrushes, let children use their custom colors to paint on wood or rocks or to make collages, as you talk together about what they are making and what colors they are choosing.

- *Memory Lane.* Talk with toddlers about events in the recent past. Ask questions that encourage them to talk about what they remember. You can also use pictures to spark their recollections.

- *Look it Up.* Answer your child's questions with words, but also with books. For example, if your child is curious about the truck that comes to collect the garbage, you can find a book on trucks or one that tells how trash is disposed of. You don't need to read all the words aloud, but you can use the pictures to help the child follow the story and learn the names of trucks, tools, and workers.

With three- and four-year-olds, parents can also introduce language and literacy games. Old standbys, like I Spy and Scavenger Hunts (e.g., find a letter in your name, find a red truck), can be adapted to children's capabilities and played on car and bus rides, during shopping excursions, or while waiting in line. Repeating favorite songs or nursery rhymes and then varying them with silly words is another way of drawing children's attention to words and their sounds. Four- and five-year-olds may enjoy a game that focuses on the parts of words. For example, Jean Ciborowski, a learning specialist at Boston Children's Hospital, teaches parents to play "the sound game." "Say 'pineapple.' Now say it again, but don't say 'pine'." When children get good at breaking apart compound words, parents can make the game more challenging by asking them to remove a beginning or ending sound or all but the beginning or ending sound. Most children learn the game easily, and love to turn the tables and make up challenges for their parents.

Dr. Ciborowski also teaches parents a simple technique for making books with their children. The child chooses a label from a can or box, a picture cut from a magazine, or a photograph, and pastes it on a page made from a folded sheet of paper. The child tells something about the picture, and the parent writes her words on the page. On the facing page, the child writes her own words, using scribbles, pictures, or invented spelling.[6]

Perhaps the most well-researched approach is a technique called "dialogic reading,"[7] developed by Grover Whitehurst and his colleagues at State University of New York at Stony Brook. This approach has been taught to both low- and middle-upper- income parents and has been shown to improve both language and emergent literacy skills.

The idea behind "dialogic reading" is to make reading a shared activity, in which the child's role becomes larger and larger as the books become more familiar. Another way to describe it would be milking a book for all it is worth. At first, a parent might read a book through so a child can hear the story, or flip through the pages and tell a shortened version of the story based on the pictures. On second, third, fourth, and umpteenth readings, the book becomes a scaffold for structured conversations that expand vocabulary, extend concepts, and encourage expressive language. Whitehurst developed a simple mnemonic (PEER) to describe his technique for using a page of a familiar book as a conversation starter.

Prompt the child to comment on the story or illustration.
Evaluate the child's response, affirming what is correct or close and correcting any errors.
Expand the child's response, adding new information or a more precise word.
Repeat. Give the child a chance to repeat the new word or information or to introduce an expansion, question, or observation of her own.

Of course, children who get hooked on a book are often eager to share their observations, story retellings, and ideas, with or without prompting, and may even prompt the parent.

For two- and three-year-olds, the prompts and conversations tend to focus on particular pictures or pages. Children are asked to name pictures, identify colors or shapes, find a character or object that is "hiding," tell what a character is doing, or say "night, night" to the teddy bear. Older children can focus on the story as a whole, predicting what will happen next, talking about characters' motivations or feelings, and drawing parallels with their own experience. Whitehurst uses another mnemonic (CROWD) to help parents remember the range of questions, or prompts, that they can use:

Completion prompts encourage children to finish sentences, usually by supplying a rhyme or chiming in with a line that is fun to repeat: *"I'll huff and I'll puff and I'll ..."*

Recall prompts ask children to recall information from previous pages or previous readings. *"Remember what the wolf did to the first little pig's house?"*

Open-ended prompts encourage children to use their own words to tell what is happening on a page or in a picture. *"What's going on in this picture? What else do you see? How do you think the wolf feels now?"*

Wh prompts ask **who**, **what**, **where**, **when**, **why**, or **what** will happen next. *"Where is that little pig going?"*

Distancing prompts ask children to make connections between the world of the book and the real world of their own experience and feelings. *"Remember when we watched the masons building that brick wall? What did the bricks feel like?"*

Setting aside time for reading and book-related conversations is probably the single most effective thing that parents can do to increase their children's exposure to words and their overall language learning. However, by itself, it won't make up for chronic underexposure to stimulating language experiences. It is not just the words that count; it's the quality of the communication. Deliberate "teaching" is in the end less important than a relationship that is characterized by warmth, active listening, and mutual delight.

Parents who take a playful approach have a decided advantage. They are likely to communicate more yeses than no's, to give children choices (within limits, obviously), to engage children as problem-solvers rather than telling them the answers or imposing a solution, to include their children in cultural celebrations and other fun activities, to use humor to smooth over rough spots, and to join with their children in verbal play. When parents make "playful parenting" a habit, their young children's language development is likely to benefit.

Some families have a culture of literacy. Conversation is constant and covers a wide range of topics. Adults do a lot of reading—not only of books but also of magazines, newspapers, instruction manuals, recipes, maps, and labels. They jot notes, make lists, mark calendars, pay bills, send e-mail, and keep records. They read for pleasure and enjoy learning. Curious children are encouraged to join in—to watch and listen, imitate, ask questions, and try to contribute.

In other families, there may be little reading and writing, but this is counterbalanced by a rich oral tradition. Children hear complex stories and extended conversations at home and also learn language through music and poetry. They participate in community gatherings and religious events on a regular basis, beginning when they are babies. In such a rich linguistic environment, children can acquire large vocabularies and rich expressive language. They may come to school lacking intimate familiarity with print, but their facility with words and awareness of their component sounds provides a firm grounding for learning to read. They may need to be taught explicitly the lessons that children who have had extensive exposure to books since babyhood have learned through repeated modeling and playful instruction: how to hold a book, that it is the print that corresponds to the spoken word, where to begin reading, that in English we read from left to right, that letters and letter combinations correspond to spoken sounds, and the names and sounds of particular letters. These alphabet skills and concepts of print are what Whitehurst[8] calls "inside-out skills," and they are as critical for learning to read as are the "outside-in skills" of background knowledge and vocabulary. But it is far easier to teach these lessons to highly verbal five-year-olds than to make up for a two-year gap in vocabulary and general knowledge.

Other families may be more isolated and less verbal. Home may be a quiet place, or a very busy, noisy one. Either way, a young child may not be included in much conversation. Reading, writing, singing, and storytelling may not be frequent or enjoyed adult activities. Reading materials may be largely absent, or kept out of sight or out of reach of young children. In homes like these, parents can be supported to adopt playful parenting habits and consciously create a home culture that supports language and literacy.

A peek at the Parent–Child Home Program[9] (PCHP) in action shows how, over time, parents can learn and practice techniques of dialogic reading, encouragement of questions, and playful parenting, until their provision of opportunities to hear and practice rich vocabulary and engage with meaningful print becomes routine.

Let's eavesdrop as a home visitor joins three-year-old Christopher and his grandmother, who is raising him.

This is Christopher's second year in the program, so he and his grandmother are old hands. When the home visitor arrives, they are all ready. The doctor's kit she brought earlier in the week is on the coffee table; their growing library of PCHP books are in baskets on the shelf behind the couch. Christopher runs to the door to greet his friend, and leads her to the couch where Grandma is waiting.

The session begins with Christopher showing off what he has learned. He puts the stethoscope in his ears and listens to his grandmother's heart. "Can you check my heart with the stethoscope?" asks the home visitor. As Christopher "listens," she participates in the play and prompts him to go further: "Lub-dub-lub-dub-lub-dub. My heart's beating fast, isn't it doctor? Maybe you'd better check my blood pressure." She then gently directs the play back to Christopher's grandmother, who needs her "pressure" taken with the "cuff" and also needs an "injection." When Christopher begins to walk away, thinking the game is over, his grandmother gently restrains him with her legs and hands him the plastic Band-Aid. "What's this, Christopher?" "Band-Aid." "You know what that's for, don't you? Can you say?"

Through many sessions like this, Christopher's grandmother has absorbed the message that children learn through play. She has learned how to engage Christopher in play and also to think of herself as his teacher. She's also learned a number of specific techniques for catching, holding, and redirecting his attention, for helping him to practice new words and feel good about what he has learned, and for getting him to think and to share his thoughts verbally.

This becomes apparent in the second part of the session, when Chris and his grandmother read a book together. Again, the home visitor begins the process by modeling her techniques, but quickly turns the task over to Christopher's grandmother.

"Where's Spot hiding now?" Grandma asks, as she lets Christopher turn the page. "Is he behind the table?" "No?" Where could he be, then? What do you think he's saying?" It is obvious that Christopher and his grandmother are enjoying dialogic reading, although not even the home visitor would use that term to describe what they are doing. She has simply shown them, by repeated example, how to support Chris's reading of a familiar book by reading some of the words, using an engaging tone of voice, cuing him to turn the pages, asking questions to direct his attention to details of the pictures and the steps in the story, and encouraging him to talk about the story characters and connect their world with his own. As they go through the story, both Christopher's grandmother and the home visitor find opportunities to reinforce some basic preschool concepts, including numbers, colors, opposites, and location words like "behind," "under," and "near."

The next part of the session is Christopher's favorite: he gets a new book to read this week. He and his grandmother will practice every day, at least once, getting more out of the book each time. The home visitor encourages them to get more books from the local library, but she also knows how important it is for little ones to have books of their very own so that they can read their favorites over and over and over again.

The Parent–Child Home Program has reached more than 15,000 low-income families since its beginnings in the 1970s. The long-term results of this program in several Massachusetts communities where it had been implemented with local funds prompted the Department of Education to recommend it as a school readiness strategy and to fund twenty sites. The state provided three million dollars to support the program in 2002, making it a separate line item in the budget.

Unfortunately, this line item did not survive the governor's veto pen when she was forced to cope with a major shortfall in the 2003 budget. The 2004 budget restored $900,000 to provide partial funding to up to twenty-two sites. Hopefully, a revived economy will make more adequate funds available for public programs that help parents to ensure that their children get the early language foundation they need. Hopefully, too, parents and grandparents, providers and educators, business, labor, and civic leaders, and all concerned with building an educational system that "leaves no child behind" will insist that all families who wish it have access to such support.

5 Supporting Early Language in Group Care

"Will you mind my kids for me while I go to work?"

"What do you mean, 'requires training'? My mother raised seven kids without any early childhood training and we all came out fine."

"It's just baby-sitting. Any teenager can do it. Why should we pay a premium?"

Statements like these, once common among parents and politicians alike, are slowly giving way to an understanding that young children need more than custodial care and that educating young children in groups is a challenging task. If you've ever tried to run a birthday party for even five or six preschoolers, then you know that keeping a group of children happy for just a few hours requires energy, ingenuity, preparation, and a lot of patience and flexibility. Imagine doing it day in and day out, for six or eight hours at a time, and you'll gain a new appreciation for early childhood teachers and caregivers. Now, imagine that you also have the awesome responsibility of supporting children's language and vocabulary development during their prime time for language learning, and that their future success in school and in life will rest on the foundation that you help them build. What education, training, and support would you need to do this critical job well, or even to do it adequately?

Let's visit a few classrooms and a family child-care setting and watch some pros at work. You will see

- how teachers and caregivers facilitate language learning through their informal, everyday interactions with children
- how they provide children with emotional support, build a sense of safety and predictability, and sow the seeds of self-esteem, resilience, and success
- how they support developing language through intentional teaching, well-planned activities, and an ever-changing environment that sets the stage for exciting discoveries and productive practice
- how they infuse both "contextualized" (tied to the here and now, to concrete objects and experiences) and "decontextualized" (dealing with

abstract concepts, or with past, future, or imagined events) language into frequent conversations with each child

- how they set up opportunities for children to converse with each other and use these interactions to facilitate social, emotional, intellectual, and academic development
- how they capitalize on individual children's interests and learning styles, expand their vocabularies, and engage and extend their expressive repertoires

You'll also see some specific strategies that have proven to make a difference in children's later academic performance.

We'll start with Elaine, the experienced family child-care provider whose home we visited to observe Jack in Chapter 1. She has invited us to join her gang for Monday Morning Meeting, a time to pull the group together, provide some instruction, and share plans for the week.

The children are gathered in a circle. Each sits on a carpet square, a device Elaine uses to keep them from crowding in too close. The youngest of the ten is turning two today; the oldest turned five over the weekend. Not surprisingly, the conversation begins with birthdays. Elaine asks the five-year-old about his party. As he begins to share the details, other children chime in with their own memories of the event. Elaine then reminds the children that today is Kayla's birthday. A couple of the others want to know when their birthdays are, and Elaine tells them, before leading the group in "Happy Birthday."

So far, the meeting has been a relatively routine warm-up, typical for child-care programs. The children feel acknowledged as individuals and part of the group. They know that Elaine cares about them and about what they have to say. Now Elaine is ready to teach. Speaking warmly to the children, she "sprinkles" each child's ears with imaginary "magic dust" to help them listen. The children giggle or smile when they get their "sprinkles." Now they are all ears, and Elaine can begin the lesson. It starts out as a review, in which the children help Elaine reconstruct last week's field trip to the airport. Most of the children have memories to share: how they saw "airplanes" and "jets," people going up steps, seats with seat belts. Using mostly open-ended questions, Elaine helps them to remember the language and reconstruct the details.

Elaine: What did they have to do before the plane could take off?
Matt: Check it.
Allie: The man had to check it to make sure everything was OK.
Elaine: That's right. The mechanic had to check to make sure nothing was broken. Was he inside or outside the plane?

Jack: Outside plane.
Elaine: And what was he checking?
Jack: Wheel.
Allie: The landing gear.
Daniel: And the propellers, to make sure they were turning fast enough.

Elaine reminds them of the song they made up, which they sing together, with appropriate hand motions so that even the two-year-olds participate, to the familiar tune of "The Wheels on the Bus." Notice how the song helps the children to remember the specialized airport vocabulary.

> The propellers on the airplane go round and round
> Round and round, round and round
> The propellers on the airplane go round and round
> All through the sky
>
> The pilot on the airplane says "Welcome on board" . . .
> The toilets on the airplane go "Whoosh, whoosh, whoosh" . . .
> The wings on the airplane help it fly . . .
> The flight attendant on the airplane says "Have a snack" . . .
> The man in the control tower says "Safe to go" . . .

Elaine then asks if the children notice anything new in the room, and they all point to the tent. "Matt brought tent" says Jack, pointing to his friend.

Four-year-old Allie, who has been angling for attention all morning, takes the meeting in hand. "You're not supposed to point at people, Jack. It's not polite to point. Right, Elaine?"

"You're right," Elaine replies. "Pointing can be impolite. Some people don't like being pointed at. But I'm thinking that was more of a friendly point. What do you think?"

"I guess it was friendly," Allie concedes, accepting the attention and the explanation.

Elaine explains that the tent will be used as a "spaceship" for the "astronaut" unit they will begin this week, as part of their study of "things that go up in the air." She pulls out some other props—a toy telescope, a nonfiction picture book about the solar system, and some large planet stickers that the children can put up in the windows. With great excitement, the group begins to brainstorm things they'd like to learn about in their astronaut unit, as Elaine records their ideas on a large sheet of paper.

Even in this brief excerpt, you can see the skill that Elaine brings to her work. She knows just how to engage the children, focus their attention, and draw out and acknowledge their contributions, without letting the conversation get too far off track or become boring to those who aren't speaking. She asks open-ended, cognitively challenging questions and responds to children's questions and contributions in ways that extend the theme and expand their knowledge. She uses and elicits a wealth of relatively rare words, using gestures, pictures, explanations, definitions, and other context clues to make their meaning clear. She integrates reading and writing in natural but deliberate ways, so that even the youngest children understand that written words provide information and help people remember things.

Research studies show that Elaine's techniques work.[1] Separately and together, they promote strong language and literacy outcomes, short and long term. Teachers who are most effective at promoting strong early language development infuse such techniques into every area of the classroom and every part of the day.

Teacher-led discussions, like the one we observed in Elaine's program, are a small but important part of the day in most preschool settings and an even smaller part in most programs for infants and toddlers. Children also spend time working or playing alone or in small groups in organized and "free play" activities, inside and outside. Each type of activity provides different opportunities for language learning, and for teachers to actively facilitate it.

Perhaps the most language-rich part of a preschooler's day is pretend play time. With dolls, action figures, costumes, and props, preschoolers love to play out scenes and stories from everyday life, from books, movies, and TV, and from their imaginations. But they aren't "just playing." Pretending with one or more friends means that language is likely to play an important role. When an adult gets involved, there's a chance to introduce new words and ideas into a context where they are welcome and likely to be practiced. Pretend play as an arena for practicing and learning language is often overlooked by policy makers and even educators who think that a direct approach would be more efficient. But research and common sense concur: play is the daily business of young children, and direct teaching is most powerful when combined with opportunities to master the lessons and extend the learning in child-initiated play.[2]

The following example is taken from David Dickinson, Patton Tabors, and Catherine Snow's Home–School Study of Language and Literacy Development, as reported in *Beginning Literacy with Language*.[3] This book presents the results of a longitudinal study of low-income children's home and school language experiences and identifies the teaching strategies that proved to be most facilitative of robust vocabulary development in the preschool years and of academic success in the early elementary grades.

In this excerpt, we see how a teacher introduces words like "daring" and "oxygen tanks" into an ongoing pretend play game, expanding the children's vocabulary and at the same time making their play more interesting.

Casey's teacher, Ann ... entered their play when the two boys were "killing sharks."

Ann: Oh. So you're going to get the sharks. Do you need to kill them, or do you move them to a different place so they can't hurt anybody?

Casey: Kill them.

Ann: Kill them. You have to kill them?

Bryan: Yeah.

Casey: There's water already in the cage.

Ann: Oh, so they're in cages that are filled with water?

Bryan: Yeah, it's a water cage.

Ann: And they don't get to eat spinach. Do you think sharks miss eating spinach?

Casey: Sharks think they could get out with spinach.

Ann: You must be very brave and daring men to go down there and take all these sharks back to the special place.

Casey: We're protecting them.

Ann: Do you have to wear special suits? What kind do you wear in the water?

Bryan: I wear climbing.

Ann: A climbing suit?

Casey: Yeah.

Ann: What do you wear?

Casey: A shark suit.

Ann: Those things on your back. Are those oxygen tanks? To help you breathe underwater?

Bryan: They can breathe underwater.

Ann: Wow, that's a special trick to learn to do.

Ann extends the boys' play by entering their fantasy as an observer and asking about what is going on. Teachers can also enter as participants, by taking on a role. Children especially enjoy having adults as "customers," and this role enables teachers to make all kinds of requests that expand both the children's play scenario and their language. For example, as customer at the gas station, the teacher might need her tires inflated, her windshield wipers replaced, the hole in her noisy muffler repaired, and her oil changed so that her engine will run smoothly.

Another way that teachers can get involved in children's fantasies and encourage their language is through puppet play. Speaking through a puppet (or a doll, stuffed animal, or mini-figure) allows the teacher to take on a persona that encourages children to speak. Puppet play is especially useful for dealing with emotional issues. A helpless or cranky baby doll can elicit comforting and nurturing; a greedy puppet who hogs all the toys can encourage children to talk about the importance of sharing. A friendly puppet can draw out a child who is feeling shy, a silly puppet can start a word play game or encourage children to put new words to familiar songs, a sad puppet can help children understand what it feels like to be teased.

Good teachers also know how to set up the space to encourage dramatic play and keep it interesting. One common technique is to provide props that suggest a scenario but don't overly define the play as TV-inspired action figures or elaborate costumes tend to do. These props can be simple and even homemade: an empty diaper box and a towel can make a fine bed for a baby or a pet. A picnic basket, pail and shovel, and a few shells can suggest a day at the beach. Two- and three-year-olds enjoy joining with others in mini-play, for example with a doll house or with toy farm animals, and in maxi-play, with child-sized props and "costumes" that they make on the spot out of old clothes, scarves, beads, hats, and tote bags.

Most preschool classrooms and many family child-care homes contain a "house corner," with a play kitchen, cooking utensils, play food, dolls, and perhaps a cradle, shopping cart, riding toy, play keys, and cash register. Children readily engage in the cooking, eating, shopping, and caretaking play that such a corner suggests. Simple additions can encourage more varied play and induce children to practice a wider vocabulary. Menus, writing pads, and trays can suggest a restaurant theme. A length of hose and some hats can turn the restaurant into a fire station; a doctor's kit or even some bandages and empty bottles can suggest a hospital, doctor's office, or veterinary; pictures, artifacts, and ethnic foods can build connections to children's home cultures or spark a trip to an exotic locale. Combining two themes—for example, setting up a home and a fire station or a store and a spaceship—can lead to exciting, language-rich interactions when the homebodies report a fire in the kitchen or the astronauts shop for supplies for their journey.

Another common classroom feature is the "block area," where children can construct their own mini-play worlds from an array of small props and building materials. Working alone or in groups of two or three, children will build race tracks, zoos, sports stadiums, dinosaur museums, and even whole fairy lands. Each project carries with it the opportunity to practice specialized vocabulary and the opportunity for a tuned-in teacher to comment on the construction, suggest new elements, and contribute new words. The sandbox and art area provide similar opportunities for children to represent their ideas and for teachers to introduce new words as they help the children explain and elaborate their representations.

But child-initiated play, even with skilled teacher involvement, may not provide enough input and practice for all children to learn the critical mass of 5,000 to 6,000 words needed by beginning readers, let alone acquire the 20,000 word receptive vocabularies that children from enriched language backgrounds typically possess by the time they are six.[4]

Perhaps the easiest way to introduce children to new words is to read or tell them stories. Story language is not quite like everyday spoken language. Both fiction and nonfiction books, even those written especially for young children, are likely to include higher concentrations of rare words than does ordinary spoken language. Children's books also contain lots of context and picture cues that explain the meaning of these words and provide opportunities for children and teachers to use the words as they talk about the pictures and the story. Well-written storybooks also use literary devices that invite children to play with the sounds of words. Rhyme, rhythm, repetition, refrains, sound effects, onomatopoeia, and surprise variations make the story fun to listen to. These devices also make it easy for children to learn the words and join in the reading.

Good teachers fill their classrooms with an ever changing array of books, including old favorites, books related to their current theme, and fiction and nonfiction books that reflect children's interests and portray children, families, and communities that are like the ones they know and also different. They choose sturdy and colorful board books for infants and toddlers, beautifully illustrated books for preschoolers, and some easy-to-read books for children who are beginning to read on their own. They encourage the children to handle the books, to "read" them to themselves, friends, or dolls by turning the pages and filling in their own words, and to request that an adult read to them. The teachers read to the group as a whole—usually at least one book a day, but they also read frequently with individuals and small groups.

Reading doesn't mean just saying the words; it means enacting the story by using different voices for different characters, asking children to chime in on a chorus line (e.g., "I'll huff and I'll puff and I'll blow your house down"), or using gestures and facial expressions to portray meaning and emotion. It means pausing at suspenseful places and letting children guess what will happen next. It means talking together about the words and the pictures, the feelings of the characters, and the real-world information. But good teachers don't stop there. They use books as jumping-off points for conversations that bring in the children's own feelings, experiences, speculations, and questions. They encourage children to treat books and storybook characters as friends—to reenact favorite stories in their dramatic play or mini-play, to quote favorite lines, to use the reading corner as a place to relax, and to share favorite books with the people they love.

Another very important way to introduce words to children is through music. Throughout the world, lullabies and nursery rhymes are handed down from generation to generation. Songs, chants, finger plays, movement games, and hand-clapping rhymes are the stock in trade of infant, toddler, and preschool classrooms. Today's children often learn songs and chants in multiple languages; they may even learn bits of American Sign Language to accompany their singing.

When you've already changed two diapers, sung three songs, read four books, wiped five noses, served ten snacks, and helped a roomful of two- and three-year-olds learn to share, use their words, play with puppets, and keep their block buildings standing and it's only 11 A.M., you might be tempted to use the "playground time" to take a break. But well-trained early educators know that playground time isn't just a time for children to get fresh air and exercise, develop their physical skills, and let off steam. It's also prime time for language learning. Some of this learning, of course, occurs as children play with their friends and negotiate issues such as taking turns on the swings, deciding what to build in the sandbox, or engaging others in a game of chase, follow the leader, or "house." Much of it, however, occurs in conversations with a teacher. Here's an example:

Teacher (pushing Jamal on the swing): Is this high enough?
Jamal (age 3): No. I want to go higher!
Teacher: How high do you want to go?
Jamal: Up to the clouds.
Teacher: Do you think you could reach the clouds?
Jamal (reaching up): Yes.
Teacher: What do you think the clouds would feel like?
Jamal: Wet.
Teacher: Why do you think they're wet?
Jamal: 'Cause clouds make rain.
Teacher: It's not raining now. Do you think the clouds feel different when it's raining than when it's sunny?

As Jamal and his teacher continue to speculate on what clouds might feel like, they use words like "soft," "fluffy," "dry," "soggy," "full," "heavy," and "raindrops." This is what's called a "teachable moment." Jamal's teacher is genuinely curious about what Jamal thinks, and her curiosity enables her to uncover and build upon his interest in "touching" the clouds. Later, she'll show him how steam comes out of a kettle and how water condenses on a cold glass, and he'll begin to learn about vapor and condensation.

Whether the curriculum is planned in advance, grows out of the children's interests and questions, or combines the two approaches, it is likely to include language challenges. For example, a toddler teacher might introduce her class to the process of making play dough. As they "pour," "measure," "stir," "knead," "pound," "pinch," "roll," and "squeeze," they'll practice the words that describe these actions. In addition, they may learn words like "powder," "moist," "gooey," "lumpy," and "springy" from their teacher and peers as they talk together about how the dough feels at each stage.

Other language challenges might come in the form of objects or pictures that puzzle children or excite their curiosity. For example, children might arrive at school one morning and find a sweet potato held up by toothpicks in a glass of water. Those who recognize the vegetable might wonder why it is sitting in a glass of water rather than in a pot or on a plate. In a few days, they'll notice white, wiggly, hair-like things coming out of the bottom, and will struggle to find words to describe what they see. As they watch the plant grow, they'll learn words like "roots," "eye," "sprout," and "tuber."

For children with language delays or communication disorders, language challenges are essential. A speech therapist can induce a child to repeat or practice words, phrases, and sentences, but only someone who is with the child for many hours each day can elicit sufficient practice to promote mastery and to make language functional. A common technique used by special educators is to set up a challenge or barrier so that the child has to use words to get what she wants. For example, crackers may be placed on a high shelf or enclosed in a plastic jar. In order to get a snack, the child will have to say "I want crackers" or "Open the jar, please."

Whether working with children with special needs or with those who are developing typically, well-trained teachers "scaffold" children's learning by helping them to build on what they know. Just as an attuned parent can read a baby's cues and know when he has had enough stimulation or activity and when he is ready for more, so an adept teacher adjusts the level of challenge and novelty to keep children learning eagerly without undue frustration.

Let's listen as Kori, who teaches a group of three- and four-year-olds, about half of whom have identified special needs, works with Ben, a four-year-old with autism spectrum disorder and a limited vocabulary who is just learning to put words together. Kori takes advantage of the fact that Ben enjoys playing with her to give him practice with the words and sentence forms he knows and to extend his vocabulary:

Kori (playing with Ben in the house corner): Should we go to McDonald's?
Ben: I go ucDonald's.
Kori: What do you want to eat?
Ben: Eat.
Kori: Do you want a hamburger?
Ben: I want amberg.
Kori (handing Ben a plastic hamburger): Here's your hamburger. Do you want French fries?
Ben: I want ench ries.
Kori (handing Ben a clump of plastic French fries): Here are your French fries. Do you want anything else?
Ben: I want i-cream.
Kori (handing Ben an imaginary ice cream cone): Here's some ice cream. You better eat it fast before it melts.
Ben (after licking the imaginary ice cream cone): I eat i-cream.

Kori used a slightly different technique with Randy, whose more severe disorder makes it difficult for him to process questions. Noticing that Randy liked to play with a bowl and spoon and would imitate her actions and some of her speech, Kori gradually taught him, over a three-month period, how to make a pretend cake like the real ones that they made in the classroom. At first, they just poured in "flour" and "water" and mixed them together. Gradually, they added other imaginary ingredients and pretend actions: measuring sugar, cracking eggs, sprinkling drops of vanilla, pouring the batter into a pan, cooking it in the oven, slicing the cake. Each new addition to the routine added new words to Randy's repertoire, words that were reinforced by their connections to real cake-making experiences.

The Family Center, a birth to five program at Nova Southeastern University in Fort Lauderdale, FL, insists that "we don't teach reading." The school goes out of its way to explain to parents that what matters for young children is curiosity, enjoyment of words and stories, and engagement in purposeful play. Late readers, like late talkers, will usually catch up to their peers, as long as they have a strong language foundation to build on. Yet year after year, nearly every four-year-old at the Family Center can look at the class "chore board," read off the names of her classmates, and tell you which child is slated to do which classroom job. Many can pick up a beginning reader or a simple, repetitive book and read it on their own. How does this program do it?

The Family Center starts with some advantages: the school is on a university campus and most of the children come from highly educated families. Parent involvement is pervasive and begins early. There are classes for parents and older siblings when a new baby is expected. Parent/baby classes provide fun activities, friendship and support networks, and access to expert guidance for children under two and their families. Toddler and preschool programs, offered half day or full school day, involve parents as volunteers, decision makers, and planners, and as partners in teaching their children. The teachers are highly trained—most have master's degrees—and have been working together for years.

The school's homegrown, research-informed curriculum centers around five C's: critical thinking, concept development, communication skills, creative expression, and cooperation and social skills development. Language is paramount and literacy is pervasive. High-interest units engage children in all of the five C's, providing multiple opportunities for exploration and play, as well as for learning and practicing new words. Teachers are constantly asking open-ended questions and encouraging children to do the same. Children's interests, questions, preferences, and discoveries drive the curriculum.

The program doesn't need to "teach" reading because the children are immersed in it. In each of the classrooms, signs on the walls tell where toys and materials are kept, what the children are "studying about," whose job it is to feed the fish, and what to do when the bell rings for a fire drill. The reading corner is well stocked and inviting, with a large stuffed bear who loves to be read to. The writer's corner is a combination office and post office, complete with bills, envelopes, greeting cards, stamps, stationary, drawing and collage materials, bookmaking supplies, a message board, and a large mailbox. Reading and writing materials are accessible in other areas as well, in case the waiters wish to write down orders or total bills, the firefighters have to take a phone message, the builders need plans or assembly instructions, the pirates conspire to draw a treasure map, the scientists want to figure out what kind of bug they found or record measurements in their lab books, the dolls decide to send out invitations to their party, or the coach is asked to diagram a play. There's a listening corner where children can hear stories on tape and "read" along in the books if they want to. In the computer center, children can read and listen to stories, control animations, play learning games, and even print out their own books.

On a typical school day, a three-year-old will hear one or two books read, learn a new song or chant and repeat a few old favorites, look at a

book alone or with a friend, make a drawing or art project and watch as
the teacher writes her name and the caption she dictates, and help choose
or arrange pictures for a homemade book or a poster that tells the story
of a class experience. On the way home, she may point out the STOP sign
that's like the one on her school playground, or pick out the first letter of
her name on a license plate. Her parents may have a note from her teacher
or a book of her drawings to talk about at home. And of course, she'll
undoubtedly hear at least one bedtime story.

Lest you think these techniques are only for affluent children whose
parents are avid readers, come visit a Head Start program that is only
a few miles away from the Family Center. The program is located on a
Seminole reservation; all the children belong to the tribe and many of them
are cousins. All speak English; a few are also fluent in a native Seminole
tongue.

The Head Start program reflects a deliberate effort by the Seminole
tribe to prepare their children for success in a modern world, while also
reinvigorating their traditional culture and language. Traditional Seminole culture does not rely on the written word. Communication is often
nonverbal. Adults, especially women, do not traditionally talk much while
they work. Yet the tribe recognized that their children would have to be
both verbal and literate—in English.

The classrooms and program have been carefully designed to promote
conversation among the children and support emergent literacy, while
bringing in the Seminole culture and its Everglades environment. The
first thing you notice upon entering one of the classrooms is the large
mural, made by the children, showing a typical Everglades "river of grass"
environment, with a small island of dry land and trees. The children have
pasted cutouts of animals in the grass, water, trees, and sky, and will happily
show you the painted turtle, alligator, egret, heron, Everglades deer, and
anhinga. Instead of the usual house corner, there is a traditional Seminole
open-sided thatched hut, or Chicki, with a communal cooking fire pit,
traditional cooking implements, a doll-sized hammock, and an adjacent
fish pond where the boys catch magnetic fish that the girls cook for dinner.
A poster depicts the Seminole clans, with their animal totems; each child's
name is written under the clan she belongs to. Tribal elders visit on a
regular basis to share their language, traditional stories, and crafts with the
children.

The class we are visiting has a mixed group of twelve three- and four-
year-olds, with a teacher and an assistant. Last week they found a snake on
the playground, and now their teacher is helping them learn everything
they can about snakes. Two girls have set up a makeshift animal hospital

by covering a table with a sheet. Today's patients are a rubber snake, a stuffed cat, and an alligator puppet, and all of them need prescriptions for medication, which the vets write out with elaborate scribbles. At the art table, a group of children are making snakes by gluing buttons, scraps of paper and cloth, shells, and snippets of rickrack (zigzag trim used to decorate traditional Seminole clothing) onto snake-shaped tagboard cutouts. As they work, they consult a guide book filled with pictures of different kinds of snakes and try to represent their markings.

In a quiet corner, the teacher and three children are playing an animal lotto game, calling out the names of the animals and noting prominent features as they seek to match cards to the pictures on their boards. The children go on to make their own lotto game, copying snake pictures from the library books that their teacher has been sharing with them. Two children work side by side with the assistant teacher. One boy arranges figures on the flannel board to tell the story of their snake discovery. His friend and the assistant teacher listen appreciatively as he narrates the events. The second boy continues the story by drawing a picture, narrating as he draws. The picture gets fuller and fuller, with later events covering up earlier ones as more and more children come to see the snake. The teaching assistant listens closely and repeats his story for him. He asks her to help him label the final image: "We found a snake on the playground and everyone came to see it." He proudly writes the word "snake" himself, copying from a sign over the "snake house" that the children made with blocks a few days ago.

As they pursue their study of snakes, the children will also take advantage of the resources in their community. The tribe's storyteller will come in to share traditional animal folktales, teaching the children the chorus lines so that they can participate as the tales are told in the traditional singsong call and response manner. She'll leave behind story tapes, so the children can hear the stories over and over again and chant along if they like. An older brother will share his snakeskin collection; a parent will take the children on a nature walk and point out good places to look for snakes, turtles, and alligators. When the children's interest broadens to include other reptiles, they'll visit the alligator wrestling show put on for tourists and talk about the similarities and differences between alligators and snakes. Words like "reptile," "cold-blooded," "slither," "jaw," "bask," "active," "river bank," "snap," and "plunge" will become part of their vocabulary.

Like the Family Center children, the Seminole preschoolers are immersed in language and literacy. As they follow their interests, they learn new words and concepts. They use books as resources; they also learn from people and from direct experience. Writing and storytelling materials are always available to them, and they are encouraged to use them in many different ways for their own purposes. Their teacher supports their attempts to read and write by pointing out words and answering their questions about what the words "say," writing what they request—either as captions and labels or as models for them to copy, helping them to find information in books, and encouraging their early efforts—including pretend reading, picture stories, and scribbles. When these children get to school, they will be eager to learn how to read "for real." Their early experiences with language and print will provide a firm foundation for formal instruction.

Techniques for supporting language and literacy are of course only part of what infant, toddler, and preschool teachers need to learn. They also need to know how to keep children safe, prevent the spread of disease, set up the classroom or home in ways that minimize chaos and facilitate learning and exploration, comfort children who are upset, plan activities that will be fun for children and at the same time extend their knowledge, help children learn basic concepts such as colors and counting, help children learn to make friends and develop a positive sense of self, and teach skills ranging from putting on a coat to using a scissors. They need to know how to assess children's abilities and understandings in all developmental areas so that they can support them to take the next steps. Indeed, "sensitivity to individual children's current competence may be one reason for the links between developmental outcomes, positive caregiving behaviors, and formal professional education that is observed in empirical research."[5]

The good news is that there are many—though not enough—college and community college programs that teach early childhood teachers what they need to know. Resource and referral agencies, early childhood professional organizations, Head Start, the U.S. military child-care system, and many other organizations also provide intensive training. There is also a lot of evidence that teachers who have had such training put it into practice. That's no surprise it makes their jobs easier. A teacher who can prevent a temper tantrum will have a far less stressful day than one who has to pick up the pieces when one child's screams distress the others. A teacher who facilitates children's language is rewarded with their curiosity and insights and finds that keeping the group happily engaged becomes less and less of a challenge.

Research shows that the teacher's general education level also makes a difference. Presumably, teachers who have richer vocabularies themselves and who have developed habits of reflective thinking and questioning are more likely to use richer vocabularies with children, to ask open-ended questions and pose interesting communication challenges, and to know how to help children find the information they are seeking. But the problem remains: in public and private programs, there continues to be a shortage of well-trained, well-educated teachers. Prevailing rates of pay are simply not high enough to attract and hold enough qualified people. And training is in shortest supply for those whose job may be the most challenging, the nearly 50 percent of the child-care workforce that cares for children between nineteen and thirty-six months old,[6] the "terrible two's" who should be bursting into language.

Responding to the research on teacher education, the 1998 Head Start reauthorization legislation called for lead teachers to have two-year Associates degrees in early childhood and classroom assistants to earn Child Development Associates credentials (generally three college-level courses covering health and safety practices, learning environments, major areas of child development, positive guidance, working with families, and professionalism, with demonstrated competency). Some states have recently upped their requirements for teachers in licensed child-care centers, and many require bachelor's degrees of teachers in state-funded programs for four-year-olds. Indeed, *Eager to Learn: Educating Our Preschoolers*, the definitive report on the research on early childhood pedagogy produced by the National Academy of Sciences, proposes as its first recommendation that "each group of children in an early childhood education and care program be assigned a teacher who has a bachelor's degree with specialized education related to early childhood."[7]

In twenty-three states (as of Spring 2004), the T.E.A.C.H. Early Childhood Project[8] provides scholarships for early childhood educators and salary enhancements for those who successfully complete their course of study and agree to stay at their sponsoring work sites. Chapter 13 will explore how such programs can be expanded to assure an early childhood workforce that is prepared to provide children in their care with the language foundation they need.

6 You Don't Speak My Language

Young children need a "critical mass" of engaging and informative language input, along with lots of opportunities to "use their words" with adults and other children. What happens if the input and communication practice come in more than one language, as is increasingly the case for young children in the United States? What happens when the language a child learns in early childhood is not the language that he will use in school? The answers to these questions are complex—and fascinating. What we as a society do with these answers is affecting more and more of our children—including many of those whose families speak English.

One Child's Ordeal

Six-year-old Jeudry Sanchez spent much of his first day of school in tears. His family had recently moved to Massachusetts from Puerto Rico, and Jeudry spoke only Spanish. His teacher was speaking in English, as were the other children, and Jeudry was overwhelmed by the cacophony of unfamiliar words.

Jeudry's teacher could have mediated the transition for him in his own language—she was a former bilingual education teacher who had been born in Puerto Rico and spoke Spanish fluently. But this was Massachusetts in 2003, where a new state law forbade primary grade teachers from using languages other than English in their classrooms. Its aim, of course, is to get children from immigrant families to become fluent in English as rapidly as possible, but that didn't help Jeudry to cope with coming to a new school in a new country—a transition that can be challenging even without a language barrier.

Under the law, Jeudry's teacher was allowed only to offer a few words of comfort in Spanish. She could not use it for teaching or for explaining procedures. This put her at a severe disadvantage in teaching children like Jeudry, for she could not build upon—nor even adequately assess—the knowledge and interests that they brought to school. Fortunately, she was able to pair Jeudry with a Spanish-speaking child whose English was strong enough to follow her lessons and who could help Jeudry understand what he was supposed to do.[1]

Families' Dilemmas

Throughout the United States, children even younger than Jeudry experience similar challenges every day, as they enter classrooms or family child-care settings where their language is not spoken. In many cases, their parents have no choice: they need to work and there are no appropriate child care or early education programs in their community where their child can learn in her home language.

When they have a choice, some families opt for places where teachers and children speak their home language, either because they want their child to learn or maintain the language, or because they believe that he will be happier and more successful in a place where he can "use his words," where they can communicate easily with his teachers, and where adults and children will understand and value his culture. Other parents reason that the sooner their children learn English the better off they will be. They place their young ones in English-speaking settings, and may even use English at home in addition to or instead of their home language. Some of these parents limit their conversations with their babies and young children, under the misconception that hearing their home language will interfere with their child's ability to learn English. Still others search far and wide for settings where their children can learn two languages simultaneously.

Conscientious parents and policy makers who study the research will not find a simple answer as to whether to place their young non-English-speaking children in settings where English is the dominant language or to seek out settings where most of the communication and learning occurs in their home language. The child's age and temperament, his vocabulary and communicative skills in his home language, the "match" of what the setting offers with the child's interests and developmental capabilities, and the quality of the relationships and of the language-related teaching that the child experiences all play critical roles in the speed and depth of children's bilingual learning.[2]

In addition, parents must consider their options for the next step—will their child be able to continue learning in his home language as he adds a second one, or will he be forced to make an abrupt transition? What level of English fluency will be required in order to fully participate in his next school? Will supports be available to help him make the transition? Will his literacy and ongoing learning in his home language be supported, either in school or in an after-school program? In their community, will their child receive better content instruction in bilingual education programs or in English-speaking classrooms?

Here is what we know:

- *Young children who hear and converse in two languages from birth learn both, and rarely confuse them, although they may "borrow" words or phrases from their other language in order to better express their meaning.* Children who hear, babble, and ultimately converse in more than one language as infants are not learning a second language—they are learning two (or more) first languages. Unlike second language learners, they store both in the same areas of their brains.[3]
- *Children who have a firm foundation in one language can build on that knowledge as they learn a second.* Children who have a rich vocabulary in their home language will also have learned a great deal of content that is not language-specific and will have developed a range of strategies for gaining new information. Children who are already good at connecting with others, sharing thoughts and feelings, and using inner language to control their behavior and talk themselves through problems do not need to relearn these skills as they add a new language to their repertoire. They bring these resources to their early childhood classrooms, and to the task of learning a second language.[4]
- *Children learn language from their peers as well as from adults; this is especially true for children three and older.* In Hart and Risley's study,[5] parents provided children with their key language inputs during the first two years, and both the quality and quantity of these inputs made a lasting difference. As the children began to talk, parents were key conversation partners. However, as the children neared their third birthdays, they more frequently sought out other conversation partners and also played more independently, using language to talk to their toys or accompany their play. Preschool play depends upon verbal interaction; children are highly motivated to use the language of their peers as they act out pretend play scenarios together.
- *Children need a basic vocabulary of about 5,000 words in order to learn to read easily.*[6] With appropriately rich early language input and conversational practice, children typically learn at least 5,000 words in their first language by the time they are five, and this oral language foundation prepares them for reading. Children who learn to read in another language can apply their knowledge to English words and use reading as a tool to support their English learning.[7] Children who are learning

to read for the first time in a language in which they are not fluent face several obstacles: they may not know the meaning of all of the words they are reading, they may not have sufficient experience with the sounds of the language to recognize common patterns of symbol/sound correspondence, they may not have sufficient fluency with grammar and common usage to recognize which of several guesses make sense in a particular context, and they will likely lack an intuitive understanding of word parts and word formation patterns that can help them to deduce the alphabetic principle and to rapidly analyze and decode new words.

• *Bilingual education programs have a mixed track record, but strong programs that support children in their home languages* CAN *help them make an effective transition to schooling in a second language.* In the United States, we have tried a variety of approaches to educating children who are not fluent in English when they enter an English-dominant school, including immersing English learners in English-only classes with little or no support, pulling children out for ESL instruction or tutoring until they achieve basic fluency, teaching children content in their home language as they learn English, grouping children with peers who speak their home language, separating children from same-language peers in order to encourage English, and discouraging children from speaking anything but English. The results have been mixed.[8] However, a study commissioned by the U.S. Department of Education found that children in programs that provide native-language content instruction for at least 40 percent of the school day through the fifth grade do better in math and English-language skills than children in English immersion or shorter-duration bilingual programs.[9] This research review has convinced some previously skeptical educators of the value of teaching children content—including reading—in their home language and in English until they have become proficient in both languages.[10]

In countries where most village children speak a native language at home and the official language at school, letting children adapt to the school situation before introducing the new language has proven to be a more effective approach than an abrupt transition. Similarly, a transitional summer program for entering kindergarteners who have spent their early years in the care of non-English-speaking grandparents is proving to be an effective support for English learners in several Massachusetts communities.[11]

Dual immersions, or bilingual/bicultural programs, have been among the most effective[12] and are gaining in popularity in the United States and around the world. In these programs, half of the students and teachers are native speakers of one language and half are native speakers of a second. Generally, half of the day is spent learning in one language and half in the other, and all of the children benefit.

- *Children who learn a language before the age of six or seven are likely to learn both its sound system and grammar as native speakers; those who learn later sometimes have continuing difficulties with pronunciation and with some grammatical forms. However, children who begin instruction or immersion in their second language earlier in their school careers do not necessarily master the language more fully or quickly than children who are exposed to it later, with the exception of its sound system.* Younger children have an advantage in that they have less of the language to learn in order to catch up with peers who learned it as a first language and a longer time in which to practice and learn in the new language; older children, however, are able to build upon general knowledge and communication skills gained in their first language, analyze grammatical forms and patterns, and, in many cases, read the new language before they are verbally fluent and learn new vocabulary through reading.[13]

Parents who do not speak fluent English at home and who want their children to do well in U.S. schools are therefore faced with a dilemma: do they maximize their child's chances for acquiring rich vocabulary, expressive confidence, and breadth and depth of knowledge in their home language, or do they prepare them to enter English-speaking classrooms by challenging them to learn English during their preschool years?

As the United States becomes more linguistically diverse, more and more families face this dilemma. In Los Angeles today, people from 100 different ethnic groups speak 70 different languages.[14] Nineteen percent of U.S. children under eighteen lived with at least one foreign-born parent in 2001, and, although this statistic is not broken down by age, the percentage was higher among the youngest children. Approximately 20 percent of all U.S. births in 2000 were to women who identified themselves as Hispanic, although they were not necessarily Spanish speakers. (Studies indicate that approximately a third of Latinos speak only or mainly Spanish, a third speak only English, and a third are bilingual.[15])

If demographers' predictions are born out, by 2010 one third of our nation's children will live in four states—California, Florida, New York, and Texas—where the majority of children will belong to groups that are today considered ethnic minorities.[16] By 2050, almost half of the residents of the United States will be non-white, and one third will be of Latino or Asian descent.[17] As more and more Americans are born into families whose preferred language is not English, we will need to develop early education programs that can meet their needs for a firm language foundation.

Educating Young Children in Mixed-Language Classrooms

Clearly, children who are not comfortably fluent in the language of play and instruction present a challenge for their preschool and elementary school teachers. Such children may be misdiagnosed as language impaired or developmentally delayed. On the other hand, problems that could benefit from early intervention may be overlooked because they are mistakenly attributed to their difficulties with a second language.[18] More important, when their teachers are not skilled at facilitating their participation, the children can miss out on important opportunities for play and learning that rely on linguistic input and communication.

Young children entering a preschool program where their language isn't widely used generally go through several stages as they learn the language of the classroom.[19] At first, they may simply speak their own language, not realizing that they are not being understood. They then may enter a period of silence, where they gather information about the new language but do not yet use it. Toddlers may babble the new sounds to themselves, just as they babbled the sounds of their home language, but preschoolers are usually too aware of social norms to use the new language in a noncommunicative way. During the "silent" phase, they are likely to rely on nonverbal communication, sometimes using words in their own language for emphasis or approximating words, phrases, and inflections of the new language as they try to make their meaning clear.

Before long, most young children will begin to pick up and repeat key words and stock phrases in the new language. They may use them as one-word labels and requests, or string two or three together in a kind of tele-graphic speech, similar to a toddler's early sentences in his first language. At times, they may incorporate words and phrases from their home lan-guages, or substitute rough approximations when they can't find the right words. At this stage they almost always get the word order right, but prepo-sitions, conjunctions, pronouns, and grammatical markers such as plural and past tense endings are more elusive. As teachers and peers respond to and expand their utterances, children begin to pick up the grammar of the new language and to use it with increasing confidence.

Each child, of course, brings a unique temperament, learning style, and set of prior skills and interests to the task of learning a new language.

Successful teachers connect with each child, bring out and build upon her strengths, and find ways to encourage and answer her questions—whatever language or nonverbal communication system she uses to ask them.

Well-prepared preschool teachers know how to support second language learners in all aspects of their development. They set up opportunities for children to demonstrate their prior knowledge and acquire new knowledge nonverbally—through drawing, block building, puzzles and games, movement activities, and pretend play. They are also adept at using techniques that facilitate rich vocabulary, expressive fluency, and emergent literacy in a child's first language, and adapting these techniques to benefit second language learners in a mixed-language setting.

- They recognize the cognitive and social–emotional strengths that children have developed through their experiences with their home language, and see their knowledge of two languages as an asset for the individual child and for the class as a whole.
- They help children learn language by talking with them a lot—providing running commentary on what they and the children are doing, encouraging children to repeat new words and to "use their words" (in both their home language and English), showing interest in what children have to say, and responding with words and appropriate clarifying gestures to children's verbal and nonverbal questions.
- They expand and elaborate the children's comments, providing good models without actually correcting grammar, just as they would for toddlers learning their first language and for preschoolers who still typically struggle with the pronunciation of certain words and with exceptions to the grammatical regularities that they have just recently mastered.
- They emphasize key words through repetition and highlight features of language, such as word endings and distinctions among similar sounds, that English learners may not hear if they are not salient in their home language. (Parentese, the way in which adults around the world tend to speak to their babies, uses repetition and emphasis in similar ways.)
- They focus on high-interest vocabulary for all children, and help them appreciate the component parts of words.
- They read frequently to children in small groups and one-on-one, choosing books carefully and using shared reading techniques that highlight new vocabulary and sentence patterns, encourage the children to chime in with repeated or predictable text, and engage the children in conversation about the story and the pictures.
- They help children make connections between written and spoken words—in both of their languages.

- They use carefully worded questions to scaffold children's learning, pushing them to draw upon prior knowledge and then go just a bit beyond what they already know and can do.
- They actively include second language learners in teacher-led discussions, facilitate their inclusion in child-centered play and exploration, and help children who do not share their linguistic background to appreciate and enjoy their contributions.
- They encourage interactions among children, especially pretend play, providing ample opportunities for children to learn and practice new words.
- They take steps to ensure that all children are comfortable in their classroom and that their development is nurtured in all domains. When possible, they use bilingual classroom aides and other children to translate, build bridges, and provide reassurance.
- They consult with each child's parents, as well as with professionals who speak her language and can explain nuances of behavior and culture-specific communication patterns.
- They make extensive use of songs, nursery rhymes, finger plays, and movement games for teaching children each other's languages.
- They bring in books and other materials in each child's home language, and, with the help of parents and other community members, incorporate her home language and culture into the curriculum for the group as a whole.
- They make a point of learning the child's language themselves, and of including words in that language in classroom conversations, displays, and play materials.

Unfortunately, too few of our preschool teachers, and even fewer of the teachers of the one- and two-year-olds who may be learning two languages simultaneously, have the level of preparation needed to employ such techniques consistently and effectively.

Losing Language

One consequence of the lack of preparation of people who work with young children is that some children may not get the input and conversational practice they need to develop a firm foundation—in any language. Another is that without the support of the teachers and peers with whom they are spending a significant amount of their time, children's first language skills may stagnate or diminish as they try to learn a second language. Scholars refer to this as "subtractive bilingualism"—the loss of the first language.

Our language is so intertwined with the way we name and know the world, the way we think and think of ourselves, as well as the ways in which we communicate with others, that it is hard for most of us to imagine "losing" our native languages. Learning a second language should mean just that—adding a new language to one's repertoire. However, language, like the neural connections in our brains, is strengthened with use and can atrophy with disuse.

For many children in the United States today, learning a new language can mean the gradual and sometimes total replacement of their first one, often within a few years.[20] As their schoolmates, neighborhood friends, and perhaps even their parents are increasingly reliant upon English, they find fewer and fewer occasions to use their native language. Unless they are spending a fair amount of time with grandparents or others who prefer their native tongue, or are enrolled in native-language classes to advance their literacy and cultural knowledge, they are likely to retain only the rudiments of the language—the basic grammar and conversational vocabulary they acquired as young children, or, quite often, only a few key words and phrases and well-rehearsed songs or sayings. Even in communities where many children speak their native language, children may pick up subtle and not-so-subtle messages that their language is not the language of learning and that their way of speaking is not the path to success. They may choose to speak English, even though this means cutting ties with family and culture.[21]

Because language is so intimately connected with culture and identity, the consequences of devaluing a child's home language can be devastating. In his autobiography, *Always Running*, Luis Rodriguez describes the linguistic challenges he faced as a Chicano growing up in Los Angeles in the 1950s and 1960s. A gifted child, he reached adolescence having repeatedly failed in school but also showing impressive talent in both visual art and poetry, along with striking resilience and leadership ability.

As he worked with teachers to prepare his writings for a national contest, Luis reflected on his linguistic abilities and disabilities:

> I had fallen through the chasm between two languages. The Spanish had been beaten out of me in the early years of school—and I didn't learn English very well either.
>
> This was the predicament of many Chicanos.
>
> We could almost be called incommunicable, except we remained lucid; we got over what we felt, sensed and understood. Sometimes we rearranged words, created new meanings and structures—even a new vocabulary. Often our everyday talk blazed with poetry.

Our expressive powers were strong and vibrant. If this could be nurtured, if the language skills could be developed on top of this, we could break through any communication barrier. We needed to obtain victories in language, built on an infrastructure of self-worth.

But we were often defeated from the start.[22]

Today, most adults working with young children know better than to "beat out" their native languages. We have seen the disastrous consequences of Bureau of Indian Affairs assimilation efforts earlier in this century. In order to promote "assimilation," children were removed from their homes and sent to boarding schools where their tribal languages were forbidden. Many returned as adolescents to find that they belonged neither on or off their reservations. Their elders called them "the lost generation." The gap that they left in the fabric of their communities contributed to the loss of tribal languages and traditions.

The practice of literally beating children in order to correct their speech is no longer accepted. Early childhood teachers are mandated child abuse reporters, and most receive some training in recognizing signs of physical abuse. Their profession considers even mild spanking to be taboo (as well as ineffective) in an early childhood classroom, even for children whose families use physical discipline. And of course, early childhood teachers are taught to value each child and each family—not to punish children for who they are.

Today, too, we realize that we live in a global economy, where the ability to speak more than one language fluently is an important economic asset. Depriving children of opportunities to practice a language and improve their proficiency and then trying to reteach it to them as a high school course seems like a waste of time. And hearing new languages from peers— perhaps even learning some basic vocabulary—benefits all children, even if they won't have an opportunity to study those languages until they are older.

Still, too often, children pick up messages that their way of speaking is not valued in school or in the larger society. Whether it is their language or their dialect, their first-language-influenced pronunciation or their regional accent, their carryover of phrases and grammatical markers from their first language or the grammatical but nonstandard usage of their English dialect, children's ways of speaking are too often misinterpreted and stereotyped as signs of lesser knowledge or lesser intelligence.[23] These pressures lead some children to hide or reject their linguistic backgrounds, while others may be inappropriately held back in their academic progress because they don't "talk right." Some children become adept at code-switching, speaking one way at home and in their linguistic community and another way at school and in the community at large.

Diversity in the Workforce

The increasing diversity of the young child population is accompanied by increasing diversity among their teachers, child-care workers, and nannies. This is in many ways a good thing: it means that families who want their children to be cared for and taught by adults who can nurture their home language learning and cultural traditions can find such adults in their communities. It means that teachers of increasingly diverse classes can find colleagues who can support their students in their home languages, translate with children and parents, explain cultural differences, and help them to avoid misunderstandings and correct miscommunications. It means that children of many backgrounds can have the opportunity to learn from adults of many backgrounds.

In the best early education and family support programs, children reap the benefits of a diverse early childhood workforce and realize the vision set forth by the Early Childhood Equity Alliance.

We envision a world where ALL children and families

- feel that they belong,
- have all aspects of their identity affirmed,
- have the resources they need to thrive,
- eagerly learn from each other across cultural and other differences,
- actively address biased behavior through open communication and willingness to grow, and
- work together to challenge and change institutionalized forms of bias.[24]

But the prevalence of close-to-poverty wages in the child-care field and the dearth of opportunities for educational advancement for those not fluent in English means that diversity tends to be greatest in the poorest paid and least trained sectors of the field. English language learners are most likely to work as nannies or caregivers for babies, as aides in center-based classrooms, as unlicensed family child-care providers, and as teachers or licensed providers where licensing requirements are lax. Some, of course, have been well trained to work with young children in their home countries—where publicly supported early childhood programs may be more prevalent and may demand higher credentials than those in the United States. Many, however, have low levels of education and literacy in their home languages and little, if any, early childhood professional training.

Child-care centers on tight budgets, unable to afford or retain staff with strong credentials, hire the best of the available applicants. This often means overlooking language. A common compromise in English-only settings is to place teachers who are English learners with preverbal children, reasoning that their limited vocabulary or difficulties reading English aloud will be less of a handicap than it would be with older children. This means, of course, that babies and toddlers are likely to hear less language, with less varied vocabulary, than if their caregivers spoke to them in a language in which they were comfortable.

This problem can be equally acute for parents seeking to hire nannies. Like Zoë Baird, President Clinton's first choice for attorney general, they may be unable to find an appropriate person to take the job who is not a recent immigrant, either legal or undocumented. Communication between the parents and the nanny may be awkward at first if they are not completely fluent in each other's language, but they will usually share enough words to make themselves understood. The child, however, needs more from his caregiver, especially if they are together for long periods of time. He needs a critical mass of rich language input and engaged conversation— and this may not be forthcoming in either language. Isolated from her own linguistic community, the nanny may use less and less of her home language as she speaks to the child in her emergent English. She may use her home language when she encounters a fellow immigrant, but the child in her charge is likely to be left out of those conversations.

On the other hand, some children are lucky enough to learn two languages—one from their caregiver and one from their parents and other family and community members. This is most likely to occur, of course, when the caregiver is a relative or family friend, or when the parents can at least speak the caregiver's language and reinforce her lessons.

Benefits of Bilingualism

For young children lucky enough to learn two languages well, bilingualism confers unique cognitive and social advantages. Children who learn two languages early in life become aware early on that the same thing can be said in different ways. They gain extensive practice in adapting their communication to the context and to the listener; often they are challenged to shift rapidly from one language to another when a new person enters the conversation or when they and their conversation partners move into a setting where a different language dominates.

Researchers have discovered an interesting phenomenon: apparently coping with the challenge of speaking two languages makes children more flexible in their thinking[25] and improves their scores on verbal and non-verbal IQ tests! In one study, researchers tested 123 kindergarteners and first graders in Puerto Rico. They found a positive relationship between the extent of children's bilingualism and their scores on a nonverbal intelligence test.[26] Studies of English-speaking Canadian children found that those who learned more French in their French-immersion elementary school classrooms made greater gains in IQ than classmates whose French language skills were less advanced.[27] Other studies found that bilingual teens used more sophisticated learning strategies than their monolingual peers.[28]

Perhaps as we both become and participate in a more global community, the United States will commit to catching up with our trading partners and competitors by educating our children in more than one language. We will provide a strong language and literacy foundation in early childhood and sustain it with later schooling. The graduates of our school systems will be able to express and appreciate complex concepts, subtle shades of meaning, technical information, and poetic possibilities in at least two languages.

Today, too many of our children are not acquiring this level of fluency and literacy in even one language, let alone in two or three. Whether they have missed the opportunity to build a strong foundation in their native language, shifted so abruptly from one language to another that they can't follow daily lessons, or "lost" their home language without fully replacing it, they start school behind and have difficulty catching up. Part II—The Quiet Crisis—examines the factors that are placing them at such an acute disadvantage.

Part II

The Quiet Crisis

7 The State of Early Care and Education in the United States

We've seen how early language learning is shaped by daily experience, and how the quality of that experience sets the stage for later achievements or difficulties. But what level of quality is a typical child likely to encounter on a daily basis? How likely is she to have experiences that are more like Jack's than like Jill's? How likely is it that the adults she spends time with will engage her in frequent conversations that hold her interest, nourish her curiosity, and build her communication repertoire? How serious are the gaps between what we would hope would be the norm for all children and what significant percentages of our children are experiencing today?

If you're fortunate enough to be born into a well-off, well-educated, child-focused family, you can get an excellent early education in the United States. As a baby, you might stay home with your mom, dad, or grandparent, who receives support in taking care of you from an array of service professionals and information providers, including nurses, pediatricians, lactation consultants, and child development experts. Or you may have a highly educated nanny who becomes a part of your family, staying with you throughout your early childhood as a partner to your parents. At some point during your first or second year, you might join a playgroup, Baby and Me class, drop-in program, or toddler story hour, where you get to interact with other kids, play with new toys, and learn songs and games while your parent or caretaker compares notes with the other adults and learns new techniques for helping you learn.

When your family decides that it's time for you to be with other kids in a more stimulating environment, they find you an excellent preschool program. Whether their choice is a child-care center or a family child-care home, it is run by a well-educated professional who has made sure that the home or program has earned national accreditation in recognition of its excellence. Your teacher(s) are experienced and reassuring; they provide support for your family as well as for you. Every day, your teachers play, read, sing, and talk directly with you. They help you to make friends, to learn how things work, to do things for yourself, and to practice new skills. They set up challenges for you and delight in your accomplishments. Your parents beam with pride as your teachers keep them up to date on your rapid learning.

Of course, you get plenty of rich language input and conversation practice. Your teachers are interested in what you want to know and what you have to say. They encourage your questions and pretend play, and, in the spirit of the game or investigation, introduce new words and ideas that make the play more fun and help you extend your knowledge. As your language becomes more sophisticated, they help you use it to carry on conversations, initiate friendships, solve problems, and tell stories.

If your family is very poor, and also very persistent or very lucky, you might get similar, high quality early experiences as part of an Early Head Start Program, or through a comprehensive early education and family support program supported with public or foundation funds or run by a university. Your state or city may have special programs to support your parents as your "first teachers" or to provide you with preschool education.

If you are born in France or Scandinavia or almost any developed country outside of the United States, you're likely to get something like the above experience.[1] Paid family leave will enable either of your parents to stay home with you for at least your first few months. When your parents are ready to entrust your care to others, they will quite likely be able to take advantage of public programs, housed in spaces specially designed for young children, with teachers or baby nurses who are well educated and well supported. In France, for example, nurses staff the crèches (nurseries) for children under three and teachers staff the ecoles maternelles (preschools) for three- to five-year-olds. Preschool teachers receive the same level of training and compensation as do elementary school teachers. About a third of the children, including most of those in districts with large poor or immigrant populations, enter the ecoles maternelles at two; the rest enter at three. Virtually all French preschoolers take advantage of these programs, whether or not their mothers are in the workforce.[2] A similar system prevails in the urban areas of South Africa, where children under three attend crèches (staffed by well-educated teachers), and three- to five-year-olds attend public preschools.

But what if you're born in the United States, to a family that is neither rich and educationally sophisticated nor poor enough to be eligible for special supports? What are your chances of getting good quality care during your early years? What are your chances of partaking of a steady diet of mind-expanding conversation when you are two, three, and four years old?

Unfortunately, recent studies of the quality of care our children are receiving are not very reassuring. Indeed, for children between one and three, the results of these studies are truly frightening.

Child-Care Programs

More than two thirds of U.S. children under five have both their parents, or their only parent, in the workforce. About a quarter of these are cared for by a parent who takes the child to work (as Jill's mother did) or works from home while caring for the child, or by parents who work opposite shifts. The rest are cared for by relatives or paid caregivers, in centers or homes, typically for more than thirty hours a week.[3] Thus, no more than half of the young children in the United States are likely to be getting the majority of their language input and practice from their parents. The rest are getting—or should be getting—a significant percentage from nonparental caregivers. Whether or not they are getting what they need depends upon the quality of their child-care settings and of their relationships with their caregivers.

The largest recent study of child-care quality, the *Cost, Quality, and Child Outcome Study*,[4] was published in 1995. In this study, child development professionals rated a representative sample of child-care centers in four states, using a nationally validated observation scale. *For children under three, only one center in twelve provided* "developmentally appropriate" care—*care that was good enough to promote strong language development.* Forty percent of the classrooms for children under three were considered so poor that they endangered children's health and safety! For children between three and five, the results were slightly better. Only 10 percent of the classrooms were rated poor; and 24 percent were good or excellent. Still, *nearly two thirds were rated "mediocre," or "minimally adequate."*

These "mediocre" classrooms tended to fall down in precisely the areas that matter most for language development: interaction among children and between children and adults, facilitation of language and reasoning, and the availability and quality of learning activities. According to one of the study's principal investigators,

> children in facilities rated "minimally adequate" are probably bored a good deal of the time, many of them learning all too soon to just put up with, if not actively dislike, school. Children in facilities rated "good" are in care that is considerate of their feelings, and that keeps them interested, and that allows them to enjoy themselves while learning. Such care is not, as some conservative critics claim, a lavish indulgence.[5]

Keeping children interested does not mean keeping them constantly on the go. Good programs provide a varied pace that is comfortable for each child. That is why the whole quality picture matters. Good programs provide times and spaces for both quiet and active play. They accommodate individual differences and support all areas of development, including health and nutrition. They keep small groups of children together, with the same teachers, and provide enough relaxed, unprogrammed time for close relationships to develop and for authentic, spontaneous conversations to occur throughout each day. They are places where both adults and children want to be.

Let's visit some centers to see how these differences in quality look from a three-year-old's point of view and the implications they are likely to have for his language development:

- Lamont spends most of his weekdays at church, sitting on the floor with twenty other kids and listening to the teacher read stories from her big book. Once in a while, she shows them a picture. Lamont doesn't know a lot of the words, and the teacher never stops to explain them, so he has a hard time following the stories. Sometimes, the teacher gives each child a piece of paper and a crayon and shows the children how to copy their letters. Lamont isn't sure what letters are for, but he tries to make his squiggles look good. Most of the time, the teacher talks to the group as a whole. She almost never talks to Lamont, unless he's doing something "bad" like standing up when he's supposed to be sitting down. Lamont, who has just learned to speak in short sentences, has few opportunities to use his new words.

- Rachel goes to a nice school with nice toys. Each morning, she gets to play with the dolls and dress-ups while they wait for all of the children to arrive. After morning circle and reading time, the children do art projects, play on the playground, sing songs, and play learning games. Rachel has learned to name all of the animals in the toy farm and all of the trucks in the puzzles. She can sing several songs all by herself, and even knows the motions to "Itsy, Bitsy Spider" and "Head, Shoulders, Knees, and Toes." She talks with her friends when they play house in the morning, but her teachers are too busy organizing activities to talk just with Rachel.

- James storms into preschool each day, full of energy, stories, and questions. Usually, he can't wait to tell his teacher about something he saw on the way to school. She listens patiently and asks James questions that help him add more information to his story. James's favorite game at school is ambulance driver. He likes to jump into the driver's seat, turn on the ignition, and sound the siren as he races to an accident scene, puts the patient on a stretcher, and zooms through traffic to the hospital. Although he's only just turned three, he knows all of those big words because his teacher reads him stories about emergency workers and talks with the children about the words and pictures. When James and his buddies play their ambulance game, their teacher helps out by suggesting new ideas and props. Sometimes, she even calls for the ambulance herself and urges the EMT's to hurry up.

Lamont, Rachel, and James all attended the same child-care center, but at different times. The younger ones were luckier; a local foundation had teamed up with a university to improve the quality of child-care programs in their neighborhood. At first, the center staff had been skeptical that the offers of help were real. Gradually, however, the donations of toys, books, and furniture and the helpful practical suggestions won them over. The center director joined a professional group, and learned how other directors managed the problems of providing quality early education on a shoestring. Teachers took classes at the university and worked with mentors who helped them apply what they were learning in their classrooms. After three years of intensive work and gradual improvement, the center was providing a good quality program and was ready to apply for national accreditation.

But centers serve only about a third of the young children while they are not being cared for by their parents. What about family child-care homes, nannies, neighbors, and relatives? Do they do a better job with infants, toddlers, and preschoolers?

Apparently not. Licensed family child-care homes tend to provide care on a par with that of centers; unregulated family child-care homes tend to provide care that is considerably inferior. The "Study of Children in Family Child Care and Relative Care,"[6] completed in 1995, found that *only 9 percent of the home child-care settings rated in three states were providing good quality care*. Fifty-six percent were providing mediocre, or merely custodial, care, and 35 percent were providing care that was so poor as to place children's health, safety, and development at risk. Only 13 percent of the regulated family child-care homes in the study were providing care this poor, but 56 percent of the unregulated family child-care homes and 69 percent of the relative caregivers fell into this category.

Similarly alarming results were reported in the "NICHD Study of Early Child Care and Youth Development," which is following 1,300 children in ten different locations from birth into middle childhood. This study looked at children who were in many different settings and assessed the quality of their interaction with the adults who were responsible for their care. The researchers found that *only about a third of the three-year-olds that they observed in centers and family child-care homes had caregivers for whom "positive caregiving" was "somewhat characteristic" or "highly characteristic."* At least while they were being observed, grandparents, other relatives, and hired in-home caregivers in this study tended to do a somewhat better job. Still, by the time the children were three, "positive caregiving" was "somewhat characteristic" or "highly characteristic" of fewer than half of their in-home or relative caregivers.[7]

The problem isn't that the teachers, caregivers, and baby-sitters don't care. It's that keeping a young child productively engaged is demanding work, and keeping a group of them happy and learning requires some special skills. Most of the people who are doing this work are doing it with inadequate training and little support. Even those who have the training and are doing an excellent job are generally paid so little that it is hard for them to stay in the field.

Indeed, according to the Bureau of Labor Statistics, "preschool teachers" (who work primarily in part-day programs with an educational focus and usually have some college-level preparation) earned an average of $9.43/hour in 1999. That was less than the average hourly wage of bus drivers ($12.72) or animal trainers ($12.39) and less than half of that of kindergarten teachers ($24.51). For "child-care workers" (who work as teaching assistants, caregivers of infants and toddlers, and often as teachers in full-day programs), the average hourly wage was only $7.42, roughly comparable to the average wage for parking lot attendants ($7.38.)! Family child-care providers, on average, earned only $4.82/hour, considerably less than the 1999 minimum wage![8]

Since 1999, efforts to address the situation have resulted in modest improvement in some states and localities. These efforts include drives to unionize child-care workers (and often parents and center directors as well), public programs that provide bonuses for those who meet education requirements and agree to stay in the field, improvements in rates paid to publicly supported providers, and increased public funds for programs that meet higher standards of quality.

Overall, however, the picture remains bleak. In 2003, the Bureau of Labor Statistics reported a mean hourly wage for child-care workers of just $8.37, essentially the same as that for parking lot attendants. Preschool teachers averaged $10.75, just slightly less than bellhops![9] In the words of a jingle popularized by the Center for the Childcare Workforce's *Worthy Wage* Campaign,[10] "parents can't afford to pay; teachers can't afford to stay."

Today, annual turnover rates for child-care teachers and assistants, as well as for family child-care providers, generally range between 30 and 40 percent.[11] Turnover creates problems for children and parents, of course, as it is hard to develop relationships with a changing cast of characters. Changing teachers can be especially stressful for toddlers who are just learning to speak, as a new teacher is likely to have difficulty understanding what they are trying to say. High rates of turnover are equally damaging to the quality of programs, causing disruptions, extra expenses for substitutes and recruitment, and challenges in terms of training and team-building.

That child-care programs in the United States are as good as they are is a tribute to the dedicated professionals who care enough about young children to work for low wages and to seek out the education and training they need. Many programs are excellent, and many children flourish. But families across the economic spectrum, especially those who are neither wealthy nor very poor, must look hard to find these excellent programs. Many have little choice but to entrust their children to programs and providers who will only partially meet the children's needs for enriching and engaging conversation during their prime time for language learning.

For low-income families, whose children stand to gain the most from high quality programs, the problem is especially acute.[12] Yes, some of these families can enroll their children in top-notch programs such as Head Start, in university-based demonstration projects, or in other special programs supported by state, local, foundation, or corporate investments. Others can use child-care subsidies to help them purchase high quality care in licensed or even accredited facilities. In a few states and communities, they can enroll their four-year-olds in public programs that provide all children in the community with a strong prekindergarten education. However, most must purchase care on the open market, with subsidies that pay far less than the cost of quality care or with no subsidies at all. Affordable care that is good or even mediocre tends to be in short supply, especially for infants and toddlers.

With such restricted choices, it is no surprise that many families make economic sacrifices or work opposite shifts so that a parent can be home with the children, especially during the first year or two.[13]

Children at Home

Do the children cared for exclusively by their parents, or nearly so, fare better than those whose families rely on paid child care or care by relatives? Obviously, some of them do. But for too many children growing up today, the care that their parents provide—without any training or support and without the partnership of teachers or child-care providers—will not provide the rich, intellectually challenging conversations needed to prime them for school success.

The best data available comparing young children who are primarily cared for by their parents with those who are involved in child-care programs or other types of nonparental care comes from the NICHD Study. The team has reported results from the first three years:

> In terms of cognitive and language development [as measured at age 3], researchers found no benefit for children in exclusive care by their mother. Among children in care for more than 10 hours per week, those in center care, and to a lesser extent, those in child care homes, performed better on cognitive and language measures than children in other types of care, when the quality of the care giver–child interaction was taken into account.[14]

In other words, it seems that young children who are at home with a parent today have similar chances of getting—or not getting—good support for their language learning as those who are spending their days in child care settings.

This result may seem counterintuitive to adults who grew up with their mothers at home and, often, with other extended family members nearby. Surely, parents are in the best position to understand their children's feelings and their first attempts at language, to know and build on their children's interests, and to provide the loving relationships and conversational opportunities that sustain language learning.

Yes, but not always. Many parents do not realize how much learning very young children are capable of. Many do not know the importance of talking with their young children, or do not talk with them very much. The importance of books and storytelling as springboards for conversation is just beginning to be widely realized. In fact, slightly fewer than half of the parents in a national study of the kindergarten class of 1998–1999 reported that a family member read or sang to their children on a daily basis.[15] In most neighborhoods, there is no longer a critical mass of mothers and grandmothers who are home during the day and can pass on folk wisdom, share child-care chores and fun activities, and learn together. Every parent needs and deserves support.

For some children, early education programs provide an essential supplement to the language experience they receive at home. For the nearly one fifth of young children whose families' incomes are close to or below the poverty line, there is substantial evidence that preschool programs make a tremendous difference in later educational outcomes.[16] Although low quality programs can exacerbate the effects of a difficult home environment, poor children with some preschool experience generally do better than counterparts with none. High quality programs, as reported in previous chapters, can produce measurable gains that persist into adulthood.

Also, about 10–15 percent of mothers of young children experience depression that is severe enough to adversely impact their child's development and language learning.[17] For mothers living in poverty the rate is considerably higher, above 30 percent in some studies.[18] Although women who are experiencing depression can still be supportive and engaging mothers,[19] many tend to fall into one of two patterns with their young children—either withdrawing and showing little energy or emotional availability or becoming hostile and intrusive. Some mothers alternate unpredictably between these two patterns.[20] Indeed, the relative silence, constrained vocabulary, limited responsiveness, and tendency to use more "no's" than "yes's" that Hart and Risley observed in some of the lower income women in their sample may have been as much related to depression as to lack of education.

Whether or not they are clinically depressed, parents at home with young children can experience high levels of stress, especially if they are living in neighborhoods with concentrated poverty or high levels of violent crime. Parents who experience chronic stress are likely to be more concerned with fostering obedience in their children than with encouraging curiosity,[21] especially when they fear for their children's safety. Thus they may be less inclined to ask their young children questions, present them with choices, and involve them in problem-solving rather than simply telling them what to do.

Good child-care programs mitigate the impact of maternal depression and stress on a child by providing the warmth, responsiveness, and stimulating interaction he may be missing at home. They can also help his mother, by reducing her isolation, providing her with a network of support, referring her to specialized services, and improving her relationship with her child.[22] But, as we have seen, too few of these supportive child-care programs are available.

What Can a Parent Do?

1. *Look for an accredited program or provider.* Programs accredited by the National Association for the Education of Young Children, the National Association for Family Child Care, or the Ecumenical Child Care Network have gone through a "self-study" process that involved parents as well as staff and have demonstrated to a trained observer that they met rigorous standards of excellence. If you can't find an accredited program, look for a licensed setting with well-trained providers or teachers. Try to find someone with a degree in early childhood or a related field, or at least a Child Development Associate credential.

2. *See for yourself.* Visit child-care centers and family child-care homes to find one where you think your child will thrive. Your local Child Care Resource and Referral Agency can help with your search. The agency can also provide a quality checklist to help you look beneath the surface and notice the features of a program that make the most difference in terms of children's language learning, emotional resiliency, and preparation for school. Finally, look at each potential setting through your child's eyes. Where would she feel comfortable, understood, and among friends? Where would she find interested people to talk with and interesting things to talk about?

3. *Get connected.* Whether you choose to stay home with your child full or part time or to place him in full-time care, look for a network that can support you and your family. Seek out other parents and family fun activities. Join a parents' group at your child-care program, place of worship, or local library. Ask your pediatrician, Child Care Resource and Referral Agency, local elementary school, or Chamber of Commerce for a list of programs for young children and their parents.

4. *Stay involved.* Signing your child or your family up for a program is only the beginning. You need to stay involved, to make sure that your expectations are being met. If your child is in full-time care, try to connect with the provider or teacher on at least a weekly basis. Speak up about things that worry you, and also about what you see as working well. Ask questions. Find ways to thank and support the professionals who are helping to support your child.

5. *Become an advocate.* As a parent of a young child, you know how important the early years are. Before you picked up this book or others like it, you had an intuitive sense of what your children—and all children—need. Join with others to articulate these needs and to spread the word. Keep your legislators informed about what is needed in your community. Register to vote, and vote with your child's interests in mind. The Appendix lists Web sites of parents' organizations and advocacy groups.

Assets to Build On

Too many of our children are not getting the stimulating experiences they need during their prime time for language learning. Too many of our families are unable to find child-care settings for their children that provide these experiences, no matter how hard they try. Yet the scarcity of settings whose quality is adequate to support learning is only part of the story. The half-empty glass is also half full. We recognize the inadequacies because we have seen what is possible.

The early childhood field in the United States is highly diverse, offering a range of different types of care, often reflecting different values, priorities, teaching approaches, and culturally based child-rearing practices. Yet within this diversity there is remarkable consensus, backed up by an extensive body of research, on the core elements of quality.

Model programs such as the Abecedarian Project and the Perry Preschool Project have demonstrated that carefully crafted early education programs can have dramatic effects, enabling many children with multiple risk factors to achieve levels of success comparable to those of more advantaged peers.

We know that college education and professional training can lead to marked improvements in the quality of early childhood settings and in outcomes for children. The evidence from a spate of studies is clear and compelling. Providing their teachers with high quality training improves children's attachment to their teachers, increases the children's involvement in exploratory play and other activities that promote language development, and results in fewer negative behaviors by children and teachers, with measurable improvements in children's social skills. Similar training effects have been demonstrated in both center and family child-care settings.[23]

Early education practitioners in all sectors of the field have banded together to create strong professional organizations.[24] These national organizations and their local affiliates regularly sponsor training conferences, develop materials for professionals and parents, and advocate for their members and for the children and families they serve. Many of these groups have developed quality standards; some accredit excellent programs. Accreditation, including the "self-study" and improvement process that leads up to it, has proven to be a useful tool for improving program quality in many states and communities. Accreditation is also a parent's best guarantee that a program provides the educational basics and is worth considering for their child.

Perhaps the best kept secret in the country is the quality of child care available to families in the military. Before 1989, the quality of care available to military families was dismal. By insisting upon quality standards, providing training and assisting providers in becoming accredited, and improving compensation to reward training and program quality, the military proved that "it is possible to take a woefully inadequate child care system and dramatically improve it."[25] Most military families can now count on care that is of sufficient quality to meet their children's needs.

Parenting education programs are another important asset. Over the past twenty years, a number of large-scale or multisite programs have been implemented to support parents. These programs have different names— Healthy Families, Healthy Steps, Touchpoints, Home Instruction Program for Parents of Preschool Youngsters, Parents as Teachers, Parent Services Project, Parent–Child Home Program, Even Start. They also have a variety of goals—preventing child abuse, improving the health and mental health of children and families, promoting positive parenting practices, enhancing family literacy. Their framers share a common belief that "parents are their children's first and most important teachers" and that providing them with knowledge and support can make a difference in how well their children do. When the services are of sufficient intensity, focus, and duration to meet the needs of the families involved, these programs can show strong, positive results.[26]

We know what young children need in order to thrive, and we know how to provide it. We just need to commit the necessary resources.

In later chapters, we'll explore these and other assets in depth, as we look at what can be done to ensure that our children do not come to school at a loss for words. We'll look at programs and policies that have been successful on a large scale, and see how they could be expanded and coordinated into systems that meet the needs of all children and families. We'll see how parents, early childhood specialists, and concerned citizens can work together to push forward workable solutions, so that every child has a good chance to be successful in school and in life. But first, let us examine how the current state of affairs came to be.

8 A Perfect Storm

T he United States is a country that values education and innovation, yet we can't seem to get our children off to a good start. Parents are increasingly frustrated by the difficulty of finding affordable child care. Professionals bemoan the low quality of much of what is available. Researchers report a dearth of settings that provide children with a strong language foundation. By the time they enter kindergarten, significant numbers of our children are already being left behind. And the problem seems to be getting worse.

Why are so many children in the United States coming to school without a strong early language foundation? Why aren't they getting the early experiences that prime them for later success? What is keeping our country from providing the services and supports that families need and that other countries routinely supply? If we're going to be successful advocates for our children, then we need to understand the changes in our society, the pressures on our families and on our early childhood service providers, and the barriers that have stood in the way of more effective public policies.

The past thirty years have been a period of rapid social change, and our public policies have not kept pace. Wider opportunities for women and an increase in the cost of raising a family have contributed to a dramatic rise in the numbers of women who are in the workforce when their children are young. Longer work weeks and increases in divorce and single parenthood have combined with these trends to increase the use of child care and to decrease the amount of time that young children spend with their parents. Parents continue to be their children's "first and most important teachers," but they are increasingly reliant on others during the critical language learning years.

At the same time, because early education has been seen as largely a parental responsibility, public supports for it have been minimal. Although child care is expensive for parents, their payments in most cases do not cover the full cost of quality. The teachers, baby-sitters, and child-care providers upon whom parents must rely to support their children's language development are increasingly underpaid, underprepared, and undersupported in their jobs. The family, friends, and neighbors who could be counted on as conversation partners in earlier eras are less and less available.

With our information-age economy demanding higher levels of education, we are asking more of our children today than ever before. The importance of an early language foundation that prepares children to meet high educational demands is increasing, even as our children's chances of getting such a foundation are increasingly in jeopardy.

In most countries with modern economies, the care and education of young children is seen as an important public investment. In contrast, policy makers in the United States have tended to assume that most parents can and should see to their young children's learning needs on their own and that government and employers should make only modest investments in family leave, family support, and early childhood education As a result, supports that are routinely available to parents in other industrialized countries are lacking or in short supply in most U.S. communities.

Currents of Change

We have entered the Information Age, a time of unprecedented global connectedness and access to knowledge. New opportunities for women, greater access to higher education, powerful new technologies, and dramatic advancements in medical care have improved our economic productivity and quality of life. It should be a time of hope. Yet the waves of economic and social change that have brought so much promise are increasingly also coming together with negative effects, creating a "perfect storm" that is imperiling too many of our children. The supports that parents and teachers need in order to provide children with a strong early language foundation are being eroded, and we are failing to take the necessary steps to strengthen or replace them. In order to understand the magnitude of the changes and of their impact on young children and their families, let's look briefly at some of these waves.

Increased Workforce Participation by Women

Women made up less than a third of the United States labor force in 1950. By 2001, there were almost as many women working as men; the labor force was nearly 47 percent female.[1] The change affected women with young children as well as those who had no children or whose children were old enough for public school. Only 39 percent of mothers with young children worked outside the home in 1975; just twenty years later, the Bureau of

Labor Statistics reported that this figure had climbed to 62 percent, nearly two out of three.[2]

In just two generations, working mothers have become the norm in all social classes. In 1996, "welfare reform" sent a new wave of poor and largely single mothers into the workforce. In earlier times, these women would have received public assistance and stayed home with their children; now they were pushed to find jobs as quickly as possible. Most states required able recipients who could not find jobs in the private sector to accept government-sponsored "workfare" jobs or to enroll in training programs. Welfare rolls dropped across the nation, as former recipients went to work and numbers of new recipients plummeted.

In half of the states, even mothers with infants under one were required to seek work or engage in "workfare" activities. States used federal funds to provide child-care vouchers, but most states had long waiting lists. Only about one in seven eligible children was served.[3] Some mothers were able to find licensed care for their children, but many used the meager stipends— or none at all—to hire friends or relatives to "watch" their kids while they worked.

For minimum wage earners, at least two jobs have become necessary to keep a family afloat. In many urban areas, the income level required for basic necessities had climbed to $40,000 or above by 2000 for a family of four with young children, significantly more than two minimum wage workers could earn working 40-hour weeks year round.[4] That meant that most single parents couldn't make it working full time unless they earned middle-class wages, and that mothers' full- or part-time earnings were an absolute necessity in many two-parent families.

Rising opportunities for women have also contributed to the increase in workforce participation by women who "could afford to stay home." Although shortages of child care of reasonable quality slowed the trend somewhat, the 1999 National Survey of America's Families reported that 61 percent of children under age four were regularly cared for by people other than their parents.[5]

Longer Working Hours

Not only are today's mothers of young children more likely to be working, they are also likely to be working longer hours.

In the boom economy of the nineties and the subsequent period of decline and uncertainty, people were working harder than ever. Whereas in 1960 the average work week was 35 hours, by 1997, full-time workers in dual-earner families were averaging nearly 49 hours per week.[6] Managerial and professional occupations typically demanded workweeks of 50–60 hours or more, and many "part-time" employees were working what used to be considered full time—between 35 and 40 hours a week. Jobs paying low or modest wages frequently demanded extended hours or mandatory overtime. In 2002, the Families and Work Institute reported that dual-earner couples with children worked an average total of 91 hours/week, an increase of 10 hours/week from twenty-five years ago.[7]

In the face of these economic pressures, parents have gone to extraordinary lengths in order to have time with their children. In some families, parents work opposite shifts so that one parent can be home with the young children at all times. Large numbers of highly educated women have given up lucrative career opportunities in order to have more time with their families. Ann Crittenden, author of *The Price of Motherhood*, estimates that the typical college-educated woman who becomes a mother pays a lifetime "mommy tax" of more than one million dollars in foregone earnings, lost opportunities, and decreased retirement benefits.[8] Crittenden concludes that the desire to give their children what they need—both economically and in terms of parent time and attention—means that mothers across the economic spectrum are giving up both leisure time and sleep. Children are spending increasing amounts of time in various forms of child care, while their parents struggle to ensure that they get enough "quality time" with their families.

The NICHD study researchers, who had been following 1,391 children in a ten-site representative sample from birth, reported their findings to Congress in 2002. "Most children begin non-parental care very early in infancy, for extensive hours, and with multiple caregivers." Most of the children began nonmaternal care by four months of age and averaged 33 hours of such care per week during their first year. At one year of age, only 35 percent of the children in the study were cared for primarily by their mothers, with another 13 percent cared for primarily by their fathers. By the time the children were three, only 21 percent of them were cared for primarily by their mothers, with 13 percent cared for by their fathers while their mothers were at work.[9]

Single Parenthood and Teen Parenthood

The divorce rate in the United States rose significantly in the 1970s and 1980s, before stabilizing and then declining in the late 1980s and 1990s. The percentage of children who were born to never married mothers also rose during this period, from less than 1 percent in 1960 to nearly 10 percent in 2000. In 1975, only 17 percent of families with children under eighteen were headed by a single parent; by 1999 the figure had climbed to 30 percent. A third of all births that year were to mothers who were not presently married.[10] In 2001, the Children's Defense Fund estimated that half of all children would live in a single-parent family at some point during their childhood.[11]

An ironic result of the 1996 welfare reform legislation, according to two national studies that followed impacted families, was a decrease in the likelihood of marriage among poor single mothers who were eligible for assistance.[12] Whether because they had less time for dating or because they were enjoying their new economic independence, these women were significantly less likely to marry than were mothers receiving benefits under old-style programs that didn't push women into the workforce.

Many people believe that the rise in single parenthood has been accompanied by a rise in teen pregnancy, but this is not the case. In the late 1980s, as more and more information became available about the health and education risks of being born to a teen mother, advocates across the political and ideological spectrum began to panic about the social and individual cost of "babies having babies." Their panic coincided with a small spike in the rate of births to females under seventeen. High schools, youth development organizations, public health departments, and faith-based groups accelerated efforts to reduce teen pregnancy and developed successful prevention approaches. At its height in 1991, the U.S. teen birth rate was lower than it was in 1960, when women tended to marry at a younger age. By 2000, this rate had dropped markedly, although it remains considerably higher than that of other industrialized countries.[13]

Child Poverty

In 1959, before the "War on Poverty," slightly more than one fifth of U.S. children under eighteen lived in families earning less than the official poverty rate. By 1969, the rate was down to 14 percent. But then our national priorities shifted. Some antipoverty programs were closed and others were allowed to slowly atrophy. The child poverty rate began to climb again. In 2002, this rate stood at 16.7 percent, a decline from its height of nearly 23 percent in 1993. Still, one out of every six children was living in poverty and one out of fifteen was living in what is known as "deep poverty," with a family income of less than half the official poverty rate.[14]

The official poverty rate underestimates the extent of suffering. Poverty is especially hard on young children. It places them at risk for undernutrition—with deficiencies in the protein, iron, and vitamins that are essential not only for their health and rapid growth, but also for their intellectual development. It places them at severe risk of living in substandard

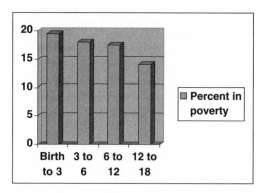

FIGURE 8.1. Percent of U.S. Children in Poverty (2002), by Age.
Source: U.S. Census Bureau, Current Population Survey, 2003. Annual Social and Economic Supplement (Single Year of Age—Poverty Status, 2002).

housing, with increased risk of exposure to lead and other toxic substances that can damage their rapidly growing brains and to indoor allergens that have contributed to a dramatic rise in asthma.[15] It increases their risk of living in neighborhoods plagued by violence or lacking in basic amenities such as safe playgrounds for young children and sources of children's books.[16]

Unfortunately, the poverty rate for young children tends to be higher than that for children in general. In 2002, as the country edged out of a recession and into what was widely called a "jobless recovery," nearly one in five children (19%) under the age of five lived in poverty (Figure 8.1).

If we look not at the official poverty rate but at more realistic figures that are closer to "sustainable" or "living" wages, the numbers are considerably larger. In 2002, 40 percent of American children were living in families whose incomes were less than twice the bare minimum level marked by the poverty line. These families had a very difficult time affording increasingly expensive child care, housing, and health care while also paying for food and other necessities.[17]

A Widening Income Gap

The persistence of poverty amid plenty is worsened by a widening gap between the incomes of those who are well-off and those who are poor or near poor. In the United States today, the richest tenth of citizens earn incomes that are about six times the size of those earned by the poorest tenth.[18] Our country has grown considerably wealthier during the past three decades, but most of that wealth has gone to those who already had an advantage.

The disparity between haves and have-nots grew dramatically during the boom of the 1990s. According to figures provided by the Congressional Budget Office, only 3.8 percent of the growth in national income between 1993 and 1997 went to the poorest fifth of households, a slightly higher percentage went to the middle three fifths, and about 70 percent went to the top fifth. The most dramatic gain—more than 50 percent of the total—went to the top 1 percent![19]

As income disparity rose, prices for necessities such as housing and health care climbed, while wages for lower income workers stagnated. Fewer people were technically poor, but more were scrimping on necessities, including child care. Using 2001 data—the latest available—the 2003 Fordham Index of Social Health, a composite of sixteen indicators of national well-being, reported a precipitous decline following a period of historic lows. Although indicators such as infant mortality, high school dropouts, and poverty among the elderly improved, two indicators hit record levels: income inequality (disparity at an all time high) and percentage of *eligible* families receiving food stamps (at an all time low).[20]

London-based journalist David Cohen, author of *Chasing the Red, White, and Blue—A Journey in Tocqueville's Footsteps Through Contemporary America*,[21] described what he saw as the pulling apart of American society.

> Since the 1970's, the average real income of the richest fifth of families has risen by 30 percent while the incomes of the poorest fifth have fallen by more than 20 percent. And with this pulling apart, equality of opportunity has been severely compromised...I wish I could report otherwise, but on my journey, talking with people at every level of society...I discovered that the haves had purposefully distanced themselves from the have-nots: geographically, socially, psychologically, and emotionally. In parts of the country, the rapidly widening gap between rich and poor had not so much frayed the social fabric as ripped it apart. "I never give poor people a second thought," was the disturbing sentiment of many young upwardly mobile professionals I spoke to.[22]

Perhaps the "second thoughts" will come when upwardly mobile professionals like those Cohen talked to have children. Perhaps, like Esther Brown, who helped to organize a lawsuit against the Board of Education of Topeka, Kansas, after she discovered the appalling conditions in the school her maid's children attended, they will be moved to action when they learn what the families of those they employ to help them care for their children are facing.

Changing Demographics

The 2000 census revealed a surge of new immigrants that surprised even those who had expected it. In sheer numbers, the increase in foreign-born residents exceeded that of 1900–1910, the decade with the previous record.

The immigrants came largely from Latin America, the Caribbean, and Asia. They generally fell into two groups: unskilled workers (or skilled workers with limited English proficiency) willing to take low-paying jobs and workers with strong high tech skills. A majority were between 20 and 35 years old, at prime childbearing age.

The influx of immigrants, combined with relatively high birthrates among Latinos and some Asian groups, meant a changing population mix that was felt throughout the country. Small towns in the South, Midwest, and West with historically homogenous populations experienced new linguistic and cultural diversity.

The increasing diversity, especially of the young child population, created both challenges and opportunities in terms of early education. On the one hand, immigrant women filled many of the gaps in the child-care workforce by taking difficult-to-fill jobs as nannies, teaching assistants, and infant room teachers. Their own children, however, were often left in inadequate or inconsistent care, and sometimes even sent back to or left in their home countries, where they could be cared for by grandparents or other relatives![23] The children who entered formal child-care programs enriched them with their cultural traditions, but also brought new challenges for teachers unfamiliar with their cultures or unschooled in working with second language learners or facilitating communication and pretend play among children who speak different languages.

Fewer Available Adults

In 1994, Dr. Felton Earls, a psychiatrist at Harvard School of Public Health, launched a ten-year study of 11,000 children in 343 Chicago neighborhoods.[24] The study explored children's lives in great detail, through direct observations, interviews with parents, and discussions with older children. Dr. Earls wanted to learn what distinguished neighborhoods where children were thriving from those where children tended to run into difficulty. Of course, there were many factors at work, and the data are still being collected. But an early, salient finding was the importance of a factor that is not usually considered: the availability of adults to children in the streets, courtyards, and playgrounds. In some neighborhoods, there always seemed to be adults around; children of different ages could play freely with adult oversight, though not necessarily close supervision.

In other neighborhoods—and these are increasingly in the majority—few adults were available to children. Dr. Earls and his colleagues found that "collective efficacy," which they defined as "mutual trust and a willingness to intervene in the supervision of children and the maintenance of public order," was a strong predictor of lower rates of violent crime and an important contributor to children's overall healthy development.

Most of today's parents and political and business leaders grew up in child-filled neighborhoods or large families, with lots of adults and older children around to keep them out of trouble. It was easy for young children to find playmates; play dates did not require elaborate prearrangement. Children heard and learned lots of words because their daily lives involved informal interaction with lots of different people.

Today, most adults are at work and most children younger than eight or nine are in programs. In some neighborhoods, family child-care providers make a habit of moving their group to the front yard when school lets out, so they can keep an eye on the teenagers. No other adults are around. In other neighborhoods, it seems as if there is nobody home, except perhaps for older children, home alone with the television in the afternoons. In such neighborhoods, parents who are home with young children can feel very isolated.

Ignoring the Warnings: Inadequate Investment to Meet Increased Need for Services

The currents of change described above have created an increased need for services. What once was done freely must now be arranged and paid for. Whether or not children get what they need depends in part upon how much their families can provide and in part upon how persistent their families are in seeking out services and demanding quality. It also depends to a large and increasing extent upon the choices we make as a society.

Unfortunately, we have not insisted that our public investments keep pace with our young children's needs. There have been some significant investments—in Head Start, the Child Care and Development Block Grant, and state-based early childhood initiatives—but they have not been nearly enough. Our investments have created islands of excellence and improvement, but, overall, the tide of mediocrity—and of dangerously low quality—continues to rise. We are treading water as fast as we can, but we are still sinking.

The results of our failure to keep pace are depriving nearly a third of the present generation of young children of the early language foundation that they require. At the same time, our failure to build an adequate early education system is creating a downward vortex. The shortage of quality services is escalating, making it more and more difficult for parents to get their children what they need.

Skewed Public Investments in Children

Whether we look at who is most "at risk" or "vulnerable," whose families have the fewest resources, whose brains are growing the fastest, whose learning curves are the steepest, or where investments yield the largest dividends, we come to the same conclusion: young children. Yet in spite of increased investment in recent years, our society is still spending far more per child on children of school age and older than it is on the very young.

Figure 8.2 depicts data from a report by Voices for America's children that examined per-child state, local, and federal investments in twelve representative states.[25] The data were collected in the 2001 fiscal year, which the report's authors called the "high water mark" of state early childhood investments. For infants and toddlers, the figures included state investments in programs to educate and support parents, such as Parents as Teachers and Healthy Families America, but these accounted for only a small percentage of each state's educational spending and averaged just $35.69 per young child. The Iowa data (Figure 8.3), which separate out the investments for children under three, provide a dramatic, and unfortunately typical, portrait of how we shortchange our youngest children.

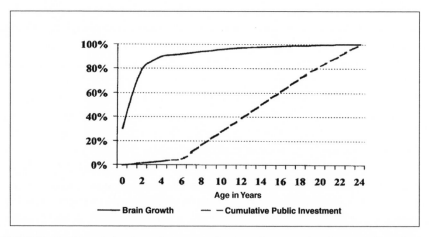

FIGURE 8.2. Cumulative State Investment by Age, Contrasted with Brain Growth. *Source:* Voices for America's Children and the Child and Family Policy Center (2004) *Early Learning Left Out: An Examination of Public Investments in Education and Development by Child Age.*

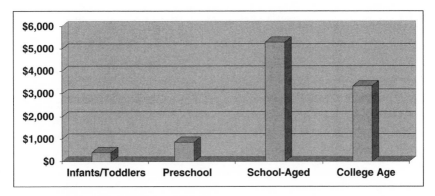

FIGURE 8.3. Iowa Spending by Child Age.
Source: Voices for America's Children and the Child and Family Policy Center (2004)
*Early Learning Left Out: An Examination of Public Investments in Education and
Development by Child Age.*

The skewed public investment pattern means that in most states a family must pay more to educate its preschoolers than it does for tuition for its college-age children at a state university, in spite of the fact that the college-age students are in a much better position to help with the payments! Even so, when public and private payments are combined, the resources available to educate a three- or four-year-old five full working days a week and nearly twelve months a year (averaging about $5,000 for licensed, center-based care in 2000) are often considerably less than those available to educate a five-year-old for only six hours a day and only nine months a year (which in 2000 averaged about $7,500 for full-day public school kindergarten)!

Static Child-Care Wages and High Turnover

In a free market that is functioning properly, when demand outpaces supply, prices go up. A shortage of workers leads to rising wages, until the imbalance is eased. That is the way it is supposed to work, but for child care, it doesn't. Wages seem frozen at an extremely low level, while demand rises and staff shortages increase. The reason, of course, is that parents are the major payers, and most of them cannot afford to pay any more than they currently do. Indeed, a family with one preschooler and an income of $50,000/year typically pays about 10 percent of its income for licensed child care; because of the high cost of infant care, this figure is likely to rise to 25 percent or more when a new baby comes along.[26]

Instead of driving wages up, the pressure of increasing demand is contributing to a downward spiral of increasing shortages and decreasing quality. With wages hovering near the poverty level—and lower than those of many entry-level jobs—child-care centers are having a terrible time holding onto workers and filling vacancies, while family child-care workers, whose earnings tend to be even lower than those of center employees, are forced out of business. As educated and experienced professionals leave the field and as vacancies remain unfilled and new hires quit after short stints, those who do stay experience increasing pressure. Many centers fall out of compliance with licensing requirements and are forced to shut down or to turn families away. Where licensing requirements are lax or ill-enforced or licensing is not required (e.g., for programs affiliated with religious institutions and for family child-care homes in some places), there is a tendency to take in more children than can be cared for responsibly—with the individual attention that they need—especially by poorly prepared staff. More children needing care simply means that scarce care of acceptable quality becomes harder and harder to find.

Child advocates refer to the conflict among affordability, adult/child ratio (class size), and teacher wages as the "child care trilemma." Adequate wages—necessary to maintain quality and prevent disruptive turnover—can't be paid without either sacrificing adult/child ratios, harming quality and also contributing to teacher frustration and therefore to turnover, or asking parents to pay higher fees, when most are already stretched past what they had thought was their limit. Similarly, making child care more affordable, without adding new resources to the equation, can only lower its quality by driving away its teachers or by making it impossible for them to do their jobs well. Unless money is added from the outside, the equation doesn't balance.

LEAP, a national leadership and advocacy training program for child-care workers, has developed a skit to help people outside of the field understand the difficulties that parents, teachers, and program directors face as they try to juggle inadequate resources. It begins with a song, set to the tune of "The Itsy, Bitsy Spider":

> The itsy-bitsy paycheck can only stretch so far
> Trying to find good teachers, we're lowering the bar
> Sad was my son when his teacher went away
> We have to work together to find a better way.[27]

An Escalating Teacher Shortage

Providers call it "the crisis in the field." There are simply not enough qualified early childhood teachers to go around, and the problem keeps getting worse. The major part of the problem, as has already been discussed, is the combination of increased demand and static, woefully inadequate wages.

But a second crisis is looming throughout the country and has already hit in some places: a shortage of teachers for children in grades K-12. The K-12 teacher shortage is primarily due to two factors: the retirement of baby boomer teachers who entered teaching in droves in the 1960s and early 1970s and the opening up of alternative opportunities for women. A third factor is child population growth, which, while less important nationally, looms large in fast-growing states with high immigrant birth rates like Florida and California. Efforts to reduce class size in the primary grades, while laudable, are exacerbating the problem. The National Center for Education Statistics estimates that 2.4 million more K-12 teachers will be needed by the 2008–2009 school year to fill the gap created by the combination of teacher retirement and expanding child population.[28]

Where will these teachers come from? Many are already being "cherry-picked" from the ranks of the early childhood education profession. The most educated early childhood teachers, those with bachelor's degrees, are increasingly taking jobs as kindergarten and first grade teachers—at double their early childhood salaries. This is generally good for older children and also good for the teachers who are "moving up" to higher paying jobs, but it leaves younger children and their families in the lurch.

Changing Course

The storm is upon us. More and more of our children are caught between rocks and hard places. Their parents can't afford to stay home with them, neither can they afford (or find) adequate child care. Their child-care providers and teachers are doing their best, but they can't make ends meet unless they take in too many children or hire poorly trained teachers and assistants who are unlikely to stay. The public, government, and workplace demand higher levels of literacy and technical knowledge, yet investment in the prerequisite early education foundation remains woefully inadequate.

Can we change course? Can we implement public policies that rescue our children from the gathering storm? The answer given by research, by comparisons with other countries, and by distinguished panels of experts is an emphatic YES!—IF we apply what we know and are willing to invest the necessary resources. With an affordable investment of less than 1 percent of our gross domestic product, we could extend supports for families and fund care that is good enough for young children.[29] We could ensure that early educators and other child-care providers have the education they need to provide young children with a strong early language foundation. We could help parents and other family members learn to engage young children in frequent, fun conversations that nourish curiosity, support emotional resilience, and build vocabulary. We could provide unhurried time so that adults can listen to children, talk with them about their interests and concerns, and share stories, songs, and experiences that expand their horizons.

The remainder of this book explains how we could apply what we know. It looks first at misconceptions and misunderstandings that have blocked our progress, and then at programs, practices, and investments that have proven to be both effective and scalable. It provides a map for policy makers and for the parents and citizens who educate them and hold them accountable. It explores multiple paths that lead to the "school readiness" goal, so that we can together chart a course of opportunity for our children.

9 Truth, Justice, and the American Way

The facts presented in previous chapters are not new: we have known for a long time that early experience makes a difference to children's later success, that the early experiences of American children are vastly unequal, and that large numbers of our children start school already "left behind." A series of national reports and White House conferences presented the facts and called for public solutions:

- In 1970, the White House Conference on Children highlighted child care as a major problem facing the American family.[1] The conference called for free comprehensive programs to meet the developmental needs of poor children, with children of single parents and working families enrolled on a sliding fee scale. These ideas were reflected in the Comprehensive Child Development Act of 1971, which was twice passed by Congress with bipartisan majorities, but vetoed by presidents Nixon and Ford.
- In 1989, President George H. Bush's national education summit highlighted the "achievement gap," set school readiness as the first of six national education goals, and called upon governors to strengthen early childhood education in their states.[2]
- In 1994, the Carnegie Foundation's *Starting Points*[3] reported research on the impact of early experiences on brain development, and called the lack of good enough child care and family support for children ZERO TO THREE in the United States a "quiet crisis."
- In 2001, Laura Bush chaired the White House Summit on Early Childhood Cognitive Development,[4] which highlighted the Hart and Risley research[5] on class differences in toddler's language development and their implications for literacy and school readiness.

And, to some extent, the nation has responded. New programs and improved public policies were launched by the federal government and by every state. But, like the differences in vocabulary between children from poor families and those from professional families in Hart and Risley's study, the gap between the growing needs of our families and the public investments to support them continues to widen.

Other countries with modern economies have faced the same social and economic trends described in Chapter 8, but they have mitigated the impact on children with paid family leaves, family allowances, and public programs that are available for all preschoolers.

- In France, where all three- and four-year-olds attend the ecoles maternelles, generous family allowances have virtually eliminated poverty among young children. Children from low-income neighborhoods enter the ecoles maternelles at two instead of three.[6]
- In Finland, all education is public, from preschool through university and professional education. After a one-year, fully paid leave, parents of toddlers can choose between heavily subsidized center-based care, partially subsidized in-home child care, or extended parental leave with a modest cash benefit, for the next two years.[7]
- In Denmark, 60 percent of children between six months and three years attend heavily subsidized infant/toddler care programs of exceptionally high quality.[8]
- In Italy, more than 90 percent of three- to five-year-olds attend preschool. Most are in public programs.[9]

In December 1995, the ERIC Clearinghouse on Elementary and Early Childhood Education compared the investments made by U.S. states and European countries in public early childhood programs. The digest concluded,

> Many OECD [Organization for Economic Cooperation and Development] countries that are far less capable financially than most U.S. states have been making far greater investments in educating their young children than have U.S. states. In these countries, there is a shared belief in the value of public investments to ensure the care of children, and strong public support for early childhood programs across a spectrum of political persuasions.[10]

Our rather minimal public investment in such programs is due less to lack of resources than to lack of public will. Our conflicts over "family values" continue to be a major reason why our public policies have not kept pace with changes in work and family life.

Beliefs That Have Blocked Our Progress

To some extent, our continuing conflicts over family values and family-serving policies are "culture wars," two sides of an ideological divide. More often, though, they grow out of ambivalence, false dichotomies, or widely held misconceptions about child care and child development. Our tendency to frame conflicts, choices, and differences of opinion in either/or terms often blinds us to a more productive synthesis. Examining our values and beliefs can clear away obstacles to enlightened policies; it can also reveal deeply held values that we want our public policies to reflect.

We may not all agree on all of these issues; on some, some of us may be genuinely ambivalent. But we need not prescribe one path for all children or all families. Instead, we can explore alternate courses, respecting the values about which people of good will genuinely disagree, while still steering clear of the "perfect storm" that is imperiling so many of our children and leaving them at a loss for words.

Here are some of the critical conflicts, cast in the either/or terms in which they have been framed in the media and in public conversation. For the sake of all of our children, let us see where we might find common ground.

Collective Versus Parental Responsibility for Children

"It takes a village to raise a child," wrote Hillary Rodham Clinton, quoting an African proverb.[11] Conservatives countered, "It takes a parent to raise a child."[12] Then First Lady Clinton was not trying to absolve parents of responsibility; she was arguing that it was difficult for most of them to do their jobs in isolation. Parents need to be able to count on support from extended family, community, religious organizations, and public institutions like schools, libraries, and hospitals, as well as from publicly supported early education and after-school programs.

Conservatives didn't mean to argue that the community, faith-based, and public institutions were unimportant. What they feared, however, were expensive programs that would cause some families to be taxed to support others. Even more deeply, they worried that government-run programs would somehow infringe on parental rights, undercut responsibilities, and pull children away from their families.

This is far less of an issue when children reach school age; public schools are a given. We may argue about their quality or how to improve them, debate issues such as local control versus accountability to state or national standards, urge parents to get involved and to act as watchdogs or bemoan parental interference in curriculum decisions, welcome legal decisions that attempt to equalize per pupil spending or complain about the unfairness of having to support other people's children at the expense of one's own. Yet few Americans question the legitimacy of the public school.

Young children, however, are more vulnerable. We see them as not yet having reached "the age of reason" and as needing parental—especially maternal—physical care, emotional support, and guidance. We worry, as parents, about letting children who can't tell us what is happening out of our sight for too long. We worry that "public support" will mean bureaucratic control, with school-like programs that are far too "cold" and "institutional" for babies.

In *The Invisible Heart*,[13] economist Nancy Folbre makes the case that healthy child development is a public good because it leads to a productive workforce and a responsible citizenry. She surfaces a set of hidden assumptions that she caricatures as "the children as pets" philosophy—parents choose to have children and therefore it is their responsibility to raise them and pay their expenses. But, of course, children aren't pets. They can't be given up if they become inconvenient. And society must pay the costs that flow from their early neglect. It would be more cost-effective, as well as kinder, if society could prevent this neglect. That means finding a way to ensure that young children receive care that is not cold and institutional, not "warehousing," "watching," or "merely custodial," but the steady diet of emotionally affirming, linguistically rich experiences that enable them to thrive.

Ironically, the Personal Work and Responsibility Act of 1996, better known as Welfare Reform, has forced many parents to place very young children in care of questionable quality, in a sense abdicating their parental responsibilities. Other parents, however, have been supported to stay home with their children or to place them in top-quality early education programs. For example, Minnesota and Montana used federal Temporary Assistance to Needy Families funds to enable poor women to stay home with their babies during the first year.[14] Rather than giving mothers vouchers for nonparental child care, these states paid them a roughly equivalent amount to care for their babies themselves. Kansas chose a different approach, combining state and federal funding streams to create Kansas Early Head Start centers that offered the same high quality care as the national Early Head Start program. These are tiny pilot projects, but they represent islets of hope.

Equal Opportunities for Women Versus Mother Care for Children

Women and men, feminists and traditionalists, conservatives and liberals have come down on both sides of the dilemma of whether to enable women to make their way in the workplace on the same terms as men or to support them in their choice to stay home with their (young) children. For example, some feminists vehemently opposed using disability benefits and sick leave to compensate women for taking time off after the birth of a child, on the grounds that this would hamper women's workplace opportunities, while others clamored for these benefits so that women could afford to take the time to bond with their babies. Conservatives argued for tax policies that would be more favorable toward the disappearing family structure of working father and at-home mother, but pushed for welfare reform changes in 2003 that would require poor women to work 40 hours/week instead of the 30 hours required in the 1996 legislation, leaving their young children in the care of others.

Our ideals of individual responsibility, rugged individualism, self-sufficiency, equal opportunity, and the work ethic are increasingly at war with our images of home, hearth, and mother love, as well as with what Drs. T. Berry Brazelton and Stanley Greenspan identify as "the irreducible needs of children."[15]

Paid Child Care Versus Parent Care

Given a choice between parental care and paid child care for very young children, most Americans instinctively favor parental care, at least for babies. Yet, perhaps because of our focus on individual responsibility, our policies point in the other direction. While most industrial countries provide paid family leave, the United States only mandates unpaid leave. Even that is only guaranteed to parents who work for companies with fifty or more employees, and then only for three months.

The United States lags behind nearly every other industrialized nation in the world in terms of paid leave. Countries throughout the world offer paid leave to new parents, based on the philosophy that parents are a child's best caregivers, new moms need time to recover from childbirth, and all families need help raising the nation's future workers and citizens.

A new mom in Chile, for example, can take up to 18 weeks off after childbirth, at full pay. French mothers are entitled to 16 weeks; German moms 14 weeks; and Italian moms 20 weeks—all at 100 percent of pay. In Norway, moms can take up to a year off at 80 percent of pay. And this year, Canadian moms won the right to take off a full year from work after the birth of a baby at 60 percent of pay. Several countries extend paid leave to both mothers and fathers.

"Other countries have long had paid and job-protected leaves for new parents, and more are including men in their policies, as a way of encouraging fathers to get more involved with their children," says Sheila Kamerman, head of the Cross-National Studies Program of the School of Social Work at Columbia University. "And the leave is just one of the components that other countries have deemed necessary support to families with young children. They also get child allowances, to help defray the cost of raising children, health insurance, and even free health care for new babies. Many also support early childhood . . . education programs."[16]

Providing paid parental leave during the first year, when child care is the most expensive and qualified caregivers and licensed settings are in critically short supply, would be a major contribution toward solving America's child-care crisis. It would also require major new public or private investment or both.

When child care is of low quality or merely custodial, there is no question that too much of it detracts from a child's development and from his relationship with his parents.[17] But good child care can be a support for parents that strengthens families, extended families, and communities. Here's how:

- *Good child care reflects parents' values.* Parents who have a choice of child-care settings pick places where they feel comfortable, where child-rearing patterns and underlying values are consistent with their own. As part of their professional training and code of ethics, early childhood teachers are urged to partner with families, support children's cultural identities, and encourage parent participation in shaping the program.[18]
- *Good child care provides children with playmates and links their families so that they can share information and fun, and support each other.* Some centers and family child-care homes provide family nights, holiday parties, parents-nights-out, guest speakers, seminars, and other programs to foster these connections.
- *Early childhood teachers help parents to see their children's strengths and support their development.* Early childhood educators are trained to observe children's emerging capabilities and interests, to exchange observations with parents, and to create classroom experiences that give each child a chance to shine. When children are not achieving developmental milestones on a typical timetable, early childhood teachers can help parents to access effective early intervention, which can be reinforced within the child-care setting.
- *Good child-care programs support parents' growth as their children's first and most important teachers.* This tenet of early childhood professional training and ethics becomes a reality as parents and professionals work together to forge a partnership. Increasingly, early childhood teachers and providers are encouraging parents to read with their children and to engage in other literacy-promotion activities.
- *Good child-care programs give parents peace of mind and reduce family stress.* Parents who are confident that their children are safe and well cared for can concentrate on work at work and on the family at home. Instability

in child-care arrangements is a significant source of stress for working parents.[19]

- *Head Start and similar programs have a track record of promoting family self-sufficiency, economic advancement, and community involvement because they support and inspire parents.*[20] Wanting the best for their children and determined to be good role models, parents go back to school, take jobs as child-care assistants and move on to teaching and administrative roles, take on leadership roles in the child-care program and then in the community at large, and find support to take on new challenges.

- *Investments in improving the quality of child care pay large dividends for families and for society.* A cost-benefit analysis of the Perry Preschool Project showed that every dollar invested yielded more than $7 worth of individual and societal benefits, including savings in welfare assistance (prior to welfare reform), special education, and criminal justice costs, savings to (potential) crime victims, and increased tax revenue from higher earnings. Program graduates had better grades through high school, were more likely to graduate high school, and were more socially and economically successful at age twenty-seven than children from comparable backgrounds who had not experienced the program.[21] A follow-up study of both groups of children at age forty showed continued benefits. With higher incomes, greater tax contributions, and less likelihood of incarceration, program children were continuing to take less and give more. The researchers determined that each dollar invested in this high quality program had yielded a return on investment of SEVENTEEN dollars, with a benefit to the public of just under thirteen dollars![22]

As long as we look at child care as a lesser alternative to parent care rather than as a supplement or support, calls for public investments to improve its quality will always evoke concerns about usurping parental functions. In reality, however, almost all children experience some mixture of parent care and care by others during their early childhood years. Even parents who "stay home" use occasional baby-sitters and are likely to also take advantage of early education opportunities for their children, including nursery schools, preschools, and Head Start programs.

Public Programs Versus Parent Choice

When we think of public programs for children, we tend to think of public schools. In most communities, parents don't have much choice about which public schools their children attend. Some large school systems have experimented with vouchers or magnet schools, a handful of states permit a small number of charter schools, and isolated localities use choice as a means of desegregation. The No Child Left Behind Act was supposed to provide options for children assigned to schools with a track record of failure, but funding has been short and very few alternative placements have been made available. Even when there is a choice, that choice is likely to be among programs that are under public auspices. If you want to send your child to a private or parochial school, you are, in most cases, on your own.

Since young children are considered their parents' responsibility, choice is seen as a must. We are deeply suspicious of uniform programs that may not fit our values, culture, or hopes for our children. If "the hand that rocks the cradle rules the world," then parents want that hand to be their own, or at least one that rocks as they would or according to their instructions.

In actuality, our public programs for infants, toddlers, and preschoolers have generally done a good job of providing choices, involving parents, and honoring parents' values. Head Start and Early Head Start offer different program models—home visits, family child care, center-based care, and various combinations. State-supported programs are likely to provide school-based, center-based, and sometimes also family child-care options. States seeking to serve all four-year-olds or to provide full-day care for Head Start children have partnered with private preschools, including those run by religious institutions. Vouchers supported with Child Care and Development Block Grant or Temporary Assistance to Needy Families funds can be used at parent discretion for center programs or family child care or to pay relatives, friends, or neighbors for baby-sitting. Following the lead of Head Start, many state-sponsored programs encourage parent involvement at the classroom level and also mandate parent representation on policy councils.

It is in the private sector where choice is likely to be limited. As the availability of affordable programs of acceptable quality diminishes in the face of rising demand, static wages, teacher shortages, and inadequate resources, parents' "choices" are increasingly constrained.

Nature Versus Nurture

Biologists have declared this dichotomy dead, but it still lingers in the public mind. It turns out that our genes respond to environmental triggers and also shape the way we respond to environmental influences. Whether, when, and how a characteristic encoded in a gene is expressed may depend upon the external environment or the environment within the body. Characteristics such as height and maturation rate, once thought to be inherited, are determined by complex interactions among genetic and environmental factors, including nutrition, overall health or illness, stress, body fat percentage, and hormonal balance. These factors, of course, influence each other and are influenced by genes, environment, and behavior. For example, what is experienced as stress and how the body responds is influenced by genetic makeup, early experience, ongoing patterns of experience, exercise, rest, learned coping and self-calming strategies, culture, nutrition, and general health. At the same time, diseases such as cancer, once thought to be caused by viruses, toxins, or other environmental insults, turn out to also have complex genetic components.

Recent advances in neuroscience have demonstrated that not only does the brain shape behavior, behavior shapes the brain![23] Young children's brains grow rapidly and develop an overabundance of connections that are strengthened through repeated use; beginning at about age three, connections that are used less frequently are "pruned" (allowed to atrophy and disappear). Thus, the brain becomes specialized with learning, enabling quick and automatic processing of routine tasks like reading. Children reared in orphanage conditions, where they are deprived of normal human contact and opportunities to explore their environment, develop small brains with few connections.

Many people still imagine child development as controlled either by nature or nurture. Those who think in terms of nature see development as something that merely unfolds, according to its own timetable, as long as the child is fed, protected, and cared for in some minimal way. In this view, being "ready to learn" is simply a matter of growing up. Some children are seen as naturally precocious, others as "late bloomers." Once a child is "ready," if he doesn't learn, it is seen as his own fault—he's lazy, or stubborn, or just plain dumb.

Those who focus on nurture may go to the opposite extreme, giving the child neither credit nor responsibility. Failure is seen as the fault of the parents, or of the neighborhood, or of the culture. Poor children, children from "dysfunctional families," and children with other risk factors may be seen as doomed to failure. Or children may be seen as infinitely malleable; a good teacher should be able to teach anything to any child, regardless of what the child brings to the table.

Both of these paradigms are appealing in their simplicity, yet in some way most of us realize that both are oversimplifications. Our folk wisdom tells us what science confirms: "as the twig is bent, so grows the tree." Children have inborn temperaments and dispositions that are shaped by their experiences, developing into habits, outlooks, approaches to learning, and abilities that influence what they gain from later experience. Early experiences have unique power because they can set the course—powerfully, but not irrevocably. The shape of the tree can still be influenced by obstacles, sunlight, rainfall, or pruning, as well as by the weight of its own fruit or the density of its leaves.

Moving Forward Together

It is time to move beyond dichotomies. Children are both a private and a public responsibility. They will always need good parent care, and, as Uri Bronfenbrenner taught us nearly thirty years ago,[24] that care will always be given in the context of communities and public policies that can enhance or interfere with parents' efforts to give their children a good start in life. Nature matters, and so does nurture. As parents, we make choices on our children's behalf, and we need good options. As citizens, we need to make sure that good options are available—not only for our children, but for all the children in our communities. Investments in children are not something that any of us can leave to others. They are not Republican or Democratic, liberal or conservative. We must all become advocates and watchdogs to ensure that these investments are both adequate and wise.

In 1996, a new organization began raising unexpected voices urging increased public investments in early education programs. The spokespeople for this organization are not child development professionals, but most of them are fathers or mothers and many are also grandparents. They care about children, but they are not known for their tender hearts. They come from many different states and both political parties, although the majority are registered Republicans. The organization is called Fight Crime: Invest in Kids,[25] and its spokespeople are sheriffs, district attorneys, and police chiefs whose job it is to enforce our laws and see that criminals are brought to justice.

As conscientious crime fighters, these activists would rather prevent crime than arrest the perpetrators after the damage has been done. They also value evidence. In this book we have been following the evidence that links early language experiences with school readiness and school success. Some of the same studies we looked at also examined the impact of early learning experiences on children's likelihood of dropping out of high school and of getting involved in crime. For children growing up in poverty, or in neighborhoods that are both victims of and breeding grounds for crime, there is overwhelming evidence that high quality early education can serve as a protective factor. It is that evidence that has led so many crime fighters to join the campaign for adequate public investment in early education.

It is time for a new discussion of family values—not one that rehashes the old controversies over who is to blame when children fail, but one that asks what we as a society can do to set all of our children upon productive paths. It's time for parents to weigh in on policy and for all of us to demand what all of our children need.

Part III

Changing Course

10 A Parent's Guide to Early Childhood Programs and Policy

The problem can be stated simply: Too many of our children are not getting the input, practice, and responsive caregiving they need during their prime time for language learning. As a result, they start school significantly behind their peers in vocabulary and language use. The ensuing achievement gap can be stubborn; it often widens rather than narrows as time goes on.

A third of our children are at risk today. If we do not change course, that percentage is likely to grow as more and more families place increasing reliance on an undereducated, undercompensated, and increasingly overburdened early childhood workforce to provide conversations, experiences, and relationships that are critical for their children's early learning and language development.

This sounds like a big problem, but it is not that difficult to solve. We have the knowledge we need. Three authoritative reports by panels convened by the National Academy of Sciences have reviewed the research and the track records of various programs and made strong recommendations to bring our public policies and on-the-ground practice into line with what we know. Each report tackled a different aspect of the problem:

- *Preventing Reading Difficulties in Young Children,*[1] published in 1998, looked specifically at reading through the third grade. The panel's first recommendations focused on the preschool period. Specifically, they called for spreading the word—among parents, caregivers, and the public at large—about the importance of building young children's language and familiarity with books through everyday activities. They urged the early identification and remediation of language delays and other risk factors, and stated that all children, especially those at risk, should have access to early childhood experiences that promote language and literacy. Other recommendations dealt with instruction, assessment, intervention, and school organization in the primary grades, education of elementary and preschool teachers, and an agenda for further research.

- *From Neurons to Neighborhoods: The Science of Early Childhood Development*[2] focused on the first three years of life. Its research review highlighted both the incredible competency and learning speed of babies and their vulnerability to environmental stressors. The panel recommended increased attention to social-emotional development and motivation to learn, concerted efforts to erase the "significant disparities observed at school entry in skills of children from different backgrounds," a guarantee that no child with a full-time working parent would live in poverty, and increasing options for parents through a combination of paid family leave and high quality child care. They called for major new investments in mental health services for young children and their families, protection of pregnant women and young children from environmental toxins, and training, compensation, and benefits for early childhood caregivers and teachers.

- *Eager to Learn: Educating Our Preschoolers*[3] focused on the years from two to five. The panel identified research-supported features of quality preschool programs: active attention to social–emotional, cognitive, and physical development as inseparable domains, responsive relationships between children and teachers, low adult–child ratios and small class size, an intentional, well-planned curriculum, and strong teacher education and supervision. Citing compelling evidence that such programs greatly increase poor children's chances, they called upon the federal government to "fund well-planned, high quality, center-based preschool programs for all children at risk of school failure."[4] They further recommended that "The message that the quality of children's relationships with adult teachers and child care providers is critical in preparation for elementary school" be widely disseminated.

These scientific reports concur in their emphasis on the importance of supportive early relationships and the opportunities they provide for language learning. All call for increased public investment in early childhood, dissemination of the existing knowledge-base to parents, caregivers, and the public at large, changes in public policy to make good quality early learning programs and supported parenting the norm, and special efforts to assure that young children don't live in poverty or that those that do get what they need.

How can we as a society achieve this vision? What will it take to act upon what we know? In one sense, the answer is obvious: public knowledge and public will. If everyone knew what children needed and that it could be affordably provided, who would say no? In a democracy, an informed and insistent citizenry should be able to ensure that its children's basic needs are met.

Yes, but there are several steps between recognizing the importance of early learning and advocating for effective policies. In order to be informed voters and effective advocates, parents, and grandparents, citizens and tax-payers need sufficient understanding of public policy tools, choices, and processes to enable us to decide what exactly we should be demanding of whom, and when and how to voice our demands.

In 2001, Market Strategies, a Republican polling firm, interviewed a representative sample of Illinois voters. They asked, "What age is most important for developing a child's capacity to learn?" Sixty-one percent of the respondents selected either zero to one or one to three. Yet when asked in the same poll "If we want to improve the learning experiences of children, what age is most important for investing public funds?" only one quarter of the respondents chose "ZERO TO THREE."[5]

Probing further, investigators discovered that the "disconnect" occurred because many people could not imagine what effective public investments for children under three would look like. Furthermore, many respondents preferred that children under three be home with their families, and were therefore wary of government action.

Many state policy makers faced a similar problem when they first learned of the "brain research" that showed how powerfully experiences during the first three years of life influenced later development, including the structure of the brain and its characteristic responses to stress. Wanting to act on this important information, they proposed new funding for early education—for four- and five-year-olds! They had difficulty imagining what state government could do to support the education of children under three, who, they felt, were too young for school.

In fact, federal, state, and local governments are today providing significant support for educational programs for children under three and their families, as well as for programs that serve children three to five. They are subsidizing the cost of child care, licensing child-care programs to ensure health and safety, providing education for caregivers in promoting language and literacy, supporting outreach to parents through home visits and resource and referral activities, supporting toddler reading programs in libraries, health clinics, and parent–child drop-in centers, sponsoring parenting classes and two-generation family literacy programs, and providing comprehensive early education programs for young children.

Our biggest problem is that we are not investing nearly enough. A secondary but still significant problem is that we are not investing wisely enough.

The vast majority of state and federal spending for children under four is going to subsidize the cost of child care, with no strings attached. Low-income parents get vouchers that they can use for any type of care they can find; middle-income families receive tax credits to cover part of their child-care costs, regardless of the type or quality of that care. But provider compensation, training, and support are generally so poor that parent payments and public subsidies to providers combined rarely pay anywhere near the real cost of quality care—care that can be counted on to provide children with the steady diet of enriching conversations that builds a strong language foundation.[6] If our goal is to ensure that children get early learning experiences that will prime them for school success, then we are not getting our money's worth if we do not invest in quality. Putting more money into the programs that *do* provide rich language experiences, investing in the education of the early childhood workforce and of parents, and providing the programs that parents select with sufficient resources to achieve and sustain quality would seem to be wiser choices.

Public Possibilities

Before we explore promising approaches to providing change on the scale that is needed, let us look briefly at the mechanisms that federal, state, and local governments have at their disposal and at some programs and policies that can serve as stepping-stones to a more effective system.

Components of Policy: Program Implementation, Regulation, and Funding

As Assistant Secretary for Children and Families in the Clinton administration, Olivia Golden was invited to speak to a group of early childhood advocates and funders who had gathered to discuss visions for the future. Ms. Golden began her address[7] by summarizing recent accomplishments: the strengthening of Head Start and birth of Early Head Start, innovative regulation at the state level that provided incentives for private programs to meet quality standards, and a significant increase in early childhood funding as a result of the Child Care and Development Block Grant.

Olivia Golden's examples illustrate the various ways that governments can exercise their power to help children and their families. The first is through operating programs, such as Head Start and public schools. These programs can be run directly by government agencies or through contracts with local service providers. Public funds can support planning, training, and evaluation to ensure that these programs succeed in their service missions.

A second avenue is through regulation of programs that are operated by others. For example, all states require that early childhood centers have a license to operate, and they periodically inspect centers to ensure that they are in compliance with the licensing requirements. States can also require credentials for individuals, such as teachers, child-care center directors, and medical professionals.

Finally, governments at all levels are sources of funding. Funds can be raised through dedicated funding streams, such as a lottery (Georgia), cigarette tax (California), voluntary tax check-off (Colorado), or a supplemental property tax levy dedicated to supporting children's services (some Florida counties). They can also be drawn from the general revenue.

In addition to flowing directly to programs and agencies, funds can also be dispersed through grants to provider organizations or government entities and through vouchers to individuals. They can also be provided indirectly, as tax deductions or credits, designed to encourage or support particular activities such as charitable giving, use of child care by working parents, or employer sponsorship of child care for their employees. Refundable tax credits are provided whether or not a person has an offsetting tax liability; they thus allow poorer families, who pay sales and payroll taxes but may owe little or nothing in income tax, to share in the benefits of an income tax credit program.

Funding and program participation can be set up as entitlements, like social security, which automatically accrue to those who meet the eligibility criteria. Government entities are obligated by law to provide these benefits. Other benefits are set up as capped entitlements, available to all who qualify, but only until the money that has been appropriated runs out. Other funding is allocated on a one-year or multiyear basis as line items in local, state, or federal budgets. Funding that flows from the federal government to the states or from the states to local entities may require a local financial contribution or "match" in order to "draw down" federal or state dollars that have been appropriated.

At the local level, programs are often supported by multiple funding streams and answerable to various government regulatory agencies. For example, a child-care center might provide a Head Start program in the mornings and "wrap-around" child care in the afternoons. For the families, it may appear to be a single place where they drop off their children, communicate with the teachers, and participate in program planning and policy. For the administrators, however, it's a complex patchwork. In addition to being answerable to their staff and to the families they serve, they must document their compliance with the regulations of various agencies that provide funding or oversight or both. The morning program is supported by federal funds through a contract with Head Start and must meet Head Start's performance standards, which cover enrollment, operations, staffing, ongoing staff development, curriculum, parent involvement, provision of health and social services, and other areas. The afternoon program—and any children who come in the morning but do not meet Head Start's very low family income guidelines—may be supported with a mix of parent payments, vouchers, and grants. The Center will be licensed by the state, and may receive extra state funding or higher reimbursement for vouchers if it can demonstrate that it meets higher quality standards, such as those required for NAEYC accreditation.

Major Federal Early Childhood Programs, Legislation, and Funding Streams

- Early Learning Programs
  - *Head Start.* Begun in 1965 as part of the War on Poverty, Head Start provides early childhood education, parenting support, and medical, dental, and nutrition services for young children whose family incomes fall below the poverty line. It also provides a career ladder for parents interested in early childhood education, as well as opportunities for all of its parents to be involved in policy decisions that impact their children's education.

    Head Start's service model is continually evolving in response to changing family needs and evaluation results. At present, it primarily serves three- and four-year-olds in half-day programs, but, in the wake of Welfare Reform, there is a new emphasis on partnering with child-care programs to provide full-day coverage for working parents. There is also an enhanced emphasis on overall program quality, staff education and continued professional development, and, especially, use of research-supported techniques to ensure that children master foundation skills for reading.

    In 2000, Head Start reported results from the first phase of a self-evaluation, as required by Congress.[8] The evaluation showed that three quarters of Head Start classrooms were providing "good" care and that none were providing care that was below "minimally adequate." This stood in stark contrast to the Cost, Quality, and Child Outcome Study findings that fewer than one quarter of child-care centers were providing three- to five-year-olds with "good" care, while 10 percent were providing care that scored below the "minimally adequate" mark.[9] The Head Start evaluation also found that the programs were, by and large, meeting children's educational needs, with notable fall-to-spring growth in language, math, and social competencies. Parents gave Head Start the highest customer-satisfaction rating of any government program. Teachers showed their satisfaction and commitment with a turnover rate of only 11 percent, far lower than the 30–40 percent rate typical of the child care and early education field.

Head Start serves only about 60 percent of the children whose age and family income make them eligible for its services.[10] *Yet its impact has transcended this narrow population group. Head Start's regional quality improvement centers (HSQICs) (closed in 2003 as part of an administrative reorganization) provided training not only to Head Start providers and their partners but also to others in their communities. The entire early childhood field has benefited from the research, curriculum materials, teacher training and credentialing programs, and family involvement models developed by and for Head Start.*

- *Early Head Start.* Early Head Start provides parenting education, family support, health and mental health, and early childhood care and education services to low-income young children and their families, beginning in pregnancy and continuing through age three. As with Head Start, community agencies or school systems apply for program grants, which are awarded on a competitive basis.

Early Head Start made its first grants in 1995 and is already proving to be a promising model for facilitating children's language and cognitive development and for encouraging parents to establish habits of reading, playing with, and disciplining children that support early language and long-term learning. [11]

When compared to similar children not in the program, Early Head Start children had higher mental development scores at age two and were less likely to score in the "developmentally delayed" range. Their parents were more likely to read to them daily, and tended to report that their children used more words and combined words in more sophisticated ways. At age three, program children had higher cognitive development and vocabulary scores and were less likely to score in the developmentally delayed range.

Furthermore, fully implemented programs had strong impacts on children's emotional development and on parenting practices such as avoidance of harsh discipline and facilitation of children's language and learning through habits such as conversation, play, daily reading, and bedtime routines.

For a new program, these results are highly encouraging. Although Early Head Start has not yet equaled the dramatic results of either the Abecedarian Project or the Parent–Child Home Program in erasing the effects of many early disadvantages and risk factors, it clearly has the potential to make a significant difference. Early Head Start served 62,000 children from ZERO TO THREE in 2002, about 3 percent of the income-eligible children who could have benefited from its services.[12] *If every community could offer Early Head Start to all families with incomes at or close to the poverty line—or even better, to all families who wanted it—we would likely see a dramatic reduction in the percentage of children who come to school at a loss for words.*

- Grants to States and School Districts
  - *Child Care and Development Block Grant.* The Child Care and Development Block Grant (CCDBG) funnels money to states to support child care for low-income working parents, especially those who may be moving from welfare to work. Most of the funds support child-care vouchers, which parents can use for center-based programs, family child care, or to pay friends, neighbors, or relatives to provide care. However, a small percentage is set aside for quality improvement activities, such as teacher training and compensation, resource and referral activities to help families find child care that meets their needs, creation of programs to serve those with special needs, and monitoring and assessment activities.

    By giving states substantial decision-making power and also requiring them to contribute money of their own, this grant has spurred innovation and coordination at the state level.

    The program was up for reauthorization in 2002. A consortium of early education advocacy groups had originally called for a $20 billion increase, with 12 percent set aside for quality. This request was scaled back as the reauthorization debates dragged on. In April 2004, after a bipartisan majority of senators had voted for a $6 billion increase to cover substantially increased work requirements, the Senate bill was again tabled.
  - *Title 1.* Title 1 of the Elementary and Secondary Education Act provides supplementary funds to school districts with large numbers of children whose family incomes are below the poverty line or close enough to it to make them eligible for reduced-price school lunch. School districts can use these funds for a variety of authorized purposes; many districts have opted to use some of them to finance preschool or full-day kindergarten programs for children considered to be at risk of starting school behind.

    Title 1 efforts are meant to be remedial, rather than preventive, and its preschool programs tend to be far less comprehensive than Head Start, which serves a similar population. Evaluation of such programs has been sporadic, and the reported results have not been encouraging. [13]
- Tax Credits
  - *Child-Care Tax Credit.* One of the largest federal child-care programs is an indirect subsidy that mainly benefits middle-class families. Families in which all parents work can claim up to $3,000 of child-care expenses for one child (and $6,000 for two or more children) as tax credits.

    Families who do not earn enough to owe this much in federal income taxes can't take full advantage of this credit, unless, as some legislators have proposed, it is made "refundable."

- Entitlements
  - *Individuals with Disabilities Education Act.* Young children with identified special needs, including sensory and motor impairments, severe emotional difficulties, and marked delays in language or other areas are entitled to early intervention services. Part H serves children under three; Part C ensures services for three- to five-year-olds. Especially in language and in related areas like speech, hearing, and mental health, the earlier the intervention the easier it is to erase delays and prevent future problems. Thus every state has a federally supported Child Find program to identify children at risk, as well as a network of supports for identified children and their families.

    It is particularly important to pick up children who may have witnessed or experienced family violence, or whose mothers have been victimized. These children are at double risk: the trauma interferes with their emotional development and learning and their mothers may not be emotionally available to them at the time when they need them most. Fortunately, early intervention for parent and child is highly effective in these cases. Coordination among agencies to identify, screen, and serve these children is thus an important policy priority.[14]
- Professional Development and Quality Improvement Grants
  - The Early Learning Opportunities Act, Early Reading First, and the Early Childhood Professional Educator Grants program have together funded approximately 100 pilot projects designed to improve early literacy outcomes for children likely to be at risk.

    These programs are a drop in the bucket. Most reach only a small percentage of providers in their communities; they can't even begin to reach the whole country. However, because each project's approach must be carefully documented and its results fully evaluated, we can expect these pilots to yield a menu of effective models from which communities can choose when an appropriate level of funding is made available.

State Early Childhood Regulation and Investment

At the state level, early childhood education is supported through a smorgasbord of programs, regulations, and funding streams that vary from state to state.

- *Licensing and Credentialing.* Every state requires child-care centers to be licensed, and most require licensing for family child-care homes that serve more than three or four unrelated children. For the most part, licensing agencies set minimal standards for facilities, equipment, adult/child ratios, teacher/provider training, and routine practices needed to maintain health and safety. Other areas of quality—particularly those that undergird language learning—are less likely to be addressed, although this is beginning to change.

Licensed care tends to be of better quality than unlicensed care, but it is not necessarily good enough to provide the language foundation that children need. Strengthening licensing requirements can be an important route to quality, but it is more likely to be effective if it comes with an infusion of funds that allows programs to maintain the higher standards. Thus, several states have developed tiered licensing programs that reward adherence to higher standards with higher reimbursement rates for serving children eligible for subsidies.

Of course, the requirements most likely to affect the quality of children's language experiences are those that relate to teacher expertise. Only twenty-one states require any preservice training for early childhood teachers who work in privately funded settings; of these, only ten require a Child Development Associate, AA degree in early childhood, or college coursework in early childhood or a related field. In 2002, only one of these—Rhode Island—met the standard recommended by Eager to Learn by requiring a bachelor's degree.[15] Massachusetts will require a BA by 2017.

- *Early Learning Programs.* At least forty states offer some state-financed early learning programs. These tend to be for low-income four-year-olds, but a few states serve all four-year-olds statewide or in designated districts, on a voluntary basis. These programs may be offered in public schools or in community sites such as churches or child-care centers, but they look a lot like kindergartens. They often set higher standards for teacher qualifications and educational programming than those that prevail in private programs; in fact, twenty states require their public prekindergarten teachers to have bachelor's degrees and several require that they use an approved curriculum or align their instruction with state learning standards. Some states also encourage or require program sites to achieve national accreditation.

- *Child-Care Vouchers.* Every state has a program that provides former welfare recipients (and, at state discretion other working parents with modest incomes) with vouchers that can be used to purchase child-care services.

  Investing sufficient funds in tiered-licensing programs can make it financially viable for centers and family child-care homes with high quality programs to serve low-income children. Generally, however, vouchers have done little to improve the quality of care in communities and the likelihood that children will get early language experiences that build a strong foundation for literacy.

- *Quality Improvement and Workforce Initiatives.* Many states have taken significant, though still insufficient, steps to improve the qualifications and stability of their early childhood workforce. In at least twenty-three states, T.E.A.C.H. Early Childhood scholarships support teachers to continue their education. In partnership with their employers, the program also provides the teachers with bonuses for completing their studies, in return for a commitment to stay on the job.[16] Several states and some localities have implemented wage-enhancement programs for experienced teachers who have met educational benchmarks.

Such investments tend to have ripple effects, improving professionalism and morale, driving up the quality of the early childhood applicant pool, increasing the demand for early childhood courses, enabling communities to secure grants for early childhood program improvement, and enhancing the overall level of quality in programs for young children and their families.[17]

- *Child-Care Resource and Referral Agencies.* CCR&Rs, supported by public and private funds as well as fees for service, help parents to find childcare and other early childhood services. They maintain databases on the supply of and demand for child care, which are used for state and community planning. They also provide education to both parents and providers and work with employers, families, state and local governments, and other entities to improve the availability and quality of early education services.[18]

- *Programs for Families.* As the importance of early experience has gained wider recognition, parent education and support programs have been growing in popularity. Most states provide some programs to help young families, particularly those who may be facing challenges such as poverty, medically fragile infants, teen parenting, or histories of substance abuse, depression, or family violence. Some programs focus on health and general well-being; others focus on providing a strong educational foundation. Parents as Teachers,[19] the largest of the education-focused programs, has more than 2,000 sites across the country, in all fifty states. The program reaches all parents in its communities, not just those deemed to be at risk. Other language-focused programs such as the Parent–Child Home Program,[20] the Home Instruction for Parents of Preschool Youngsters,[21] and AVANCE[22] provide services to targeted populations.

- *Local Partnerships.* Just as the federal government has "devolved" funds and decision-making power to the states through block grants, so many states have initiated similar devolution initiatives to encourage local planning, program design, and coordination of services. For example, North Carolina's Smart Start is a public–private initiative that provides early childhood funds to local partnerships in all 100 North Carolina counties. Within broad limits, these funds are used at local discretion to "improve the quality of child care, make child care more affordable and accessible, provide access to health services and offer family support." Smart Start, as it proclaims on a Web site[23] that provides resources for parents, professionals, and potential donors, "has achieved tremendous results in these areas and continues to strive to reach all children in North Carolina." The model has been adopted or adapted in several other states.

Pulling the Policy Levers

In her talk to early childhood leaders and funders, Assistant Secretary Golden focused on the challenges ahead: closing the gaps in quality, affordability, equity, and sustainability of needed programs for young children. In order to address the magnitude of these gaps, the Assistant Secretary urged her audience to identify and work for "large incremental steps" and to articulate these steps in ways that would inspire public support. She closed with a simple piece of advice: "Pull the policy levers." It is generally easier, politically, to expand or modify an existing program than to create one from scratch. Legislatures debate relatively few of the bills that are considered by their committees each session. They often attach time limits to programs and policies, especially when appropriations are involved. A new proposal is more likely to get out of committee if it can be incorporated into an existing law or program that is up for reauthorization because its time limits are approaching, or if it is related to a chief executive's initiative.

Pulling policy levers is what advocacy organizations do. They know when a program is due for reauthorization, and cultivate relationships with members of key committees and their staffs so they can help shape proposals for change. They also track budgets. They know when to mobilize their constituencies to press for action or to thank friendly policy makers, and how to hold legislators accountable at election time by reporting their positions on key votes. They know how to build coalitions with organizations whose agendas and constituencies are different from theirs, but who recognize a common interest. They also know how to use the initiative petition process that is enshrined in many state constitutions to bypass the state legislature and enact a law through direct voter approval.

Advocates have another asset: their belief that where there's a will there's a way. When the legislative climate is friendly or the governor shows an interest, they can help to shape new laws and initiatives. When these paths are blocked, they can work behind the scenes to form alliances with state administrators or to build coalitions that can tip the electoral balance or put an initiative petition on the ballot.

In November 2002, Pennsylvania parents joined with early education providers in a "virtual strike." Through a weeklong series of activities, they explained to their employers and elected representatives what would happen if early educators could no longer afford to keep their jobs. "If this were a real strike," parents informed their employers, "I would not be able to come to work." Their letters pointed out that the persistence of low salaries, averaging just over $16,000 for child-care teachers and considerably less for assistant teachers and aides, contributed to annual turnover rates of 30 percent for teachers and 50 percent for aides. "In effect," they explained "this turnover amounts to an *actual walkout*.[24]

The "strike" was the capstone on the five-year efforts of a broad coalition of activists to improve the quality of child care throughout the state. In 2002, this coalition prevented early childhood cuts in a tight budget year and won two of the three increases they asked for: expansion of the T.E.A.C.H. program and a tiered reimbursement and compensation enhancement program known as "Keystone Stars." These programs had been recommended by the Department of Public Welfare, whose leaders had been engaged, convinced, and supported by the activists. The coalition, which had strategically pushed their issues with gubernatorial candidates in the primary election, also secured the support of the incoming governor for additional early childhood investments.

Great Leaps Forward

Most of the time, change comes gradually. Government programs develop incrementally, through the tweaking of existing laws, expansion of pilot programs that have proven their worth, and redeployment of resources. But sometimes, such incremental change seems just too slow, and a major policy shift is enacted. The leadership for such change often comes from a governor or president, but it can also come from agency heads, legislators, and grassroots advocacy groups.

The following examples illustrate three different ways in which significant advances in early childhood policy have been brought about.

- *Agency Planning.* In 1994, Congress reauthorized Head Start. Responding to the "quiet crisis" facing families with infants and toddlers and the scientific evidence on the importance of the first three years of life presented in the Carnegie Foundation's *Starting Points*[25] report, as well as the track record of success achieved by Head Start's pilot Parent Child Centers (which served infants, toddlers, and their families), Congress set aside 3, 4, and then 5 percent of Head Start funds for each of the next three years for children under three. In order to implement this directive, Secretary of Health, Education, and Human Services Donna Shalala convened an Advisory Committee on Services for Families with Infants and Toddlers. The Advisory Committee brought together experts from universities and highly successful parent–child programs across the country to design a program that would promote positive outcomes in terms of child development, family development, staff development, and improved community capacity. Thus Early Head Start was born.[26]

- *A Governor's Leadership.* In 1990, Zell Miller ran for governor of Georgia on an education platform. His proposal for early childhood was simple and profound: provide a public prekindergarten education for every four-year-old in the state whose parents chose it, and fund the program with proceeds from a state lottery.

  The Georgia Prekindergarten Program was launched in 1993, as a lottery-funded pilot serving low-income four-year-olds. Under Governor Miller's leadership, the program continued to grow, until by 1995 the program was open to all four-year-olds. Conceived from the beginning as an academically oriented "school readiness" initiative, the program required the use of an approved, nationally recognized curriculum and provided training for teachers. Private child-care and early education providers were encouraged to participate.

  Governor Miller made sure that the program worked. He actively promoted the lottery and the benefits of preschool education. He insisted on expanding the program to serve all four-year-old children rather than including low-income three-year-olds, because he knew that a high quality program would only be sustainable in his increasingly conservative state if it had a broad, middle-class constituency. When differences with the elected State Superintendent of Schools imperiled his program, Governor Miller took steps to remove it from her jurisdiction as head of the Department of Education by creating an Office of School Readiness that reported directly to him. He appointed a top-notch director who streamlined administration, actively marketed the program and its educational value, introduced a client service approach to encourage the participation of private child-care centers and preschools, and upped teacher qualification requirements and ongoing training.[27]

  Zell Miller's example and that of other governors who made early childhood education a priority was so persuasive that a 2002 report by the Governor's Task Force on Early Childhood Care and Education in Pennsylvania made gubernatorial leadership and vision its first recommendation. They justified this choice with the statement that "In achieving the school readiness goal, only the governor can provide the leadership that blends agendas across agencies and ideological divides, creating a comprehensive and coordinated approach that reduces inefficiencies and builds public support."[28]

- *Citizen Action.* In 1997, famed actor and director Rob Reiner appeared on the public stage in a new starring role—as champion of children. Swayed by research like that presented in the earlier chapters of this book, Rob Reiner made it his mission to improve options, opportunities, and outcomes for very young children. He founded the *I Am Your Child* Foundation http://www.iamyourchild.org [29] and served as spokesman for a statewide campaign. California's Proposition 10, enacted by initiative petition in 1998, imposed a fifty-cents per pack tax increase on cigarettes to provide funding for early childhood health and education programs. Eighty percent of the money flows to county-level Children and Family Commissions, who determine its use in their communities. Twenty percent supports the work of the statewide Children and Family Commission. Since its implementation in 1999, Prop 10 (now called First Five) has provided more than $700 million for new services and program enhancements to promote the education and healthy development of children from before birth to age five. First Five funds have supported early childhood teacher training, stipends to attract and retain qualified teachers, consultants to help teachers work more effectively with children with challenging behaviors and other risk factors, accreditation of family child-care homes and child-care centers, and other quality-improvement efforts.

Charting a New Course

We saw in Chapter 7 that a disproportionate share of public educational funds is spent on school-age children and college students as compared to preschoolers. It is also true that a disproportionate share of public early childhood funds is being spent on four-year-olds as compared to younger children.[30] Most states have public prekindergarten programs for low-income four-year-olds, and a growing handful have public programs for ALL four-year-olds in at least some districts. Few, however, make significant investments in early learning programs or supports for children three and under, and most of the programs take the form of home visits or parent–child programs for at most a few hours a week.

Four-year-olds are important, and we need to be spending more on them, not less, if we are to achieve the goal of having all children begin school primed for success. But, in order to achieve this goal, we must also invest significantly more and more wisely in our zero- through three-year-olds, to ensure that they develop the language foundation that will make later educational investments more effective.

If we are to meet the needs of our youngest children for a steady diet of experiences that nourish their language development, then we must stay ahead of the societal trends that are leaving so many of them at risk. Our progress toward a sustainable system that supports parents and provides high quality programs for children must be dramatically accelerated. We need to shift resources and policies from investments and regulations that have proven to be ineffective or marginal to those that have proven their worth, and ensure that evidence-supported programs and policies are implemented with the resources, quality controls, and leadership required for sustainable results.

There is unlikely to be one best solution that everyone can agree upon. Rather, there may be multiple, convergent paths, each with a series of milestones, that together lead to the goal. We need to look for:

- opportunities to provide targeted programs known to be effective with those known to be in need of them or highly likely to fall behind without them
- opportunities to provide ALL children with early experiences of sufficient quality, intensity, and duration to prime them for school success
- opportunities to support parents as their children's first teachers
- opportunities to support teachers as language and literacy experts that parents can count on
- ways to spread the cost of early learning programs equitably and widely enough so that all private and public payers can afford their share
- ways to build systems that can deliver services affordably and sustain quality.

As we examine promising approaches, we can ask several questions:

- What is effective?
- What can be implemented at scale?
- What is cost-effective?
- What is affordable in the short term?
- What is politically achievable?
- What preserves cherished values, such as local and parent choice?
- What is sustainable?

Finally, we need to recognize that any solution will require many partners. Parents, grandparents, business and community leaders, teachers, and those who prepare teachers all have roles to play. But government must also play a significant part. Raising the next generation is a collective responsibility. It must be taken on at the local, state, and federal levels with the best knowledge we can muster and with sufficient resources to apply what we know.

The next three chapters will present solutions that are proving to be effective and cost-effective on a fairly large scale. Each chapter focuses upon a different approach: supporting parents, improving programs for children, and building systems that can sustain effective programs and strategies. Taken together, they provide a menu of options for aligning what we do with what we know. Whether you believe in public programs that provide a common experience or favor parent choice, embrace women's entry into the workforce or wish that more mothers would stay home with their young children, long for national educational standards or value local decision making and innovation, you should find in these chapters proven and promising approaches that match your vision, values, and political viewpoint.

11 Supporting Parents

Parents are their children's first and most enduring teachers.[1] When a child is thriving, we say she is a credit to her family. When a child is failing or not getting what she needs, it is often the parents who are blamed. When too many of our children are coming to school with too few words, requiring disproportionate resources of money and teacher attention and often continuing to lag behind in spite of remedial efforts and repeated grades, it makes sense to include parents in the solution.

Parents help their children to build a sturdy language foundation for later learning in several ways:

- they interact directly as they talk, read, and play with their children
- they choose caregivers, programs, and activities for their children and set up learning opportunities
- they supervise, monitor, and partner with people to whom they entrust their children's care and education, to be sure their child's individual needs are met
- they notice when their children are lagging behind peers in reaching critical milestones and seek help for speech and language delays or other difficulties
- they scout out resources and information and join with other parents to exchange ideas and provide mutual support
- they support, advocate for, and sometimes create programs and policies to meet the needs of their children and of all children in their communities

Supporting parents in all of these roles can improve children's chances of getting the kind of early and ongoing experiences that prime them for success.

Supporting Parents as Nurturers, Playmates, and Language Teachers

T. Berry Brazelton, who has been called "the nation's pediatrician,"[2] believes in parents. He loves to watch a newborn baby turn toward the sound of her mother's voice and to see the joy in her parents' eyes when he shows them what she can do and tells them how special she is.

"What a beautiful baby!" he tells parents on a typical first visit, in a voice that shows that he is already falling in love with their child. "Look how that baby looks in your face and smiles, and look how you look back at her." He urges other doctors to use similar introductions, and to begin "right from the start to help the parent see the responses the child makes, and the stages the child is going through."[3]

Dr. Brazelton has worked with thousands of families in his forty-year career. He knows that every parent of a young child has questions. And because for all of their wonderful uniqueness children traverse a common series of developmental challenges, many of these questions can be anticipated. Dr. Brazelton has identified a series of expectable transitions, when children are likely to regress, act up, or show signs of distress as they prepare for a developmental spurt. He calls these transitions or challenges "touchpoints"[4] because they are times when parents are most appreciative of professional guidance and of reassurance that they and their child are OK. They are also opportunities to provide parents with information on what to expect and with insights and resources that help them fully support their child's emerging abilities.

Dr. Brazelton has reached out to parents through books, television shows, and one-on-one consultations, and has trained other health professionals in his methods of behavioral assessment, relationship-building, and anticipatory guidance. The Brazelton Touchpoints Center[5] reaches out not only to individual professionals but also to communities, training health care and family support professionals, early childhood educators, community elders, and others who touch young children and their families to work together to ensure that every child gets a good start. Essentially, Touchpoints strengthens the culture of the village, with the community coming together to support families so that families can support their children.

Dr. Brazelton's faith in parents and his determination that they get the information and attention they need are shared by policy makers throughout the country. In Missouri, these convictions have sustained Parents as Teachers (PAT),[6] a parenting education program that has become a national model. PAT brings information and education to families, visiting them in their own homes or in other places where they feel comfortable, providing information for parents, activities for parents and children together, screening for vision, hearing, language, health, and overall developmental problems, and connections to providers of health, early childhood education, nutrition, and other family support services.

Like Touchpoints, PAT works to empower parents with child development knowledge. Its mission is "to provide the information, support and encouragement parents need to help their children develop optimally during the crucial early years of life." The program, which started in Missouri in 1981, expanded nationally beginning in 1986, and is now international, provides parenting education on a weekly, biweekly, or monthly basis until the child reaches kindergarten age. PAT support is generally offered to all parents in a community, not just those whose children are considered at risk, although families with greater needs may be offered more frequent visits and more intensive services.

In Missouri, PAT is offered by law in every school district, and serves nearly half of the families of preschool-aged children in the state. About 40 percent of the children served are considered "high need" and receive more intensive services.

The program has a strong language component, and the results reported on its national Web site are impressive. Studies done in Missouri, New York, California, and North Carolina[7] showed that PAT parents successfully implemented the practices that the program encourages and that their children developed strong language skills. Special needs and developmental delays were addressed and often remedied before kindergarten. Children's gains in early language development relative to peers whose families have not had PAT visits persisted as higher reading scores in the early elementary grades.

A summary of Missouri results from 1985 through 1995[8] concluded the following:

> Independent evaluations in Missouri show PAT parents are effective in their role as their child's first and most influential teachers.
> - PAT children were significantly more advanced in language development, problem solving, and social development at age 3 than comparison children.
> - 99.5% of participating families free of child abuse or neglect.
> - Significant cost savings to school district by
>   reduced placement in special education
>   fewer retentions
>   less remedial education.
> - Early gains maintained in elementary school, based on standardized tests.
> - Significantly more PAT parents took an active role in their child's education.

In 1999, PAT updated its parent information component. The new *Born to Learn*[9] curriculum incorporates the latest neuroscience research and helps parents to take advantage of "windows of opportunity" when their children are most likely to show interest in particular types of learning pursuits. Parents across the economic spectrum report that they are intrigued by the science and find the new information helpful for understanding and supporting their children's learning. PAT currently offers programs in 3,000 communities in the United States, Canada, and other countries.

The Parent-Child Home Program (described in Chapter 4) has achieved even more impressive results. This multisite program has taken on the especially challenging task of working with parents with low levels of

---

Parent-Child Home Program Research Results

- Parent–Child Home Program (PCHP) replication graduates, from low-income families, had reading scores of 54 in second and fifth grades, and of 51 in seventh grade, above the national norm of 50 on the California Achievement Test (CAT).[10]

- PCHP replication graduates had mathematics scores of 52 in second grade, of 51 in fifth grade, and of 55 in seventh grade, above the national norm of 50 on the CAT.[11]

- A follow-up study of graduates of the original Parent–Child Home Program found that they maintained their 17-point short-term gain in IQ, to above the norm of 100, up to age ten.[12]

- A study of participants found that PCHP parents' verbal interaction with their children was 50 percent higher than that of non-Program mothers when measured at the conclusion of the Program.[13]

- A follow-up study of PCHP parents found that their verbal interaction with their children maintained its 50 percent superiority to that of non-Program mothers when tested two years later, after their children had entered school.[14]

- PCHP parents' verbal responsiveness to their school-age children, two years after completion of the program, correlated with the children's scores in reading, arithmetic, task orientation, social responsibility, self-confidence, and cognitive skills.[15]

- A study of a long-running PCHP replication found that low-income children who had completed the program graduated from high school at higher rates than similarly-situated children who had not been in the program and at rates equal to those of middle-class students.[16]

- PCHP graduates, all from low-income families, exceeded state norms on the Cognitive Skills Assessment Battery given to all South Carolina first graders. When a small group of children who exhibited severe developmental delays in infancy were excluded, nearly 93 percent of PCHP graduates scored "school ready," as opposed to fewer than 83 percent of children in the general population.[17]

literacy, education, and income. Some of these parents are unlikely to use rich vocabulary in everyday conversations with adults, let alone to use it with their children.

The program gets parents and children playing, reading, and asking questions together. It thus encourages the kinds of conversations that tend to support rich vocabulary development and varied language use. Parents not only come to appreciate their children's learning—they enjoy participating in it. The results of numerous studies conducted by outside observers indicate that the Parent-Child Home Program is effective both in promoting parent and child behaviors that facilitate language development and in giving children with initial risk factors academic advantages that persist through the elementary grades. Few programs can boast this level of success!

Like the Parent–Child Home Program, the federal Even Start program works with the most challenging families. Taking a two-generation approach, it aims to foster the parent's literacy and educational progress while also supporting the child's. Community-based grantees integrate literacy or GED (high school equivalency) classes for parents with parenting education and early childhood education.

A national evaluation completed in 1998[18] found that some grantees had more success than others, and offered clues as to what made the program most effective in promoting positive outcomes for the children involved. Four points were highlighted:

- *Literacy-Based Parenting Education Is Important.* Even Start began as a federally administered program, with grantees required to implement a high quality literacy-focused parent education component. Later, when program administration was transferred to states, rules for parenting education were often relaxed to allow a broader focus on the range of challenges faced by these multiproblem families. Children in the first evaluation study (of federally administered programs) made greater gains in vocabulary and kindergarten readiness than did those in later years.
- *Intensity of Services Matters.* First, the length of time that children and their families were involved in the program made a difference: "an analysis of growth rates of children who remained in Even Start for more than one year shows that children who remained in Even Start for longer periods of time may grow at a faster-than-expected rate both on the Pre-School Inventory and on the Pre-School Language Scale."[19] Secondly, the first study (where the parenting education component was literacy-focused) found that children made significantly greater gains in

vocabulary when their parents participated in a more intensive parenting education program.

- *Service Location Matters.* Children in center-based programs had larger learning gains than those receiving only home-based services.
- *Parent–Child Time Matters.* When projects emphasized parent–child activities, providing large amounts of time for parent and child together, families did a better job of supporting children's language and early literacy with reading and play materials, learning activities, and positive approaches to discipline.

Looking across programs, we can see that it is possible to improve language and literacy outcomes for children by supporting parents in their teaching role. If the intervention is intensive and focused enough and continues throughout the key language-learning years, these improvements can be quite significant, with an impact that extends into elementary school and beyond. The especially strong results of the Parent–Child Home Program, which typically provides two home visits per week for two years, suggest that the key might be to involve both parent and child in repeated, frequent opportunities to practice the rich, engaging conversations that research shows make a difference. But even this may not be enough for children spending the better part of their days away from their parents. In these cases, the caregivers may also need the repeated, frequent opportunities to practice these rich and engaging conversations and the supportive environments that enable them to occur.

The Missouri Department of Elementary and Secondary Education completed a School Entry Assessment Project in 1999. This careful study of 3,500 entering kindergartners from eighty schools throughout Missouri[20] shows the power of combining a high quality, intensive parent education program with good early education programming. Forty-two percent of the children in the study had participated in PAT. Of those, half had been involved for more than two years.

Kindergarten teachers were trained to assess children's skills, knowledge, and behavior in the domains of symbolic development, communication, mathematical/physical knowledge, working with others, learning to learn, physical development, and conventional knowledge, using a sixty-five-item School Entry Profile. Six weeks into the school year, the teachers filled out the forms based on their observations of the children.

The results of this snapshot of children's capabilities at kindergarten entry were consistent with those of the Abecedarian Project research in indicating that early education can overcome disadvantages of birth so that children are not "left behind" before they even start school. As stated in the School Entry Assessment Project's Report of Findings:

- When Parents as Teachers (PAT) is combined with any other pre-kindergarten experience for high-poverty children, the children score above average on all scales when they enter kindergarten.
- The highest performing children participate in PAT and preschool or center care. Among children who participate in PAT and attend preschool, both minority and non-minority children score above average. Children in both high-poverty and low-poverty schools who participate in PAT and attend preschool score above average when they enter kindergarten.
- Among children whose care and education are solely home-based, those whose families participate in PAT score significantly higher.
- Special needs children who participate in PAT and preschool in addition to an early childhood special education program are rated by teachers as being similar to the average child.
- Head Start children who also participate in PAT and another preschool score at average or above when they enter kindergarten.

Supporting Parents as Choosers of Child Care

Choosing child care is a complex task, especially when good choices are limited. Parents must balance cost and convenience with many dimensions of quality. As parents search for a setting where their child will feel comfortable, the quality of the early education program vies for consideration with practical concerns like the length of the car or bus ride, hours of operation, and expectations and opportunities for parent contribution.

Parents want places where they themselves feel comfortable—where they can trust the caregivers to appreciate their cultural background and uphold their deeply embedded values, to understand and look out for their children, and to communicate clearly about their child's progress and any problems that may occur. Immigrant parents may want their children to learn English rapidly, to be sustained in their home language, or both. Parents whose children are unusually active or inquisitive, who tend to be shy or sensitive or easily overstimulated, or who are precocious or delayed in particular areas of development look for settings where their child's strengths will be accommodated and encouraged and caregivers who are attuned to their child's style. For parents with limited resources, finding care that is affordable, reliable, and close to home may be so much of a challenge that questions of educational quality or temperamental and cultural attunement are not even raised.

Studies of parents' and experts' perceptions of "quality" reveal large gaps.[21] This is due in part to parents' vested interest in believing that the programs in which they place their children are good or at least good enough, and in part due to differences in priorities. In part, however, the gaps occur because experts have expertise that parents may not share and so tune in to key indicators of quality that are not readily apparent to the untrained eye or ear. Curricula and teaching practices that effectively support early language may be evident in programs where they are openly espoused and intentionally pervasive, but their absence or uneven implementation is more difficult to spot.

Can consumer education make a difference? Clearly, better-informed parents are in a better position to choose care that meets their child's needs and to point out any problems that need correction. Pressure from informed consumers can also encourage programs to improve quality—to the extent that they can with the resources they are able to obtain.

Resource and referral agencies are the primary consumer educators for the families of young children. Because they help match families and child-care providers, they can also convey parents' desires and help providers develop the capacity to meet them. In their early days, CCR&Rs were reluctant to share judgments about quality with parents because they had no objective way of determining whether one program or setting was better than another. Today, however, there are good tools. In addition to receiving mandatory licenses that certify a basic "floor" level of quality, centers and family child-care homes can earn professional accreditation from NAEYC[22] or NAFCC.[23] These badges of excellence subsume and transcend the state licensing requirements and include rigorous standards related to the educational program and the interactions among teachers, children, and parents. They are awarded after a thorough self-study process involving all staff and at least a representative group of parents, correction of any weaknesses, and an observation by a professionally trained validator or observer. Many providers have found accreditation to be an effective marketing tool.

Recognizing that quality costs, Arkansas and Maine provide a double tax credit to parents who choose accredited programs for their young children. The hope is that this will help spur and sustain quality, as parents demand that programs achieve accreditation and accredited programs are able to increase their fees.

Some states have also begun to use licensing to help parents be more informed consumers. For example, the Illinois Department of Children and Family Services (DCFS) operates a Day Care Information Line that provides parents with licensing compliance information about child-care programs.

Supporting Parents as Partners to Professionals and Supports for Each Other

Child-care providers may be paid like parking attendants,[24] but child-care programs are not parking lots. Parents can't just drop off their children and pick them up at the end of the day. They need to be involved. The younger the child, the less she is able to speak for herself, the more essential is the parent's role.

This is one reason why Head Start puts so much emphasis on family involvement. In Head Start and other high quality child-care programs, the partnership often begins during the enrollment process. Providers find out as much as they can about the child, as parents assess whether what the program can offer will be a good fit. A transition plan, with the teacher making a home visit or the child visiting with his parent, can help ease a young child's entry into a new situation. Ideally, the child's teacher or caregiver develops a relationship with the parent that helps the child to feel secure. When the child develops new interests or traverses important milestones, parent and provider share the joy. When concerns arise at home or at "school," parent and provider address them together.

Programs that are truly family-supportive go beyond partnership to build community. The Parent Services Project (PSP),[25] which has been adopted by many child-care, Head Start, and prekindergarten programs, is an effective model.[26] The project usually begins simply, with fun activities for parents and children. As families get to know each other, they plan activities to address their needs—respite care on Saturdays so that parents can shop without two-year-olds in tow, a revolving loan fund for family emergencies, lectures by experts on issues such as discipline, sleep problems, and early literacy, workdays to paint the classrooms and fix up the playground, and holiday celebrations. Some parent groups start craft co-ops, provide support in seeking employment, or take on community-improvement or advocacy projects. When a parent needs advice, baby-sitting coverage, or help in a crisis, she can call upon other parents as well as on her child's teachers.

PSP has been so successful at reducing parent isolation and depression and improving family well-being that the state of Delaware funds the program as a child abuse prevention measure. Like PAT, PSP is an effective support both for families in trouble and for families facing the ordinary and expectable challenges of parenting young children today.

PSP and other programs like it might also be called parent empowerment projects. Within the center or program, they invite parent participation in policy making, staff evaluation, curriculum selection, and long-range planning and educate parents to take on these roles. Furthermore, they provide incubators for activism, teaching parents to speak up so that their children's needs will be addressed, to access information and community resources, to build supportive networks with other parents, and to deal with professionals and bureaucracies as effective partners.

These lessons are especially important for parents whose children have special needs, and those parents are often the first to learn them. Just forty years ago, educational programs for children with handicapping conditions were few and far between. In South Florida, for example, there were NO preschool or kindergarten programs for children with normal intelligence who could not walk, and the elementary schools looked askance at their inclusion.[27] Parents were urged to place such children in institutional care, or in day programs for children with multiple handicaps and severe intellectual impairments. Today, of course, the situation is very different. Because previous generations of parents insisted that the schools take their children, educated themselves and their children's teachers about what their children could do and what help they needed, started programs where none existed, and lobbied school committees, state legislatures, and Congress, children with a variety of handicapping conditions now routinely participate in educational and recreational programs with their nondisabled peers. Individual Educational Plans, constructed each year with parent input, provide guidance for their teachers and assure their access to needed therapeutic services.

When a child is ill or has an obvious handicap, parents become fiercely protective. Parents whose children are subtly falling behind because they are not getting the language input, practice, or early intervention treatment they need must learn to be equally fierce protectors and equally savvy consumers.

Supporting Parents as Advocates

We often think of advocates as pests, constantly banging on closed doors to plead their case with legislators and other decision makers who would prefer not to listen. The persistence that has earned advocates this reputation has been important to their success, but it is only one of many ingredients. Effective advocates are more likely to build alliances with legislators than to badger them.[28] They thank legislators for favorable votes and help bring out supporters at election time. Most important, they provide legislators with information on an ongoing basis that helps them to do their jobs.

Connecticut lawmakers place so much value on input from parents that the General Assembly's Commission on Children actually sponsors a course to develop parents' leadership and advocacy skills. The Secretary of State presents graduates with their diplomas on the state house steps! Connecticut's Parent Leadership Training Institute[29] is now offered in eight other states. No government can parent a child, but governments that are responsive to parents can make it easier for parents to access the resources they need to nurture the next generation.

"*If parents only knew what they were entitled to in a civilized society, they would demand it.*" David Lawrence, Jr., father of five and grandfather of one coined this sentence and repeats it often. As publisher of *The Miami Herald,* David Lawrence had become increasingly alarmed about what was happening to children in his hometown and throughout the state of Florida. He knew the statistics,[30] many of which were featured prominently in his newspaper:

- *In Miami-Dade,* one of every four children under age six living in poverty; almost half living in poverty or near-poverty
- At least 50,000 children under age five with no health insurance
- More than one third of children coming to kindergarten unprepared to succeed
- 21,000 new cases of juvenile delinquency each year
- Fewer than 20 percent of the over twenty-five population holding a college degree, as compared to 31 percent nationally
- *Statewide,* one million Floridians between zero and five years old
- 150,000 reported cases of abuse or neglect annually
- Almost 900,000 children hungry or at risk of hunger
- Child-care workers earning a median income of $6.15/hour, averaging far less in earnings than dental assistants, auto mechanics, or roofers
- Forty-six percent of fourth graders scoring "below basic" on National Assessment of Educational Progress reading test
- State ranked in the bottom 10 on death rates for children, arrest rates for juveniles, percentage of children living in extreme poverty, and percentage of children without health insurance

He soon found out that his community was filled with experts who had been quietly making a difference through their work with children, families, and child-care providers. Several universities provided excellent early childhood education courses, model programs for children and families, and outreach to child-care centers and other community organizations. Head Start and resource and referral programs (called Central Agencies in Florida) also offered extensive training and support services for child-care workers serving low-income populations and for parents seeking appropriate care for their children. In addition, foundation and corporate funders had made significant investments in initiatives to improve the quality of early education. Still, only 17 of the more than 1,400 child-care centers and licensed family child-care homes had achieved professional accreditation. Dave Lawrence and the experts he consulted suspected that many of the rest were not providing children with the rich conversations they would need in order to enter school with the robust vocabularies that would prime them for success. The large numbers of children from non-English-speaking backgrounds were a special concern, as they would need a critical mass of English words in order to learn to read in English,[31] along with a richer conceptual vocabulary in their native language or in English to sustain their curiosity and provide a context for more advanced learning.

David Lawrence knew that radical change was called for. He quit the newspaper job he loved and went to work full time to help parents in his community learn what they and their children should be entitled to—and to help them get it.

Miami-Dade's community engagement campaign to promote school readiness began with a broad vision. With leadership from Miami-Dade Mayor Alex Penelas, hundreds of people discussed and committed to its mission statement. The next step was the formulation of a strategic plan. Nearly two hundred professionals in education, early childhood, health, and human services met in a three-day retreat to create the first draft. This draft was then taken out to various sectors of the community, through twenty-one community meetings where participants asked questions and offered critiques and supplementary ideas. This was followed by a daylong Children's Summit, convened by Mayor Penelas. The Summit combined aspects of an old-fashioned town meeting with twenty-first-century technology. There were workshops for parents, grandparents, and professionals, activities and gifts for children, meetings of newly forming task forces, and an opportunity to vote electronically for the three first priority tasks in each area of the Strategic Plan (early development and education; child health and well-being; parent and family skills, services, and information; and prevention of and intervention in child abuse, neglect, and family violence). Sessions were offered in four languages—English, Spanish, Haitian Creole, and American Sign Language. Hundreds of the more than 4,500 community residents who attended volunteered to join a task force to work on next steps.

Three years later, most of the issues that the community had prioritized were being effectively addressed. A 24-hour hot line provides answers to parents' questions and referrals to services and financial supports. A "Welcome" kit greets every newborn and provides her parents with information on community resources. A trilingual Web site[32] and monthly newsletter provide information for parents on enhancing their children's learning, choosing quality child care, identifying problems and concerns, and accessing community resources. Local universities have won major grants to educate child-care providers and improve the quality of their programs. Voters have passed a new property tax levy for children's services, with 50 percent of the funds earmarked for early childhood.

In November 2002, with major leadership from David Lawrence and his growing coalition, Florida voters passed a constitutional amendment to provide every four-year-old with a high quality publicly funded prekindergarten education, without taking resources from programs for younger children.[33] Voters understood that a "universal," publicly supported program could give families a choice, not only about whether to send their four-year-olds to preschool but also what kind of preschool to send them to. Classes could be offered by public, private, or faith-based providers, in family child-care homes or in centers, but they would have to meet quality standards in order to receive state support. The constitutional amendment passed overwhelmingly, by 59–41 percent! The program is slated for statewide implementation in 2005.

It is too soon to judge whether the *Teach More/Love More* campaign and related efforts in Florida will produce the level of change that David Lawrence hopes for. What is clear is that the lives of many children and families have been improved and that a powerful cadre of change agents has been galvanized.

Growing Up Together: The AVANCE Model

Uri Bronfenbrenner, a Cornell University professor, enshrined the notion of a "village" that raises children and supports their families (or doesn't) in academic theory.[34] He pioneered what he called the "ecological model" of human development, explaining that the trajectory of a child's life could only be understood by looking at the complex interactions among biological and environmental factors, including the interplay of family, community, schooling, culture, and public policy.

In 1972, Dr. Bronfenbrenner and several of his graduate students conceptualized an intervention model based on his theory, and put it into practice in a small program in Dallas, TX. The program brought together parents of children under two and provided them with a structured program of parenting education, toy-making workshops, and information on accessing community services for themselves and their children. At the same time, it provided their children with high quality child care.

In 1973, Gloria Rodriguez brought the model to her hometown of San Antonio and founded AVANCE.[35] Gloria had grown up in the barrios of San Antonio, across the street from the housing project from which she would recruit AVANCE's first class of mothers and babies. At first, these mothers seemed a dispirited group—frightened, undereducated, isolated, and living in conditions of extreme poverty, accompanied by neighborhood dysfunction and violence. In all of the roles described in this chapter, they were providing poor support for their young children's language development.

The program that Dr. Rodriguez started grew up with its clientele. GED courses, leadership and advocacy training, fatherhood programs, and employment counseling provided avenues of advancement. AVANCE also hired some of its graduates and supported their professional development. As the community grew—and grew up—new links were added: Head Start, after-school and tutoring programs, youth leadership opportunities, community action, college scholarship funds for both adult and child graduates. When twenty-three of the thirty-one original AVANCE moms came together for a seventeen-year reunion, the long-term results were apparent. Thirty of the thirty-two "AVANCE babes" had graduated high school or were on track to finish and 43 percent of the high school graduates were in college. The mothers had furthered their own educations as well. More than half of those who had dropped out of school had completed their GEDs, and nearly two thirds of that group had continued on with college or technical education.[36]

Today, AVANCE has ten chapters in Texas and one in Los Angeles. It serves more than 20,000 individuals annually and is supported by both public and private funds. AVANCE's core programs for parents and babies continue to foster the parenting practices that build a robust language foundation. In a rigorous evaluation study,[37] AVANCE parents talked more with their children, spent more time teaching them, used more developmentally appropriate speech, and were more encouraging of their children's vocalizations than mothers who had not experienced the program.

AVANCE is a particularly successful example of what Mary Belenky, Lynn Bond, and Judith Weinstock[38] call "a public homeplace." It provides a community where children can flourish, and where the adults who sustain them also sustain each other as they grow and advance through their mutual investment in their children and their community. Such places have sprung up in many neighborhoods, and some, like AVANCE, have endured for decades. They are part of "a tradition that has no name."

This tradition has strong roots that can anchor themselves in all kinds of soil. But it cannot bear fruit without nourishment and support.

12 Improving Programs for Children

The majority of young children in the United States are spending significant parts of their days in the care of people other than their parents. Bringing these programs and settings up to a level of quality that is good enough to support robust language development for most children has become a national necessity. It is also surprisingly easy. It has been done many times, in many places, using many different strategies. It has been done one center or child-care program at a time, and it has been done on a national scale. Let's explore some examples.

Building Models of Excellence

In Allegheny County, PA, a consortium of foundations and public and private agencies took on the challenge of providing early education programs for the vast majority of poor children in their community, programs that would be good enough to enable them to start school on a par with their wealthier peers. Before launching their Early Childhood Initiative, this Pittsburgh-area consortium mapped out the "business case." Drawing on the research in child development and early learning, they sketched a model program. They figured out what training the teachers would need, what salaries would attract and hold them, what equipment and learning materials would be necessary, and what it would take to create appropriate facilities. They estimated the level of use in their county, figuring that about 80 percent of the low-income families would take advantage of free, high quality early education programs. Then the number crunchers went to work. They calculated that the per-child difference between the state child-care subsidy and the cost of a good program was just $13 a day! Armed with this information, they asked local businesses and philanthropies to join their consortium and help fund the gap.

The first Early Childhood Initiative centers opened their doors in 1997. It soon became apparent that the planners had been correct: children were happy and learning. Their parents and teachers were thrilled with their progress. A formal evaluation[1] documented that children were gaining about one and half months of development in language and cognitive skills for every month they spent in the program. Children who entered at three were on track to make up their initial deficits and enter school primed for success.

The Allegheny County project never reached its goal of making good enough programs the norm for its poor children. Two things stood in its way. First, the planners had underestimated the need. Their planning had been done prior to Welfare Reform; their implementation occurred just when large numbers of former welfare recipients with young children were entering the workforce. The part-day, Head Start-like programs they had planned would have to offer full and even extended day care to accommodate parents' work schedules. Extended hours, community involvement in planning these new programs, start-up and recruitment delays, and administrative oversight soon pushed the per-child cost to triple the original calculation.

The second, unexpected problem was a shortage of public funds. The funders, led by the Heinz Endowments, had made a five-year commitment. Their goal was to demonstrate the success of the experiment and to persuade the state government to create a dedicated funding stream, not just for Allegheny County, but for counties throughout the state that wanted to provide high quality early education to the children who needed it the most. The coalition included powerful business leaders who had the governor's ear; they and other advocates worked tirelessly and strategically to secure a public commitment.

Unfortunately, the initiative planners overestimated their persuasive powers. No amount of documented success or documented need could convince the governor to make early education a top priority, and the legislature was not prepared to push for it without his leadership. In the context of welfare reform, many legislators saw the Allegheny County model as "expensive child care," rather than as a foundation for lifelong learning. Reluctantly, the coalition scaled back the Initiative after its third year of implementation, when it became clear that public funds would not be forthcoming and the initiative's ambitious benchmarks could not be met. In the end, Allegheny County got excellent new programs for about 10 percent of the children that they had targeted. The rest remained out of luck.

A RAND Corporation study of the Early Childhood Initiative[2] called it "a noble bet" and sought explanations for its failure to achieve its program and policy goals. The study identified three major problems: "a cumbersome management structure," "mistaken planning assumptions that raised costs to unsustainable levels," and "an inadequate strategy for securing state funding." These are correctable factors: with an up-front commit-ment from state government or a public/private partnership and a stream-lined administrative structure, this bold experiment could be repeated for a reasonable cost. The investment would be well worth making: a research team from Children's Hospital of Pittsburgh[3] found that only 2 percent of the program graduates needed to repeat kindergarten or first grade, in districts that typically retain 21 percent of their kindergarten and first graders! Furthermore, the 18 percent of children in the study with identi-fied mental health conditions progressed at average rates, entering school without marked behavioral or social difficulties. Special education referrals in the schools the children entered dropped from 21 percent to only 1 per-cent. For the 834 children in the study, the "noble bet" was an unqualified success!

The Allegheny County Early Childhood Initiative is one of many demonstration projects that have proved the power of early education. But the question posed by the Initiative was not "Does good early educa-tion work?" but rather "Can good early education be made the norm for "at risk" children in our community?" Despite the failure of their initial attempt, the coalition members know that the eventual answer must be "yes."[4]

Comprehensive, intensive, zero through age five programs that can level the playing field for children with multiple risk factors are few and far bet-ween. But good programs are available throughout the country. Reaching the vast majority of young children with programs that are good enough to provide them with a strong early language foundation can be accomplished in several ways:

1. Create large-scale programs—like Head Start or the Allegheny County dream
2. Bring effective programs "to scale" by replicating them in multiple sites
3. Make existing programs effective

Each route has its own strengths and challenges. And, of course, they can be used together.

Creating Large-Scale Programs

Since 1999, the French-American Foundation[5] has been bringing U.S. policy makers and early childhood experts to France to show them a sys-tem that provides all children with a strong early education, beginning at birth. Always, the visitors come away impressed—by the quality of the nurseries and classrooms, the commitment and expertise of the teachers, and the fact that virtually all French families with young children take advantage of the early education programs their government offers. There are cultural differences, of course, and not all of the French practices are seen as appropriate for American children.[6] But the trips inspire confidence that we could—if we chose—create public early education programs that parents across the economic spectrum would embrace.[7]

In the United States, our biggest success in creating a public program that nurtures robust language development is Head Start—a program that serves the poorest of the poor, and still, after nearly forty years, reaches less than two thirds of the children who are eligible for its services! Head Start began as a large national program, serving half a million children in the summer of 1965. Benefits were evident almost immediately, as children who had never seen a doctor got medical and dental care, children who had been going hungry got nutritious meals, and children who had no books in their homes began learning the alphabet and enjoying story time.[8] The program quickly expanded to provide full-year services, and soon educational benefits were apparent as well. Children were coming to kindergarten or first grade better prepared to learn the standard curriculum.[9] Early studies showed short-term IQ gains, which tended to "fade out" by third grade. Later studies showed broader and more long-lasting impact, as programs became more systematic and consistent in their approach and researchers looked at a range of outcomes in additions to short-term cognitive gains.[10]

Anecdotally, parents reported that their Head Start educated children were becoming chatterboxes and that their curiosity was infectious. Years later, a Florida mother described the results to the director of her son's Head Start experience[11]:

> I've got three kids, and the two older ones have done OK. But my youngest, you remember, he was in your program. Once he started Head Start, he had so much to say we just couldn't shut him up. He kept at me with questions—always wanted to know "why this" and "why that." You know, he was the only one who went on to college. Now he's a doctor, and he's still full of questions.

Today, Head Start educates approximately one million young children, with programs in all fifty states. Although Head Start serves an especially challenging population, its classrooms generally provide better opportunities for language learning than are found in the majority of privately funded full-day programs.[12] As a national program, Head Start provides its teachers and administrators with ongoing training. It also requires the sites it contracts with to meet its performance standards, which are more stringent and educationally focused than the state licensing requirements that the programs must also comply with. Within these standards, individual sites are given leeway to choose curriculum materials, activities, and teaching approaches that work for the children and families they serve. As more is learned about what children need to build an optimal foundation for later learning, Head Start trainers update practitioners' knowledge. The new insights can then be incorporated into revised performance standards.

One of the major insights supported by Head Start's programming and research is the benefit of starting as early as possible. Historically, Head Start included a small group of child and family programs that began early in life. Lessons learned from these Parent and Child Centers and Comprehensive Child Development Programs helped shape the new Early Head Start program. The wildly successful Abecedarian Project[13] provided additional compelling evidence that starting in infancy could enhance the effectiveness of later interventions.

Unlike Head Start, Early Head Start was not launched on a massive national scale. Instead, it started with a relatively small number of carefully selected grantees, trying out different mixes of parenting education and direct services for children and of home-visiting and center-based delivery systems. As described in Chapter 10, the program has inched forward with year-by-year expansion to serve more children in more communities. National training, provided by ZERO TO THREE[14] and WestEd,[15] as well as ongoing evaluation and quality-improvement assistance have enabled the start-ups to move quickly toward ensuring that children with multiple risk factors build a sturdy language foundation. Now many communities are clamoring for Early Head Start programs; unfortunately, the available funding can barely begin to meet this demand.

The strengths of a large-scale program can also be seen at the other end of the economic spectrum. For-profit child-care programs have historically earned a "bad rap" with early childhood experts, who accused companies of putting profit above children's needs. But a relentless focus on quality—as it is defined by early childhood professionals—can enable a national network to deliver excellent early education services in multiple sites, and a reputation for excellence can garner the additional resources from a well-off client base that make quality sustainable and investment profitable. Bright Horizons Family Solutions,[16] which operates more than five hundred programs nationwide, is an example. It pays its employees top dollar, 20 percent above the going rate,[17] and invests in their professional development. It supports centers and family child-care programs in its network to achieve national accreditation, and most have. Its *World at Their Fingertips* curriculum incorporates best practices and provides strong support for early language through teacher–child relationships, book reading and learning activities, and opportunities for exploration, pretend play, and social interaction—using techniques and materials similar to those that are widely used in Head Start classrooms and successful Early Head Start programs.

Bright Horizons succeeds where other for-profit programs have struggled, because it has both an understanding of how to build quality and resources that are adequate for the job. Many of Bright Horizons families are middle and upper income, but the company's major corporate clients also subsidize the programs to close the gap between what parents can pay and what quality costs. Indeed, about 20 percent of the company's revenue comes from employer clients.[18]

Exporting Excellence: Expanding Effective Programs

The Head Start story shows that it is possible to build a large-scale language-supportive program from scratch. With today's knowledge base, implementation of effective practices and achievement of predictable quality can be quite rapid when adequate resources and staff are available. At the same time, however, building from scratch can be costly, as was true in the Allegheny County experiment.

A second approach is to start with a proven program and expand it, or to train others to reproduce it at their own sites. Montessori Schools[19] are a well-known example of an early education program that has been successfully replicated on an international scale. The High/Scope approach is another example. Though less well known outside of the early childhood field, it has been widely adopted by both public and private programs in the United States and in other countries.

High/Scope[20] is the Michigan-based nonprofit organization that developed the Perry Preschool Project. You probably heard of it before picking up this book: it is the focus of the oft-quoted longitudinal study[21] that showed that a high quality preschool program could prevent criminal involvement, welfare dependency, and school dropout, as well as promote high school and college completion and higher adult income, and that every dollar invested saved society $7.16 by the time the participants were twenty-seven years old, and $12.90 by the time they were forty!

High/Scope's name reflects its ambition: to provide programs with quality that is *high* enough to achieve significant results, with a *scope* that is wide enough to have significant impact on the level of need. To this end, High/Scope has developed, tested, and refined comprehensive programs for infants, toddlers, and preschoolers. Its research and development team has created tools and intensive training programs for implementing the

High/Scope teaching approach, setting up learning activities, tracking children's progress, partnering with parents, and targeting teaching to each child's developmental needs.

High/Scope's methods are similar to those described in Chapter 4, emphasizing exploration, play, warm relationships between children and teachers, book reading and discussion, and activities that prompt children to ask interesting questions and share discoveries. High/Scope is also known for its Plan/Do/Reflect methodology, in which children intentionally select activities, actively engage in play and projects, and talk with their teachers and peers about what they have learned. This approach gives even very young children lots of practice in sharing thoughts and feelings, asking questions, making predictions, and drawing conclusions—using an ever-expanding vocabulary to share genuine interests.

Research on the effectiveness of High/Scope's continuously evolving methods and models shows strong short-term impact on language and cognitive skills as well as overall development and long-term impact on the social–emotional well-being and educational aspirations of low-income children. Evaluation of its training programs show that the High/Scope methods can be successfully taught by trained trainers.[22]

High/Scope's 1,300 certified trainers have trained 32,500 early childhood practitioners since 1992, serving 325,000 children each year in programs that have implemented the High/Scope approach. Today, High/Scope programs serve low-, middle-, and upper-income children with programs that incorporate an effective learning model that provides strong support for all aspects of language learning.

Programs like Head Start and High/Scope work at scale because they don't get stale. Both have a central organization that maintains an ongoing program of quality-monitoring and research and a strong system for communicating with practitioners.

Making Existing Programs Effective

The High/Scope strategy of providing extensive training, coupled with continued research, evaluation, and product development, assures high quality. But it is also relatively expensive and requires a serious commitment by the programs involved. Can more modest per program investments bring a wide range of programs up to quality, so that the vast majority of children are no longer left out?

The answer is "yes," and the proof comes from some of our nation's largest employers—the U.S. armed forces.[23] In 1989, a Congressional oversight committee was alarmed by the dismal state of the child care provided for military families. Some called it "a disaster;" others referred to it as the "ghetto" of American child care. There had been a few high profile instances of gross neglect; overall, quality was poor, morale was low, and parent dissatisfaction was high enough to jeopardize the recruitment and retention of military personnel.

Congress acted. The Military Child Care Act of 1989 mandated reforms in licensing standards, oversight, and child-care worker pay, and allocated significant resources to address the problems. A series of improvements over the next decade brought military child care from the bottom of the barrel to a system that many states are looking to as a model. This feat was accomplished through the synergistic application of five key strategies:

- *Tough minimum standards.* New licensing standards raised the bar in all areas of quality, including the critical areas of teacher qualifications, staff–child ratios, group size, and use of a planned curriculum.
- *Professional accreditation.* A pilot project to help fifty centers achieve NA-EYC accreditation proved so successful that when the Military Child Care Act was reauthorized in 1996, it mandated that all centers become accredited. A complementary effort has begun to accredit family child-care providers, including a pioneering effort to align family child-care licensing and compensation standards with the NAFCC accreditation.
- *Strong and supportive oversight.* Unannounced inspections occur four times a year to ensure that programs are in compliance with licensing standards and that centers maintain their eligibility for accreditation. If concerns arise, inspectors provide suggestions and help programs access the resources needed to correct any deficiencies.
- *Making pay commensurate with qualifications.* Military child-care workers and family child-care providers are compensated on a military scale, where jobs requiring comparable levels of prior education and experience receive comparable compensation. As a result, the starting child-care wage in the military is equivalent to the average civilian child-care wage, with far better benefits and opportunities for advancement.
- *Using public funds to fill the gap between what parents can pay and what quality costs.* Military families pay for child care on a sliding scale. Their employer funds the difference between what they can pay and what the programs cost.

As this multipronged strategy was implemented, improvements in staff performance, morale, and retention as well as in classroom quality, parent satisfaction, and children's healthy development became increasingly obvious. It came as no surprise when, in 1998, a study by the RAND Corporation[24] reported that 61 percent of the child-care centers serving military families were excellent, another 35 percent were good, and only 4 percent were fair. None were rated as poor.

The Armed Services are large employers with the resources and clout to demand and sustain excellence. But most programs for young children are small operations: mom-and-pop family child-care homes, faith-based centers serving local congregations, nonprofits operating on a shoestring, or barely profitable "for profits." How can these programs be brought up to a level of quality that is good enough to support robust language development for children?

There are many successful approaches. Accreditation is one way. The process of earning accreditation[25] is a process of self-study and self-improvement that involves all stakeholders—staff, parents, director, and community supporters. Already excellent centers and family child-care homes benefit from identifying strengths and establishing procedures to maintain them; weaker programs benefit from identifying and working on areas that need improvement. States, localities, corporations, philanthropic foundations, community service clubs, and early childhood professional or-ganizations have all made significant investments in helping centers and family child-care homes achieve accreditation. As they build the overall quality of their offerings, programs seeking accreditation put in place the teaching approaches, learning materials, settings, and activities that sup-port early language. They also establish workplace policies, parent com-munication patterns, and business practices that can help sustain these quality elements.

Tiered licensing programs, such as Illinois's Great START and Pennsylvania's Keystone Stars, provide financial incentives for programs that serve subsidized children to become accredited. They also provide a ladder that programs can climb, rewarding partial success and then provid-ing a larger award for further improvement. Such programs may have as many as five levels, ranging from basic licensure through full accreditation.

Another approach is targeted training. Throughout the country, child-care programs are teaming up with universities or other training organiza-tions to get specific training that will improve the quality of their programs and their support for language and emergent literacy skills. In Florida, for example, Nova Southeastern University (NSU) has started a training pro-gram for directors of centers serving infants and toddlers. Teacher turnover is quite high in their area, but the directors have been more stable. Us-ing the training materials that were developed for Early Head Start, NSU trained directors to train and mentor their teaching staff. They also pro-vided coaching in classroom observation and supportive supervision. In an evaluation study,[26] the twelve-week intervention brought the quality of infant and toddler classrooms up from the mediocre average that is typical of the field to the good to excellent range.

With a federal Early Childhood Professional Educator grant, NSU is also working with programs serving infants, toddlers, and preschoolers in a more targeted way.[27] The university is providing courses for teachers and directors in supporting language and emergent literacy, with mentor coaches who can help them apply the material in their own classrooms. At the same time, the grant supports the centers to develop family lending libraries and to conduct workshops to help parents read with their children and encourage the children's questions and vocabulary development.

Even without major grant funding, many centers and family child-care homes are finding ways to upgrade their support for language and emergent literacy, incorporating practices supported by recent research. They are taking advantage of courses offered by local universities and community colleges, of workshops provided by child-care resource and referral agencies and other training organizations, of sessions at professional conferences, of distance education provided on-line or through broadcast or satellite television, and of commercial teacher training products and classroom curricula (see Appendix for examples). They are teaming up with libraries, community foundations, United Way, corporate sponsors, and local service clubs to get the materials, financial support, and assistance they need. They are working together to form learning communities, write grant proposals, and advocate for improved public investments.

One particularly innovative distance education program is being offered by the National Head Start Association, in partnership with the Council for Professional Recognition and RISE Learning Solutions, with funding from nine states and seven private foundations. HeadsUp! Reading[28] uses satellite television and the Internet to enable early childhood teachers and parents to learn from and interact with the top experts in the field. The eight-month course, which consists of weekly satellite broadcasts with an opportunity to phone in questions, facilitated live discussions, on-line readings and discussions, and written assignments, can be taken for college credit at more than 140 colleges nationwide.

Because the network is so large and so well organized, this top quality training can be delivered at a cost of about $70 per participant. Because the participants work in learning teams, with on-site facilitators, these teachers have the support they need to incorporate what they are learning in their daily practice. Indeed, an early evaluation[29] by top reading experts found that participating teachers had significantly increased their use of recommended practices to support language and emergent literacy after only sixteen weeks.

"Just throw money at it" has been universally panned as shortsighted strategy for improving anything. Yet, in early childhood as in other arenas, better-funded programs have gotten better results.[30] Indeed, it seems as if most programs for young children are so underfunded that any money they get is immediately put to good use.

A study of the first two years of North Carolina's Smart Start program,[31] which allocated funds through county partnerships to improve early childhood services in their community, found that the partnerships employed a number of complementary strategies. The researchers collected data from 180 child-care centers, and found that they were engaged in an average of five and as many as fourteen quality improvement activities. Most of the partnerships supported training—through workshops, on-site consultations, scholarships for college courses, and/or substitute coverage for teachers engaged in training activities—and most provided funds for new equipment and materials. About half of the counties funded lending libraries for teachers, parents, and children. Other strategies included improvements in provider compensation, tiered licensing, and support to obtain accreditation. Two years into the program, the percentage of centers earning a quality rating of "good" or "excellent" had nearly doubled—from 14 to 25 percent. Though not approaching Head Start's 75 percent "good to excellent" record[32] or the military's achievement of nearly 100 percent accreditation,[33] this still represented important progress on a broad scale, achieved through modest and flexible investment.

Florida achieved a similar jump in the percentage of quality programs between 1992 and 1994 by strengthening its licensing requirements and providing modest support for teacher training. For children between zero and two, the new requirements, which went into effect in 1992, mandated lower staff–child ratios that came close to professionally recommended levels. The state also increased required preservice training from 20 to 30 hours and mandated that, by 1995, there be at least one person on site with a Child Development Associate Degree or its equivalent for every twenty children enrolled in a program. The state invested in CDA programs and provided scholarship funds to help teachers obtain this credential. Even before the law was fully implemented, a study conducted by Families and Work Institute[34] documented dramatic results. For infants and toddlers, the percentages of centers in the study's representative sample receiving good or excellent ratings jumped from 25 to 36 percent. For programs serving older children, the gain was even more significant: from 27 to 44 percent! Hiring a teacher with a CDA degree or its equivalent not only improved classroom quality, but also increased the children's functional language scores and the complexity of their play with peers. As would be expected, the highest classroom quality, the most sensitive and responsive teachers, the most sophisticated peer play, and the most advanced use of language were found in the classrooms where the teacher held a BA in early childhood education.

Bringing existing programs up to quality through targeted training, support and incentives for improvement, and modest investments to retain, retrain, or upgrade staff may be our most powerful short-term remedy. However, it needs to be supplemented by more comprehensive approaches if the gains are to be sustained. Quality costs, and it costs more than most parents can pay.[35] Unless we can create an "infrastructure" that provides for the cost of quality and that continually infuses both new ideas and enduring principles, we will be frustrated in our attempts to make a lasting difference.

13 Building Systems that Sustain Quality

Early childhood education in the United States is often described as a "nonsystem," a patchwork of public and private programs that meet the needs of some children but allow many to fall through the cracks. Unfortunately, the children most likely to receive inadequate supports are those under four, especially if they are from families with modest incomes.

If our goal is to provide every child with a sturdy early language foundation, then we must address the systemic barriers that keep parents, providers, and programs from getting the supports they need to succeed. We don't need to put babies into public schools, but we do need a public system to support their learning.

Not By Chance

In 1994, the Carnegie Corporation released its *Starting Points*[1] report, calling attention to the "disconnect" between the emerging scientific consensus on the importance of the first three years of life for brain development, language, and social–emotional resilience and the data on the lack of appropriate stimulation, nurturance, and even basic health and safety practices in the settings where most young children were spending most of their time.

Alarmed at their emerging findings, the Foundation began in 1993 to convene experts who could figure out how to improve the quality of early care and education in our nation—and how to ensure that adequate quality would be sustained. The group and its goal were called Quality 2000; the aim was to achieve sustainable quality in time for the new millennium. When it became clear that this goal was unrealistic, the group set a target of 2010 for the implementation of reforms.

The Quality 2000 experts identified five aspects of the "infrastructure" that would have to be robust if quality were to be assured. These were

- parent information and engagement
- professional development and teacher and administrator credentialing (individual licensure)

- facility licensing, enforcement, and accreditation
- funding and financing
- governance, planning, and accountability

The group had lots of ideas for improving each area, which they eventually consolidated into eight recommendations:

1. Use a wide range of approaches to achieve quality in family child-care and center-based programs for young children and their families.
2. Focus on goals and results for children.
3. Place parents and families at the core of early care and education programs.
4. Require staff to be licensed.
5. Expand the content of training and education.
6. Eliminate exemptions and streamline and enforce facility licensing.
7. Raise new funds and set aside 10 percent for quality and infrastructure.
8. Create local and state early care and education boards.

They entitled their report *Not By Chance*,[2] and stated in its foreword: "Its eight actionable recommendations are predicated on, and dedicated to, the proposition that we can and must do better by American children—that we must create an early care and education system—because children matter—and because what we do for them matters immensely."

As Sharon Lynn Kagan, lead author of the report, traveled the country to share its findings, she emphasized the word "system" and cautioned her audiences that "EIGHT MINUS ONE EQUALS ZERO." In other words, the recommendations should not be implemented piecemeal; each was important, but their power came from their synergy.

State and local boards would be ineffective without adequate resources, or without a system of evaluation and oversight to guide their efforts. Resources deployed poorly were unlikely to achieve the desired effect. A system that was unresponsive to parents would be doomed to failure, no matter what professionals thought of its quality. But even the wisest parents and best-organized advocates couldn't push programs up to quality if they couldn't hire and retain teachers who had been well prepared. Raising the standards for teachers would enable them to command higher pay—but only if the financing was available and an accountable distribution system in place. Without a strong and accessible training system, teachers could never reach the higher standards. Even the best-trained teachers would not succeed and even the best-paid teachers wouldn't stay if their tasks were impossible or their workplaces substandard. If one element were left out, the structure could still crumble.

"System-think" was the essential message of the Quality 2000 group—and it excited the field. Advocates and state administrators had already begun to look at programs, policies, and political opportunities through a systemic lens and to work together to create blueprints for quality. They struggled to keep parts of emerging systems in balance as they tackled issues such as how to distribute child-care subsidies, how to use licensing and accreditation to improve program quality, appropriate reimbursement for providers serving subsidized children, which community college courses and community-based trainings could "articulate with" (count toward fulfilling requirements) university programs, offering scholarships for providers and financial incentives for completing education and training, and coordination of programs and funding streams to meet the needs of families at the local level.

Step by Step

No state has chosen to implement all of the specific *Not By Chance* recommendations, but several have made significant strides toward building systems of financing, standards, oversight, professional development and compensation, results-based planning and accountability, and parent involvement that provide incentives and supports for sustained quality.

Here are just a few of the states' innovations to improve quality through professional development and facility accreditation:

- The first step on *Maine* Roads to Quality is "core knowledge" training, delivered by certified instructors, for early childhood educators who are beginning their educations. The state supports further advancements through scholarships for CDA, BA, MA, and doctoral programs, an accreditation support project, and a leadership institute for center directors. The state also provides an extra tax credit to families who choose accredited care for their young children.
- The *Massachusetts* Department of Education supports a network of local Community Partnerships, who provide child-care subsidies and links to health and family support services for low-income three- and four-year-olds and ongoing professional development, health and mental health consultation, and other supports to the early education programs that serve them, with the requirement that these programs achieve accreditation within three years and maintain it thereafter. As a result Massachusetts leads the nation in its percentage of accredited centers and family child-care providers. Massachusetts has raised its education standards for early childhood teachers, and will require an AA degree in 2010 and a BA by 2017. Its Advancing the Field initiative is helping

higher education institutions to improve their offerings and make them more accessible. The commissioners of education, child-care services, and public health are working together to design an integrated system.

- *Maryland,* like Maine, has created a registry of certified early childhood instructors, but it also provides a financial bonus to early childhood workers who complete each level of training. In addition, the state funds a number of model, comprehensive early childhood centers (known as Judy schools). In order to build a results-driven education system that begins in early childhood, Maryland trains early childhood and primary grade teachers to use the Work Sampling System[3] to collect observational data on an ongoing basis. These data are used to improve instruction, communicate with parents, and track each child's progress toward educational results that will be measured by standardized tests at the end of third grade.

- *North Carolina* Smart Start is a state/community partnership model that has been copied by other states. The national T.E.A.C.H. program of scholarships and salary enhancements linked to training and retention was also pioneered in North Carolina. The state's Child Care Wages program provides salary supplements to qualified early education providers, linked to their education levels.

- *Georgia* Pre-K is supplemented by the Georgia Early Learning Initiative (GELI), which provides support for improving quality to programs serving children under four. In addition, the public/private Incentive$ program, which supplements the salaries of teachers who have achieved its educational benchmarks, has helped Georgia achieve a remarkably low turnover rate of only 9 percent in participating centers.[4]

- *Oklahoma,* like several other states and some localities, encourages quality through a tiered licensing program. Programs earn "stars" for meeting increasingly stringent requirements, with accreditation as the highest level. They are rewarded with higher voucher reimbursement rates and other benefits.

Still, across the nation, turnover remains too high, salaries remain too low, and, in many places, the level of preparation that early childhood teachers bring to their jobs has actually declined.[5] Why? EIGHT MINUS ONE EQUALS ZERO. The one that has been most lacking is, of course, adequate funding.

But this pessimistic assessment is not the whole story. In many states and localities, determined advocates, professionals, and policy makers have found ways to make progress through state and community-level initiatives and public/private partnerships. The state innovations listed above and similar efforts across the nation are providing important lessons about what works and what doesn't. What we are learning?

Resources, relationships, and quality matter. These basic tenets are serving as a framework for planners in Ohio in their efforts to coordinate several statewide early childhood initiatives and local demonstration projects into a birth to five school readiness system.[6]

State/local partnerships can implement systemic change in a way that is responsive to local needs, builds buy-in, and leverages support. Some decisions are best made in local communities, by people who are in tune with local needs and emerging issues and who can marshal local resources. Others are best made by people who can see the big picture. After reviewing state/community partnerships in California, Colorado, Florida, Iowa, Kansas, Kentucky, Massachusetts, North Carolina, and South Carolina, a 2002 Children's Defense Fund study concluded that "comprehensive early childhood initiatives hold great promise to expand supports for children and families and improve the delivery of existing services, but only if states make adequate investments, maintain statewide standards, and sustain investments in multiple strategies to support children and families."[7]

Expertise is essential and should be built into the system. Vouchers, tax deductions, and general tax credits help families afford child care, but, unless they are coordinated with other approaches, they do little to improve its quality. More effective approaches target funding toward offering high quality programs, bringing programs up to quality, or making quality programs affordable. They employ experts not only in designing the system, but also in aiding implementation, evaluating results, supporting success, and holding partners accountable. Participants at all levels of the system share "lessons learned" and have ongoing access to professional development opportunities.

Compensation initiatives, tied to education and experience, are an effective investment. Well-planned initiatives have resulted in reductions in teacher turnover, increased education and professional development, increased credentials of applicants for early childhood positions, an improved sense of professionalism and commitment to the field, and greater demand for early childhood courses.[8] Coupled with higher standards, they have also led to improvements in classroom quality and in children's language, pretend play, and academic skills.[9]

Unfunded mandates may succeed short-term, but they fail in the long run. States that impose more stringent licensing standards produce higher overall quality in their licensed programs and better results for the children who attend them. However, when improved standards are expensive to implement and no new resources are provided, the strongest, best-funded programs are likely to benefit, while weaker programs with less access to resources are forced to close. Similarly, teachers who can't afford to pursue mandated further education may go underground or leave the field. As a result, families with fewer resources may have a more difficult time finding adequate care for their children. Those who need the best programs may be least likely to get them.

Reforms need champions—and a base that can sustain support. Champions of successful systemic reforms have come from obvious and unlikely places. Governors, legislators, business leaders or coalitions, early childhood experts, converts to the cause, parent/provider advocacy groups, and state agency directors have taken the lead in different places. But political leadership changes with election cycles, and often reforms are enacted in one session only to be weakened, defunded, or reversed in the next. A broad base of support, with many highly engaged stakeholders, can keep the issues "on the table" and assure continuity.

Piecemeal can be problematic. When each community, program site, family, employer, or state agency is on its own, effort and funds may be wasted on false starts, seeking hard-to-find information, reinventing the wheel, or duplicative and inefficient administrative procedures. For example, when states offer tax incentives to employers to set up on-site child care, few take advantage and those who do often have a difficult time producing and sustaining quality programs.[10] On the other hand, significant strides have been made when employers have come together, with expert guidance, to improve offerings in their communities, work with state agencies, and address policy barriers.[11] Similarly, many states have implemented multiple programs to provide or subsidize early care and education, support families, or improve provider training and compensation. Although each may be strong in its own right, the multiple options and funding streams create extra hurdles for families and providers, who must juggle different eligibility requirements and accountability systems.

The Movement Toward Universal Pre-Kindergarten (UPK)

In spite of the successes, systems that support young children and their families remain fragmented and underfunded. Some children are eligible for programs like Head Start, Early Head Start, Title I Preschool, or state-funded prekindergarten classes, based on their family's income and their place of residence. Some get vouchers that their families can use to purchase child-care services, based on family income or former welfare status. Some are served in public preschool programs because they have handicapping conditions that make them eligible for special education and therapeutic services. Various private and public programs are subsidized by employers, universities, faith-based organizations, local and state governments, United Ways, and foundations, each with its own service population and entry requirements.

Many experts have come to believe that a universal program—one that is open to all children—is necessary because quality can only be assured through the inclusion of a middle-class constituency that is in a position to demand it. An active campaign can instigate change, but ongoing attention, dependable funding, and continuous quality improvement require vocal, voting consumers who can hold policy makers accountable, year in and year out. Furthermore, the costs of training, adequate staff compensation, quality assurance, planning, and intensive service to those with special needs are affordable if and only if they can be spread across a wide base of support that includes a substantial public contribution.[12] While poor children tend to gain the most when high quality programs are made available and affordable, higher income children also benefit significantly. And programs that serve all children reach a far higher percentage of poor and near-poor children than do those that employ a means test.[13]

A few states have created universal programs—though only for four-year-olds. In Georgia and New York, public prekindergarten is offered throughout the state. As explained in Chapter 8, the Georgia program was the result of one governor's vision, and it thrived because he kept it under his wing until it had strong community support and was ready to fly on its own. In New York, the program came into being during a last-minute legislative compromise, but it built upon years of work by advocates who were thinking as system-builders.

In both New York and Georgia, some UPK funds come from the state but are administered locally, and the state sets standards for teacher credentials, facility licensing, curriculum, parent involvement, class size, and inclusion of children with special needs. In New York, system-think has been taken to the local level as well: school districts must apply for funds, and their plans receive thorough scrutiny from early childhood experts.

Georgia's program requires teachers to have either a Child Development Associate (CDA) degree or a BA in child development or a related field. The state provides ongoing training and technical assistance and requires the use of an approved curriculum. Workforce development has been a bigger challenge in New York, where a BA is required of UPK teachers. Colleges and universities have stepped up to the plate with new courses and night, weekend, and summer classes, but, as of the third year of implementation, there aren't yet enough qualified teachers (nor enough state money) to offer programs in every district.

In both states, classes occur in both public schools and private settings, and a range of providers have become part of the system. In New York, school systems are mandated to use at least 10 percent of their funds to support services in nonschool settings; most systems exceed this target because space in the schools is limited. In Georgia, Head Start, nonprofit, family child-care, and for-profit providers were invited to participate along with public schools. In the 1999–2000 school year, more classes were offered by for-profit providers than by public schools.[14]

An evaluation of Georgia's Pre-K program,[15] conducted by a team from Georgia State University, found that the program was providing learning experiences that equaled or exceeded those available in either Head Start or private programs. It effectively promoted school readiness and decreased, but did not close, the achievement gap.

The evaluation study compared fall to spring and fall to fall gains on a battery of vocabulary, problem-solving, and literacy tests between four-year-olds who attended Head Start, Georgia Pre-K, and private programs. The Head Start children were all low-income and more than half were black. The private population was of course more affluent, and two thirds of the children were white. Georgia Pre-K served the entire range; the study sample was evenly divided between white and black children, and the average income was considerably higher than in the Head Start sample but lower than the private program average. The programs were similar in their staff/child ratios, but the Georgia Pre-K teachers were better educated than the teachers in the other two programs. On measures of observed classroom quality, both publicly funded programs were significantly superior to the private schools.

At the beginning of their pre-K year, children in the public programs scored below national norms on vocabulary and problem-solving, while the private program children scored close to the national average. Both the Pre-K and the private groups scored slightly above the national average on word and letter recognition, with the Head Start group scoring below it. All groups averaged significant gains on these measures from fall to spring, though only the Head Start group continued to gain in vocabulary over the summer. Both the Head Start and Pre-K groups improved their vocabulary scores at a faster rate than did the private group, but the Head Start children had started way behind and were still significantly behind the other groups by the beginning of kindergarten. At that point, however, the Georgia Pre-K group had exceeded the national norm on the problem-solving test and had nearly caught up with the more affluent private school group on all of the standard measures.

When background variables were taken into account, it was clear that Georgia's Pre-K program benefited all children and narrowed, but did not close, the achievement gap. For disadvantaged children, those in the Pre-K group started out slightly ahead of those in Head Start in vocabulary and problem-solving, as well as in other literacy and communication skills. Learning new words at a faster rate, the Head Start children caught up in vocabulary, but in other areas the gap widened as Pre-K children made the greater gains. For children with more educated and more affluent parents, the Pre-K program provided a better learning experience than could generally be obtained in private programs.

In Oklahoma, the third state to offer a free public program for four-year-olds statewide, UPK is a school-based program, although services are sometimes delivered in Head Start and child-care programs that collaborate with public schools. It grew by extension from state-funded programs for the poorest four-year-olds, which had served only about 10 percent of the population. Enabling legislation was introduced and shepherded by two Democratic legislators and signed into law by a Republican governor. It was "funded by dilution," with state funds pulled from other areas of the education budget and given to school districts at a time when revenues were growing and K-12 enrollments were shrinking. A complicated formula provided extra resources for children with special needs or free-lunch eligibility. Both half- and full-day options were made available in most districts, and within three years the majority of the state's four-year-olds were taking advantage of these offerings. The requirements, in terms of teacher and assistant preparation, child/staff ratios, and group sizes, are far more stringent than those for private programs, in line with the expert recommendations embodied in the NAEYC accreditation standards. In addition, teachers, who are required to have BA's, were compensated at kindergarten-teacher levels.

Unlike Georgia and New York, which pulled school and community programs into an emerging Pre-K system, Oklahoma simply added a grade to its school systems. In Tulsa, the state's largest city, the district's testing policies enabled researchers to conduct a rigorous evaluation of the new program. The results from the program's first-year evaluation[16] were encouraging.

- Overall, children averaged a 16 percent gain in test scores attributable to the program, with most of the increase resulting from spurts in language and cognitive development.
- Children who were poor, non-white, or from non-English-speaking backgrounds benefited the most—no surprise, since these children generally have less access to high quality programs and supports in their infant and toddler as well as preschool years and are more likely to

face ongoing challenges because of lack of family and neighborhood resources. (The researchers also note that the instrument they used may not have picked up all of the gain made by the 35% of white children, 24% of black children, and 15% of Hispanic children who obtained perfect scores.)
- Hispanic children, in particular, showed large (54%) gains; the difference in language and cognitive development between those entering UPK and those who had completed it suggested that Hispanic children were learning English rapidly in their UPK classrooms.

These findings add support to two conclusions that are backed by a large body of other research, including the Georgia findings:

1. High quality public education programs for all four-year-olds in a community can accelerate their language and cognitive development, and are especially beneficial to those who need them most.
2. Four is already too late to prevent the achievement gap; if we want all children to begin school primed for success, we need to start earlier.

The Tulsa results confirm that a well-crafted school-based program can educate all four-year-olds, and that extending public school downward can help to level the playing field. Georgia's and New York's experiments also point in another direction—to the possibility of bringing the existing mix of public and private early childhood programs together in a system that can effectively serve all young children, prepare and support their teachers, and offer supports and choices to their families.

Accelerating Change

The promise of universal programs and integrated systems has excited some of the major U.S. foundations, and their efforts and investments are helping to push the movement forward. Most have defined UPK as including both three- and four-year-olds, although some of the efforts they have supported have begun with four-year-olds only (see Table 13.1).

But What About the Babies?

Forty-nine percent of the early childhood direct care workforce is involved in caring for children between nineteen months and three years[17]—prime time for language learning. Yet most of the training opportunities—and dollars—are focused on the 22 percent who work with three- to five-year-olds. About 80 percent of the caregivers of toddlers work in family

TABLE 13.1. Major Foundation Initiatives to Promote Universal
Pre-Kindergarten Programs

Foundation	Goal/Activities	Results (as of Spring, 2004; some initiatives had just begun)
Lucent	Provide grants and technical assistance to help four states to design and implement UPK programs	• *Alabama*: pilot program implemented • *Massachusetts*: see Schott Foundation, below • *New Jersey*: UPK for four-year-olds implemented in poorest districts, as a result of judge's decision (Abbott Districts) • *Oklahoma*: UPK for four-year-olds implemented statewide
Pew Charitable Trusts	Foster UPK for three- and four-year-olds by providing information for policy makers, building public will and key stakeholder support for federal and state efforts, and supporting promising initiatives and partnerships	• National Institute for Early Education Research collects and disseminates policy-relevant research related to UPK • Trust for Early Education educates stakeholders through listservs, Web site
Foundation for Child Development	Document and encourage effective practices and policies related to UPK implementation process, teacher preparation and compensation, curriculum, and program standards; frame UPK as part of a prekindergarten through grade 3 continuum	• National Universal Pre-Kindergarten Center • Working Paper Series (commissioned papers) • Research agenda
Early Childhood Initiative Foundation	Implement UPK for four-year-olds in Florida; improve early education and parent support programs for zero- through five-year-olds in Miami-Dade County; galvanize parents	• UPK adopted statewide by initiative petition • *Teach More/Love More Campaign* provides outreach and support to parents and providers
Schott Foundation	Early Education for All three- and four-year-olds, as part of a birth through five system	• Campaign supported by a broad and active coalition • Early Education for All framing legislation enacted, with a goal of full implementation by 2012
Joyce Foundation	Make progress toward implementation of UPK in mid-western states.	
David and Lucille Packard Foundation	Implement UPK for three- and four-year-olds in California by 2013	

child-care homes or in private arrangements among relatives and neighbors; many of them are beyond the reach of public support and public regulation.

UPK efforts in Georgia and New York have brought some benefits for younger children,[18] even though the emphasis has been on the next years' kindergarteners. Emerging efforts in many states have a similar preschool focus, but their planners are also looking at how to build programs and supports for infants and toddlers into the system. In addition to workforce education, compensation, and strategies to improve center-based care, they are looking specifically at the roles that well-supported and accredited family child care can play in serving infants and toddlers, children with special health needs or developmental or behavioral challenges, children from new immigrant groups, and others whose families prefer the flexible hours, mixed-age groups, home settings, and opportunity to remain with the same "teacher" for several years that are hallmarks of family child care. In launching its Preschool for All initiative, the Packard Foundation stated on its Web site, "Preschool for all is the cornerstone of our larger vision of quality early education for all children from birth to five years of age in California and the nation."[19]

But, as ZERO TO THREE stated in the title of its 2003 annual training conference, "Babies Can't Wait." Those who care for them—who have the awesome responsibility of helping them build the language foundation that will under-gird their lifelong learning—need and deserve support.

Requiring anyone who accepts a voucher to care for children to be licensed, and providing incentives for compliance in the form of support, mentorship, information and training, children's books and toys, access to the federal child and adult care food program, or loans for facility improvement, can bring many providers of infant and toddler care "into the system." But it may not be the best method for supporting grandparents and other "kith and kin" caregivers or for helping parents who care for one or two of their friends' children in addition to their own. For caregivers who do not think of what they do as a job or career, or whose past experiences or immigration status make them wary of government agencies, it can often be more effective to extend a helping hand.

This helping hand can be extended by parents' employers, public agencies, or a wide range of community organizations. Working together, such groups can weave a community-level infrastructure—a network of community supports for families and caregivers that improve the odds of children getting safe, stimulating, responsive care that spurs their language development.

Having collected examples of promising strategies from around the country, the *Sparking Connections*[20] initiative, a collaboration of Families and Work Institute and the NRF Retail Work Life Forum, is working with employers, media, local and state government, and nonprofit organizations to create such networks in several communities. Efforts focus on

- *reaching out to families and caregivers* in social and community settings where people naturally gather
- *disseminating information* through multiple channels, including word of mouth, and in multiple languages
- *connecting caregivers* for mutual support, intentional learning, recognition, and to voice concerns
- *developing partnerships* with libraries and museums, places of worship, health care organizations, housing and neighborhood associations, child-care resource and referral agencies, and other groups
- *creating community connections* to support convening, resource sharing, outreach, and community education.

But a network of voluntary supports will never be enough unless we also address the quality of licensed care, which every national and state-based study has shown to be of lower quality for infants and toddlers than it is for preschoolers. Part of the problem is one of resources—babies cost more because they need higher staff/child ratios. In the event of a fire or other emergency, the caregiver needs to be able to get her charges out of the building. And, on a daily basis, babies need caregivers who can speak and respond directly to them, one-on-one, in a nurturant and engaging way. Three-year-olds can play with peers, but younger children need trusted adults as very frequent interaction and conversation partners.

Cost is not the only issue. There is also a problem of perception and policy. Too many of us make an assumption that is not borne out by the facts: that the younger the child, the less expertise is required to provide good education and care. Because of this bias, applicants with the lowest levels of education, training, and experience, as well as those least fluent in the language of instruction, are disproportionately assigned to "the baby rooms." The same bias obtains in many institutions of higher education. Early childhood education courses, and those focusing on infant/toddler development in particular, are less likely to be available than those focused on K-12 education. In addition, except where there is a specially designed program or institutional early childhood focus, such courses are more likely to be taught by adjunct faculty who may have lower qualifications and receive lower pay and less support than those with regular appointments.[21]

The *Better Baby Care Campaign*,[22] launched by Joan Lombardi, who served as the first Associate Commissioner of the U.S. Department of Health and Human Services' Child Care Bureau, provides a simple, twelve-point blueprint for efforts to build systems that ensure better care for children under three.

Better Baby Care Campaign Goals

Safe and Healthy Care

1. Ensure that all child care meets state and local licensing requirements and that standards follow the recommendations in the National Health and Safety Standards for Out-of-Home Care.

2. Provide every infant/toddler program with access to health and mental health consultation and support.

3. Promote the inclusion of children with special needs and provide ongoing support to parents and providers.

Family-Centered Care

4. Help parents understand how to select and monitor the quality of care for their infants and toddlers.

5. Promote parent involvement, parent education, and family support through child care and services that reflect the cultures and languages of the families served.

6. Create networks of support for family child care and kith and kin providers.

Developmentally Appropriate Care

7. Ensure that infant/toddler providers have specialized training in child development and family support, and receive adequate compensation.

8. Develop the capacity of all higher education institutions in the community to offer courses in infant/toddler care and supervision.

9. Provide an infant/toddler specialist to work with providers and parents in every Child Care Resource and Referral Agency.

Critical Investments

10. Expand the supply of quality infant care through direct investments and higher reimbursement rates for accredited care.

11. Ensure that all eligible children have access to Early Head Start.

12. Provide families with paid parental leave for the first year of a baby's life.

Working from this twelve-step platform, Voices for America's Children[23] and its affiliate child advocacy organizations have launched campaigns in several states. They are educating the public and policy makers on what babies need and why, and are urging them to put into place the key building blocks of a system that can support the families, caregivers, teachers, and institutions that are responsible for sustaining their development.

The campaigns scored some early victories[24]:

- *Comprehensive planning*: strategic plans for early learning and mental health systems that begin at birth, Early Learning Councils and related legislation to coordinate state policies and programs, and legislative task forces on issues such as paid family leave
- *Reversing budget cuts and proposals to relax standards*: maintaining home visiting programs, child-care quality standards, reimbursement rate increases, and health insurance benefits for providers
- *Garnering new resources*: for birth to three programs, child-care subsidies, and increased reimbursement rates for infant/toddler care.

Pulling It All Together

If we could start from scratch, we would create a logical, efficient system to serve our diverse array of families and communities, ensuring that they could all provide their children with a strong beginning and a sturdy foundation for later learning. Our current patchwork of efforts doesn't fit together easily. It is fraught with inefficiencies and inequities, often enshrined in programs with similar or overlapping goals that compete for the same inadequate resources. Still, we have made good beginnings on many fronts. Now our progress toward Worthy Wages and appropriate education for child-care providers, Universal Pre-K, community-based family support networks, and Better Baby Care needs to coalesce into stable early childhood development systems.

The BUILD Initiative, funded by a consortium of fifteen national and regional foundations, is supporting efforts in Ohio, Illinois, New Jersey, and Pennsylvania to build systems of birth through five services. BUILD is different from the UPK efforts in that babies are included. Grants to coalitions in individual states, coordinated through the Civil Society Institute, support work to reform existing systems, test new models, connect programs and services, and expand access to learning systems that promote school readiness. Health, mental health, and family support services are being pulled into the mix along with early learning programs, as states recognize the emotional foundations of school readiness and the critical role of early relationships. With BUILD funding and shared expertise serving as a catalyst for coordinating and accelerating preexisting efforts, BUILD states—and other states that are learning from their efforts—have identified and begun to achieve measurable outcomes in areas such as infrastructure development, quality improvement, evaluation, financing, and public engagement.

Citizen Action

Building state and national systems that achieve and sustain quality can be complicated—especially when you don't control all of the pieces that need to be integrated. But there is one piece of the puzzle that is easy to understand: in the long run, you get what you pay for. If you keep paying substandard wages, it is going to be very difficult to attract and retain qualified teachers.

In Boise, Idaho, a small group of parents, providers, and other citizens came together to improve services for children in their community. They realized that good quality child care was getting harder and harder to find—and to provide—because trained teachers couldn't afford to stay and new recruits had no incentive to get appropriate training. The parents couldn't pay more, but neither could they continue to ask the people who gave so much to help them provide their children with a good start to keep shouldering the burden. The group formed a local chapter of Stand for Children,[25] and, with the support of the national organization, found a concrete step that they could take in their community. They drafted a proposal to use city funds to improve provider compensation, education, and retention by providing stipends to teachers and quality-improvement resources to programs. Their plan was patterned after the CARES model, which had been developed by the Center for the Childcare Workforce and implemented in several California counties.[26] They took their case to the city council and won—a three-year, $200,000 initiative.

Other communities identified the same need, and other Stand for Children chapters pushed for similar legislation. Over the next two years, three Oregon counties passed similar initiatives. In 2003, as the Boise CARES initiative entered its third year, Idaho Stand for Children chapters convinced their Department of Health and Welfare to incorporate the CARES model into their newly developed statewide early childhood professional development system!

Our children's early language development is too important to be left to chance. Parents and grandparents, policy makers and private funders, civic groups and corporations, researchers and program administrators, caregivers, teachers, and those who teach caregivers and teachers—all have roles to play and a stake in the outcome. But we can't keep reinventing the wheel, or, like Sisyphus, getting the rock to the top of the hill only to have it roll back. We need intelligent policies at the local, state, and national level that create an infrastructure for quality that we and our children can count on. Working together, we can shape such policies and insist that they are fully funded and intelligently implemented.

14 We Can Get There from Here

In 1989, President George H. W. Bush convened the nation's governors to set educational goals for the nation. The summit led to the adoption of six educational goals, which Congress later expanded to eight. These goals were codified in the Goals 2000: Educate America Act,[1] signed by President Clinton in 1994. The National Educational Goals Panel, made up of governors, state legislators, members of Congress, and representatives of the administration, was charged with monitoring progress toward the goals.

In 2005, we have not yet achieved Goal 1: "All children will come to school ready to learn and succeed." Yet this goal is, in Lisbeth Schorr's words, "within our reach."[2] The key is language development, fostered in caring relationships through frequent, engaging, vocabulary-stretching conversations when children are between one and four years old. By applying existing knowledge and allocating appropriate resources we can assure that all children have access to the rich experiences that build a foundation for learning. With wise and affordable investments of public and private dollars, we can assure that children do not start school already having been "left behind."

The tools we need and the evidence that they can succeed have been explained in earlier chapters of this book. Table 14.1 summarizes what researchers, practitioners, policy makers, and funders have learned about what works and what doesn't work to build a solid foundation for language, literacy, and school success.

We know what our children need, and we know how to provide it. We also know that we are falling short. In the richest and most powerful country in the world, at a time when so much is known about what young children need and what they are capable of learning, no child should languish for lack of language.

TABLE 14.1. Building a Solid Foundation for Language, Literacy, and School Success

What Works	What Doesn't Work

Practices

- Talking with babies and young children—a lot![3]
- Positive discipline and playful parenting[4]
- Using words that stretch children's vocabularies in contexts that make their meaning clear[5]
- Asking children open-ended questions and encouraging their curiosity[6]
- Using language to reassure children, explain events and processes, and help them predict what will happen when[7]
- Using "decontextualized language" that goes beyond the here and now; talking about the past and future as well as the present[8]
- Encouraging and expanding pretend play[9]
- Reading books and telling stories with children many times a day, beginning in babyhood, in ways that hold their interest[10]
- Using books as springboards for interaction and discussion—"dialogic reading"[11]
- Playing with words, sounds, and word parts[12]
- Use of music, rhythm, and action games to teach vocabulary and play with language[13]
- Print-rich environments[14]
- Early identification and treatment of hearing, visual, and language difficulties, developmental delays, mental health and behavioral problems, nutritional deficiencies, and exposure to violence, abuse, neglect, or chronic stress[15]

- Waiting until children are ready to talk to them[16]
- Too many "no's" and too few "yes's"[17]
- Using limited vocabulary with young children so they will understand everything you say[18]
- Lack of explicit instruction or planned activities for children in a group setting[19]
- Overly didactic drill or instruction that doesn't consider young children's preferred modes of learning[20]
- Keeping books out of reach[21]
- Focusing too narrowly on specific skills like ABCs[22]
- Waiting until school age to teach book-handling skills, phonemic awareness, and ABCs[23]
- Teaching a child to read in a language in which he is not fluent[24]

Program Design

- Providing parents with frequent practice in engaging their young children in rich conversations and fun learning activities[25]
- Combining parent support and education with good early education programs, especially for poor children[26]
- Beginning as early as possible, even before birth, to provide parents with education and support and to assure that any nonparental care supports robust language development[27]
- Using child-care programs, family centers, and other community-based organizations as hubs for supporting families, building community, and encouraging parenting practices that support language[28]

- Parent education programs that lack a strong language or relationship-building focus[34]
- Short-duration programs that enroll families for less than one year or children for less than two, especially for children with risk factors[35]
- Waiting until age four or five to provide early education programs for children and/or support for their parents as first and most important teachers[36]

TABLE 14.1. Continued

What Works	What Doesn't Work
Program Design (continued)	
• Assuring that family child-care and center-based programs meet a "good" standard of quality, especially in areas of staff qualifications, staff/child ratio and group size, interactions among adults and children, and learning activities;[29] professional accreditation[30] • Training for caregivers and teachers through classes, distance education, mentorship, and on-site consultation; CDA and BA[31] • Hiring teachers with college degrees who can also "speak the language" (literally and figuratively) of the families they serve[32] • Higher pay for teachers, commensurate with their education and responsibilities[33]	• One size fits all. Programs shaped by community input can match methodology and delivery systems to the needs, strengths, and cultures of their constituents.[37] Programs that work well for many families can be ineffective or even harmful for others.[38]
Policies and Systems	
• Dedicated funding streams, such as lotteries and special taxes • Strong performance and/or licensing standards and a centralized capacity for training, technical assistance, and oversight[39] • Requiring that state-funded child care and pre-K programs meet Head Start's performance standards, or more demanding ones[40] • Providing incentives and supports for early childhood programs to achieve and maintain professional accreditation[41] • Community-based planning and resource allocation—in the context of high standards and a strong professional development infrastructure[42] • Workforce improvement and stabilization initiatives, such as T.E.A.C.H.,[43] wage enhancements tied to education and qualifications, and tiered reimbursement[44] • Public/private partnerships and employer collaboratives that invest in improving child care and family support in their communities and address policy barriers[45] • Universal programs that have a broad-based constituency and can spread the cost of training and oversight[46]	• Lax licensing standards, especially in areas of teacher preparation, staff/child ratio, group size, and provision of educational activities[47] • Setting high standards without providing additional resources that enable programs to meet and maintain them[48] • Investing in quantity (e.g., more subsidized slots) at the expense of achieving and maintaining adequate quality[49] • Tax credits to businesses to establish child-care centers[50] • Relying on market forces to balance supply and demand[51]

Applying What We Know

Applying what we know, we can build a system that helps every family support their children's language development, in both home and child-care settings. Supports will follow the child, so that all of the family members, caregivers, and teachers who are responsible for a child on a daily basis understand the importance of language development and have the tools, training, social supports, and time to engage that child in rich conversations and fun learning activities.

For families choosing center-based or family child care, the system will provide affordable options in professionally accredited settings.

- Teachers, directors, and assistants will be well trained and appropriately compensated.
- Training will include general education and specific child development and early childhood education content, with a strong emphasis on teaching and caregiving practices that build a strong foundation for language, literacy, and school success.
- Classrooms will be well equipped with books, pretend play materials, and a changing array of items to stimulate children's curiosity, engage their imaginations, and increase their knowledge about a wide variety of real-world phenomena.
- Teachers will have time to converse with each child, facilitate conversations among small groups of children, meet with parents, and plan together.
- Training and ongoing professional development will help teachers to be effective partners with parents, supporting families in the multiple roles they play in fostering their children's healthy development and preparing them to succeed.
- Children learning two languages will receive support in both, through books, stories, and conversation.

For children spending much of their time at home, or in home settings with caregivers who are not professionals, the system will provide a network of support for both the children and the adults.

- Home visitors will bring resources, answer questions, and model effective techniques for supporting language and literacy through play, using proven models adapted for different linguistic and cultural communities and for families with different levels of need.

- Community-based playgroups, family centers, and drop-in programs will provide opportunities for children to interact with others and for both adults and children to learn in group settings.[52]
- Libraries, health clinics, community-based agencies, and early childhood programs will collaborate to ensure that all families can access a rich supply of children's books (in their home languages as well as English) and play materials.

Strong and supportively enforced requirements, ongoing professional development opportunities, serious parent input, and an adequate financial base will sustain a level of quality that keeps children safe, happily engaged, and actively learning.

It's not rocket science. We can get to our goal by many paths. Federal systems, state systems, local efforts centered around public schools, libraries, pediatric clinics, or community-based organizations, public/private partnerships, and targeted investments in the education and engagement of parents and teachers can all take us there.

Big Dreams

The Gross Domestic Product of the United States was about ten and a half trillion dollars in 2002.[53] The federal budget for that year was nearly 20 percent of that figure, or close to two trillion dollars.[54] Total public spending for K-12 education—state, federal, and local—was about $420 billion, an average of $7,574 per child.[55]

Suppose we decided that it was equally important to invest in our twenty million zero- to five-year-olds. What would it take to implement the practices, programs, policies, and systems that we know can work to build a firm foundation for language and learning? If our goal is to meet the needs of ALL OF OUR CHILDREN, how much might we need, and how might we channel these dollars efficiently and effectively? What existing systems might we build upon and what innovations would we add?

A National Commitment: Early Head Start for All

Between 1965 and 2003, the United States built high quality Head Start programs of national scope, with adaptations to meet the needs of very diverse communities and of individuals with a broad range of backgrounds and needs. These programs have used proven training materials and methods and have developed a robust infrastructure with national reach.

Across the board, Head Start classrooms maintain higher levels of professionally assessed quality than most privately funded programs.[56] Though serving only the poorest of the poor, and only a fraction of that group (about two thirds of eligible three- and four-year-olds at its peak), Head Start has demonstrated that a large-scale program with national performance standards can deliver the quality and flexibility needed to educate children growing up in challenging circumstances.

But most of the children who enter Head Start are already significantly behind their more advantaged peers. Although they will tend to catch up somewhat during their one or two years in the program, they are still likely to enter kindergarten lagging behind in essential language, pre-reading, and mathematical skills.[57]

Early Head Start, a Head Start program that serves children ZERO TO THREE and their families (who are encouraged to enroll even before the child is born), was created to PREVENT this achievement gap. Though not yet a mature program, Early Head Start has already demonstrated significant gains for children across all areas of development, as well as success in teaching parents effective techniques for supporting their children's learning. Services are provided in children's homes, child-care centers, and family child-care homes. Fully implemented programs that meet all of the program performance standards and offer a menu of home-based and center-based services have shown the strongest results.[58]

What if we built upon this federal model and offered Early Head Start services in every community, to every family who wanted them? We could take advantage of Head Start's administrative, research, and training capacities and proven performance standards to ensure that the programs were of sufficiently high quality to support robust language development. We could also build upon Head Start's current community-based linkages to health, nutrition, and family support providers for families seeking more comprehensive services.

State Programs for Young Children: Toward Universal Early Education

States have been running prekindergarten programs since the 1980s, largely geared to low-income children. In the 1990s, several states moved to make these programs universal, so that all four-year-olds could participate on a voluntary basis. Georgia, the leader in this area, serves just over 60 percent of its four-year-olds in its School Readiness program.[59] Many of the classrooms are in public schools, but others are run by nonprofit, for-profit, and religious organizations that buy into the state standards and curriculum and receive public money under contract with the state.

State pre-K programs can be expanded both outward, to serve a larger percentage of children—and downward, to serve younger children. Both of these directions have clear advantages. The evidence on early language development argues for making downward expansion the priority. Even where licensing standards are strong, the majority of programs for infants and toddlers are not of high enough quality to build a strong language foundation.[60] Strong state pre-K programs hire certified teachers, pay them higher salaries than they would earn in private programs, support their professional development, and often mandate particular curricula or alignment of curriculum with state education standards.[61] All of these mechanisms could provide programs of improved quality for younger children. A program beginning at birth, or even at age two, would provide continuity for children and their families. Programs that start earlier and enroll children longer have been shown to have greater impact, both short and long term.[62] That impact is greatest for the neediest children.

On the other hand, many advocates and policy makers feel that it is better to spend limited funds building a robust system for ALL four-year-olds before including younger children.[63] Educational programs for four-year-olds, or even for three- and four-year-olds, tend to be more saleable to politicians who think very young children should be at home rather than in school than do programs for zero- to three-year-olds. Furthermore, a program that serves middle class as well as poor children gains a constituency that is more likely to vote, and is thus more likely to be sustained.

State/Community Partnerships: Making Devolution Work

With federal, state, and specially raised funds, states have served as laboratories for innovation. Though some, like Georgia, have created centralized state programs, many have devolved considerable decision-making power to the local level, with county or community boards charged with creating early education plans and overseeing allocation of funds for basic services and/or supplementary professional development and other quality improvements.

State/local partnerships can work spectacularly—leveraging local commitment to produce improved and expanded services with better outcomes for children.[64] Sometimes, though, they encounter a rockier road. Turf battles, duplicative infrastructure, unsophisticated or self-interested decision makers, and unfunded mandates can all hamper progress. At times, such partnerships have merely transferred inadequate resources from one jurisdiction to another.

States could create efficient and effective systems by combining the best of varied models and heeding the lessons learned from implementation efforts. Revenue would be collected at the state level and distributed to local entities according to the number and neediness of young children in their jurisdictions, with guidelines to ensure that the neediest children were accommodated. This revenue would be adequate to fund high quality early education and parent support programs with appropriately trained, credentialed, and compensated staff and to support local planning, oversight, program evaluation, and quality-improvement initiatives. Local entities could raise additional funds for community projects.

Licensing, higher education, and credentialing of staff and of professional trainers would be state functions, with accountability to high standards and an efficient, accessible system of introductory, community college, university, and professional in-service education for providers at all level. A statewide program of scholarships and incentives would encourage workers to enter the field and reward their continuing education. The state could also set minimum compensation standards, tied to qualifications and responsibilities, and provide access to health insurance and other benefits.

Resource allocation and planning would occur locally. Boards composed of individuals who were knowledgeable about child development and connected to diverse constituencies would assess needs for services and training, assure the efficient coordination of programs serving the same families, create linkages with public schools, and allocate supplementary resources.

The local boards could decide upon the mix of parent support and early education services that would best serve their community and the settings where these activities would occur. They would have the freedom to invest in quality programming, even if that meant that fewer children would be served through public funding. They could also invest in service expansion to fill identified gaps.

Local Solutions: Schools of the 21st Century

In 1988, Ed Zigler, professor at Yale University and one of the architects of Head Start, launched a new initiative, the transformation of the public elementary school to meet the needs of twenty-first century families. Schools of the 21st Century[65] begin at birth, providing high quality early education services and information and supports for parents through an on-site or linked center and an associated network of family child-care homes. Parent workshops, home visits, and playgroups build the community and help parents to provide experiences that promote robust social, emotional, and language development. Family-centered programming continues through the elementary school years, with before- and after-school and vacation activities, parent support and information groups, and strong parent involvement in shaping the educational experience. The school is linked to comprehensive health, mental health, and social services so that its programs promote the overall well-being of children and families and referrals can be made when outside services are needed.

There are now more than 1300 Schools of the 21st Century, located in at least seventeen states. Funded through private grants and public appropriations, they have improved reading and mathematics scores of children, resolved developmental lags so that children enter school primed to succeed, reduced parental stress, improved school climate, and built bonds among families and between the family and school.

Obviously, there are additional costs involved in creating such schools, but there are also savings associated with preventing school failure, reducing the need for special education services, and consolidating programs for children and their families. State or federal grants, ongoing financial support, or willingness to match start-up costs (as is done for school construction) could accelerate the implementation of Schools of the 21st Century.

Consumer Choice: Graduated Vouchers

In *America's Childcare Problem: The Way Out*,[66] economists Suzanne Helburn and Barbara Bergmann examine what it would cost to provide an affordable early childhood education—of sufficiently high quality to support robust language development—to all children zero through age five in the United States. Their calculations take into account both the cost of running high quality programs and the infrastructure of training, oversight, and financing that would be needed to sustain them.

In order to take advantage of the various kinds of programs that now exist and the diversity of parent preferences, Helburn and Bergmann propose funneling most of the money through a system of vouchers for families. To ensure an equitable system, they suggest a sliding scale, giving larger vouchers to poorer families so that no family has to pay more than 20 percent of its above-poverty-line income for child care and even the poorest families can purchase high quality services. The value of the vouchers would also be adjusted to take into account the age of the child and any special needs that would make care and education more costly.

Such a system might be tweaked in several ways:

- Families could be given additional, refundable tax credits (or more valuable vouchers) for choosing licensed care that meets or exceeds the standards used in the military (accreditation) or Head Start (performance standards), with the credits allocated on a sliding scale. This could help drive quality improvements through consumer demand, and would enable programs and individual caregivers to charge higher fees for excellent service.
- Centers, family child-care homes, and community-based programs like libraries and drop-in centers might be given funding directly for facilities, equipment, learning materials, start-up costs, and quality improvement.
- Additional money might be appropriated for community-based family support and parent/child services, using models such as the Parent—Child Home Program, AVANCE, and Parents as Teachers. These could be attached to early education programs or be funded separately through grants, additional vouchers, or both.
- Families who chose to care for their children at home could receive income or tax credit of equivalent value to the vouchers for which they would otherwise be eligible. For the first year of a child's life, this might take the form of partially paid family leave, with incentives to participate in parenting education and parent/child programs.

Calculating the Cost

Can we afford these big dreams? Helburn and Bergmann calculated that it would take $89 billion, or $69 billion more than we are currently spending, to fund their voucher system. That's less than 1 percent of our gross domestic product, less than 4 percent of our federal budget. Extrapolating from existing state, Head Start, and school-based programs yields similar figures.

In 2003, Head Start and Early Head Start served 900,000 children and their families with a $6.54 billion budget,[67] a cost of $7,267 per child, comparable to the cost of public kindergarten or prekindergarten. (The added cost of Head Start's comprehensive health, nutrition, and family support services, a key to its success, is offset by offering only part-day educational programs for children.) We'd expect to pay a higher price for the better-educated teachers that will be demanded in the future. Even at $8,000 per child, it would cost just $128 billion to serve all of our one- through four-year-olds, or about $90 billion for the 70 percent who would be likely to participate. For only $38.4 billion—an annual increase of just $18 billion—we could serve the neediest 30 percent.

Thus, a relatively modest investment of about $20 billion would fully fund Head Start—a dream of the program since its inception as a pilot in 1965. It would enable Head Start to provide services to children and their families beginning at age one, and to include children whose family incomes are just above the poverty level. If, instead, we chose to fully fund Early Head Start, which currently costs about $10,000 per child, we could serve one third of our nation's zero- to three-year-olds for $40 billion.

Extrapolating from today's costs, however, still leaves us with the underfunding that characterizes our current public programs and especially our private ones. Using sophisticated mathematical models that take into account the costs of training and infrastructure, the recommendations of experts in the field, and the levels of compensation needed to recruit and retain a qualified workforce, Drs. Sharon L. Kagan and Richard Brandon calculated the cost of a publicly funded school readiness system that could serve all children. Incorporating this work, the Policy Matters Project, a partnership of the Center for the Study of Social Policy, the National Center for Children in Poverty, and Child Trends, recommends a public investment in early care and education programs of between eight and twelve thousand per enrolled child for three- and four-year-olds, and between ten and fifteen thousand per enrolled child for children under three.[68] The costs vary by state and locality, reflecting local differences in wages and cost of living. Taking the average figures, it would cost nearly $180 billion to provide free, high quality, language-enriching programs full-day, full-year for ALL of our one- through four-year-olds. This cost could be divided among state, federal, and local governments. Part of it could be borne, as it is today, by families who can afford to pay some portion of the cost to give their children an excellent start.

Promising Innovations

During the boom years of the 1990s, child advocates dared to dream big dreams and to take steps toward their implementation. In times of more constrained public resources, it is helpful to consider less comprehensive reforms that could still propel us forward in large incremental steps. Some of these steps are already being taken; others are on the drawing board. A few have been tried and found successful, but rolled back or frozen in place because of funding shortages.

National Resources

- *Increased CCDBG with quality set-aside of at least 10 percent.* The funding provided to states through the Child Care and Development Block Grant (CCDBG) has helped many families to afford child care; it has also financed some improvements in child-care services and systems. But the amount set aside for these quality improvements is not sufficient to move the system toward a level of quality that builds a sturdy language foundation. An increase in the quality set-aside to a percentage that would at least cover the training and regulation costs of a quality system could assure some of our neediest children of early education services that are good enough to prepare them for school.

- *Scholarships and loan-forgiveness for early childhood teachers.* Such programs are already in place for K-12 teachers, as well as for low- and middle-income group students who follow a traditional path and enroll in college full time. They could be easily extended to serve early childhood teachers who made a commitment to continuing in their jobs during and following their education.[69]

- *Literacy corps.* The corps would include early childhood educators who worked in centers, family child care, home visiting, and drop-in programs, or in parent education and support programs in libraries, health clinics, places of worship, and community-based organizations. Corps members would complete a relatively short but demanding course of training, such as the HeadsUp! Reading[70] program. In return for applying what they've learned and sharing it with others, they would receive a salary supplement for three years, as long as they remained active in the early childhood field. Such a program could improve the skills of the parents and providers who work with young children while at the same time addressing the challenge of recruiting and retaining a qualified early education workforce.

- *FOCUS Act.* This bill, introduced in 2001 but not yet passed, would provide $1 billion per year to help states cultivate and retain a qualified early childhood workforce. The funds would provide stipends for qualified early childhood teachers and scholarships for those seeking to further their education.[71]

- *Ongoing program of research, linked to practice and policy.* Evaluations of federal programs and research on the effectiveness of different approaches with particular groups of children and families have informed resource allocation, program improvement, and the design of new programs. Efforts to generate and evaluate new models, such as the Early Learning Opportunities Act, Early Reading First, and the Early

Childhood Professional Educator grants, should be continued. Successful projects should be refunded, expanded, replicated, and adapted.

State Investments

- *UPK Plus.* So far, universal prekindergarten, like most state-run pre-k programs, has been only for four-year-olds. Yet both universal and limited-eligibility public pre-k programs can open the door toward improved services for two- and three-year-olds and can lay the groundwork for a three-year program, supported by a mix of public funding and parent copayments, that educates all children during their prime time for language learning.
- *Parents as Teachers.* Missouri offers this in every community, and at least 40 percent of its young children get involved. Other states could do the same.
- *Parent–Child Home Program (PCHP).* In terms of outcome for the money, the PCHP is an outstanding buy, yet few states offer it. The program also has unique adaptability for immigrant groups, as it doesn't require a lot of prior training for someone to offer services in the family's home language. Ideally, PCHP visits would be offered not only to parents, but also to caregivers, including relatives, neighbors, and family child-care providers.
- *Strengthened resource and referral (R&R) network.* R&Rs connect families with service providers and build connections among providers. Most engage in training, needs assessment, and supply-building activities. With a modest infusion of resources, R&Rs could hire experts in language and literacy, infant/toddler development, and working with families. These teams could train trainers and serve as the hub of a training and consultation system.
- *Workforce initiatives.* Recruiting and retaining a qualified early childhood workforce continues to be a challenge. A comprehensive approach would combine promising initiatives, including accessible and well-developed higher education programs, supports and financial incentives for course and degree completion, wage supplements for qualified teachers, tiered licensing to reward programs that hire qualified teachers, and programs such as T.E.A.C.H., which subsidize and reward continuing education for workers who stay in their jobs.[72]
- *Public/private partnerships.* States can provide tax incentives for businesses to enter into long-term strategic partnerships to improve and expand services for young children in their communities. These partnerships should focus on filling the gaps that leave some children with inadequate support for building a sturdy early language foundation.

Community Action

- *Public engagement, education, and social-marketing campaigns.* Get people throughout the community talking about the importance of early learning and the need for public support. Use appropriate media, methods, and messengers to reach parents, grandparents, providers, business and civic leaders, and other community members.
- *Asset-based strategic planning.* Every community has resources that can be brought to bear to help young children learn their language(s) well. In 2003, the National League of Cities issued a "100 City Challenge" to encourage cities to develop long-term strategic plans, coordinating their assets so that more of their young children would receive a steady diet of engaging experiences that would prepare them to succeed in school.
- *Model programs.* Establish a cluster of excellent programs serving zero- to five-year-olds from low- and moderate-income families, with well-trained and appropriately compensated staff and the resources needed to sustain excellence. Use these as demonstration and training sites and hire their staff as mentors as you bring other programs up to quality.[73]
- *Family support networks.* In an age where most adults are in the workforce and commerce is increasingly transacted through large corporations, the "village" that "it takes" to "raise a child" is disappearing. Yet, especially during evenings and weekends, neighborhoods can create spaces where families with young children can come together, engage in fun activities that support early learning, get information about child care and other resources, access emergency aid, share personal and public concerns, and get children's books in their home languages and in English. Child-care programs, public schools, libraries, places of worship, roving vans, playgrounds, housing projects, community-based organizations, pediatric clinics, and police officers can all be part of this twenty-first-century village.
- *Public/private partnerships, endowments, and special taxes.* Dedicated funding streams for essential services for young children can be established at the local level, where families, voters, and employers can see and reap their benefits.
- *Mobilization of volunteers, advocates, and philanthropy.* Service clubs, religious groups, and private philanthropy can provide scholarship funds for early childhood teachers and for young children, sponsorship of early education programs, and a network of advocates who can be called upon to support child-friendly policies and public investments.

Sustaining Progress

As we push for large, incremental steps, we shouldn't forget to pull the policy levers whenever we get the chance. Providing children with a strong language foundation saves money down the road in education, mental health, special education and support for people with disabilities, and crime control; it therefore makes sense to direct a small percentage of these budgets toward improved early learning programs for children and supports for their parents. Food programs, higher education programs, public libraries, maternal and child health programs, and full-service schools are already contributing to the quality of early learning opportunities; it makes sense to strengthen and coordinate these efforts. And for some children, language learning will continue to be compromised unless more pressing issues of housing, nutrition, health and mental health, substance abuse, or domestic violence are also addressed.

Early childhood education is an essential industry, as important to our nation's social and economic welfare as higher education, K-12 education, transportation, health care, or retirement security. It deserves the same public subsidies, incentives for expansion and improvement, workforce recruitment and support, and comprehensive planning that we invest in other sectors that produce "public goods."[74]

Many of the nation's mayors agree. In 2002, Mayor John DeStefano of New Haven took over the presidency of the National League of Cities. Building on that group's prior work, he issued a challenge to 100 cities to develop three- to five-year plans for improved early childhood programs in their communities. The League would provide an Action Kit on "Supporting Early Childhood Success,"[75] tools for assessing community needs and assets, leadership training, and technical support. By the end of 2003, 107 cities had signed on.

Establishing a network of high quality early learning and parent support programs in a community may not be as glamorous or dramatic as building a sports stadium or convention center, but it is likely to have a more immediate and powerful payoff and make a stronger lasting contribution to the public welfare. The following excerpts from an article by officers of the Federal Reserve Bank of Minneapolis argue in hard-nosed business terms for an endowment that will support such a network in Minneapolis. The article "Early Childhood Development: Economic Development with a High Public Return" draws upon research done by High/Scope on the Perry Preschool Project,[76] which is described in more detail in Chapter 12.

High Quality Child Care as an Economic Investment

The High/Scope study conducted a benefit–cost analysis by converting the benefits and costs found in the study into monetary values in constant 1992 dollars discounted annually at 3 percent. The researchers found that for every dollar invested in the program during the early 1960s, over $8 in benefits were returned to the program participants and society as a whole.

While 8-to-1 is an impressive benefit-to-cost ratio, policymakers should place this result in context with returns from other economic development projects. Perhaps another project can boast a higher benefit-to-cost ratio. Unfortunately, well-grounded benefit-to-cost ratios are seldom computed for public projects. However, an alternative measure—the internal rate of return—can be used to more easily compare the public, as well as private, return to investments.

While program participants directly benefited from their increase in after-tax earnings and fringe benefits, these benefits were smaller than those gained by the general public. Based on present value estimates, about 80 percent of the benefits went to the general public (students were less disruptive in class and went on to commit fewer crimes), yielding over a 12 percent internal rate of return for society in general. Compared with other public investments, and even those in the private sector, an ECDP seems like a good buy.

The returns to ECDPs are especially high when placed next to other spending by governments made in the name of economic development. Yet ECD is rarely considered as an economic development measure.

For example, tax increment financing and other subsidies have recently been used to locate a discount retail store and an entertainment center in downtown Minneapolis, and to relocate a major corporate headquarters to suburban Richfield and a computer software firm to downtown St. Paul. Can any of these projects, which combined represent an estimated quarter of a billion dollars in public subsidies, stand up to a 12 percent public return on investment? From the state's point of view, if the subsidy is simply moving businesses within the state, the public return is zero. If the subsidy is required for the business to survive, the risk-adjusted public return is not merely small but could be negative.

As our lawmakers review proposals to build or improve the state's major professional sports stadiums, let's not make the same mistake. The various proposals to build new baseball and football stadiums and improve the current basketball stadium total over $1 billion. Can new stadiums offer a comparable public return on investment as an ECDP? How does a new stadium reduce crime, increase earnings and potentially break a chain of poverty? We propose that this $1 billion plus be invested in a project with a much higher public return.

(excerpted from "Early Childhood Development: Economic Development with a High Public Return," by Art Rolnick, Senior Vice President and Director of Research, and Rob Grunewald, Regional Economic Analyst, Federal Reserve Bank of Minneapolis, 2003[77])

So, how can we get there from here? With a lot of local efforts and a few big ideas. With patience, and with impatience. With small projects that grow and with bold state and national initiatives. With wise political leadership and with grassroots parent power. With determination to leave no child behind, and with understanding that we cannot achieve that goal unless we begin well before age three and invest wisely, adequately, and equitably. Most of all, with the unwavering conviction that where there's a will, there must be a way.

It is up to each one of us to make our visions for children a reality:
by talking with young children
and teaching others why this is so important

by supporting early childhood teachers and caregivers
by asking questions of our public officials and candidates for office
and by voting in the interest of children

by joining and contributing to organizations working for change
by working for change at the national, state,
local, and neighborhood level

by sharing our knowledge
and by spreading the word

. . . so that every child begins school
with a wealth of words.

Appendix

Resources and Connections for Parents,
Policy Makers, and Advocates

AVANCE (www.avance.org)

AVANCE serves predominantly poor Latino families in underserved communities. Its Parent–Child program supports parents of children aged ZERO TO THREE as their child's first teachers through parenting education, parent–child activities, and adult literacy, English, and GED classes. In sites throughout Texas and in Los Angeles, CA, the core program is supplemented by a host of other activities that build ongoing community support for families. AVANCE's methods and materials have been adapted by other programs that serve predominantly Latino families.

  301 South Frio, Suite 310, San Antonio, TX 78207; (210) 270-4630

Better Baby Care Campaign (www.betterbabycare.org)

The Better Baby Care Campaign is a nationwide effort to improve the early care of infants and toddlers while their parents are working, in school, or in need of out-of home services. The campaign works in collaboration with national, state, and local organizations to bring attention to the issues and to improve the policies that govern child care, support and education for families, paid family leave, and related areas. Its Web site provides fact sheets, research reports, and other resources for parents and advocates.

Brazelton Touchpoints Center (www.touchpoints.org)

The Brazelton Touchpoints Center gives health care, child care, education, and family support professionals "effective and proven tools to support infants and parents at the beginning of their lives together." Developed by Dr. T. Berry Brazelton, the Touchpoints model "aims to build alliances between parents and providers around key points in the development of young children." These predictable issues and milestones "can disrupt family relations, but can also provide an opportunity for practitioners to connect with parents." The Center trains professionals working in a variety of settings to incorporate Dr. Brazelton's relationship-based, anticipatory guidance model into their individual practice and to infuse it in their communities.

  1295 Boylston Street, Ste 320, Boston, MA 02215; 617-355-2297

Center for the Childcare Workforce   (www.ccw.org)

The Center for the Childcare Workforce, a project of the American Federation of Teachers, works to improve the quality of early care and education for all children by promoting policy, research, and organizing that ensure that the early care and education workforce is well educated, receives better compensation, and has a voice in their workplace. Its Web site provides information on the compensation, retention, and education of early childhood teachers and resources that can be used at the program, community, or state level to reduce turnover and improve program quality.

American Federation of Teachers Educational Foundation, 555 New Jersey Avenue NW, Washington, DC 20001; (202) 662-8005

Child Care Services Association   (www.childcareservices.org)

The Child Care Services Association supports local and state efforts in North Carolina to improve the quality of child care. It also supports other states in the implementation of its successful T.E.A.C.H. Early Childhood® Project and Wage$ Plus to improve the education and compensation of early childhood teachers and caregivers and the retention of qualified professionals in these roles.

1829 East Franklin Street, Bldg. 1000, P.O. Box 901, Chapel Hill, NC 27514; (919) 967-3272

Children's Defense Fund   (www.childrensdefense.org)

The mission of the Children's Defense Fund (CDF) is "to *Leave No Child Behind*® and to ensure every child a Healthy Start, a Head Start, a Fair Start, a Safe Start, and a Moral Start in life and successful passage to adulthood with the help of caring families and communities." CDF develops fact sheets, outreach campaigns, and other resources to educate the nation about the needs of children and about opportunities to effectively address these needs through preventive investments and enlightened public policies. Its Web site and e-mails keep advocates informed of upcoming legislative decisions on a range of children's issues.

25 E Street NW, Washington, DC 20001; (202) 628-8787

Connect for Kids   (www.connectforkids.org)

As "an alternative news source on the Web," Connect for Kids helps adults become aware of and join campaigns to make their communities better places for families and children. Their Web site provides solutions-oriented coverage of critical issues for children and families, bringing together meaningful information, success stories, and ideas for action.

Ecumenical Childcare Network   (www.eccn.org)

Ecumenical Childcare Network (ECCN) is a national interdenominational network of individuals who work from a faith perspective to strengthen early childhood care and education programs offered by religious organizations and to garner congregational support. ECCN's members advocate "serving families by offering options, celebrating diversity, and assuring high quality, affordable, and equitable care and education for all God's children."

P.O. Box 803586, Chicago, IL 60680; (800) 694-5443

Every Child Matters   (www.everychildmatters.org)

With a special focus on making sure that all children "get the right start," the Every Child Matters Education Fund works to push children's many needs to a higher place on the country's political and policy agenda. To this end, the Education Fund conducts polls, publishes reports, works with reporters and state children's groups, runs advertising, and conducts campaigns on behalf of children.

440 First Street, NW, Fifth Floor, Washington, DC 20001-2080; (202) 393-0504

Family Support America   (www.familysupportamerica.org)

Family Support America (FSA) is an umbrella organization for programs and organizations that provide support and information to families. With its bedrock belief that parents need to be involved as equal partners in crafting solutions and systems to serve their children, families, and communities, FSA serves as the "catalyst, thought leader, and clearinghouse" for the family support movement.

20 North Wacker Dr. Suite 1100, Chicago, IL 60606; (312) 338-0900

Fight Crime: Invest In Kids   (www.fightcrime.org)

Fight Crime: Invest in Kids is a bipartisan, nonprofit anti-crime organization led by more than 2,000 police chiefs, sheriffs, prosecutors, victims of violence, and leaders of police officer associations. Its mission is "to take a hard-nosed, skeptical look at the research about what really works—and what doesn't work—to keep kids from becoming criminals" and to share that information with policy makers and the public in the form of reports, policy recommendations, articles written by its members, and resources for journalists.

2000 P St. NW, Suite 240, Washington, DC 20036; (202)776-0027

High/Scope Educational Research Foundation
(www.highscope.org)

High/Scope Educational Research Foundation is a research, development, training, and public advocacy organization whose mission is "to improve the life chances of children and youth by promoting high-quality educational programs." The High/Scope approach is based on the belief that "children learn best through active experiences with people, materials, events and ideas."

600 North River Street, Ypsilanti, MI 48198-2898; (734) 485-2000

HIPPY (Home Instruction for Parents of Preschool Youngsters)   (www.hippyusa.org)

HIPPY is a home-based program that helps parents prepare their three-, four-, and five-year-old children for success in school and beyond. The program was designed to "bring families, organizations, and communities together and remove any barriers to participation," including limited education and lack of financial resources.

220 East 23rd Street, Suite 300, New York; (212) 532-7730

National Association of Child Care Resource and Referral Agencies (NACCRRA)   (www.naccrra.org)

"NACCRRA is the national network of more than 850 child care resource and referral centers (CCR&Rs) located in every state and most communities across the US. CCR&R centers help families, child care providers, and communities find, provide, and plan for affordable, quality child care." NACCRRA provides training, resources, and best practices standards to local and state CCR&Rs and promotes national policies and partnerships that facilitate universal access to quality child care.

1319 F. Street, NW, Suite 500, Washington, DC 20004-1106; 202-393-5501

National Association for the Education of Young Children
(www.naeyc.org)

With more than 100,000 members and a network of 450 local, state, and regional affiliates, the National Association for the Education of Young Children (NAEYC) is "the nation's largest and most influential organization of early childhood educators and others dedicated to improving the quality of programs for children from birth through third grade." NAEYC and its Affiliate Groups work to improve professional practice and working conditions in early childhood education and to build public support for high quality early childhood programs. NAEYC accredits early childhood centers and programs for early childhood educators, publishes materials for educators, parents, and policy makers, holds training conferences, and issues position papers that set standards for the field.

1509 16th Street, NW, Washington, DC 20036-1426; 800-424-2460

National Association for Family Child Care   (www.nafcc.org)

The National Association for Family Child Care (NAFCC) works to "promote quality care by strengthening the profession of family child care." NAFCC accredits family child-care programs, supports family child-care associations, provides training and technical assistance to providers through outreach, conferences, and materials, and provides an advocacy voice for the profession.

5202 Pinemont Drive, Salt Lake City, UT 84123 (801) 269-9338

National Association for Bilingual Education   (www.nabe.org)

As "the only national organization exclusively concerned with the education of language-minority students in American schools," National Association for Bilingual Education (NABE) supports the education of English language learners by providing publications and professional development opportunities for their teachers, advocating nationally for strong bilingual education programs, and "collaborating with other civil rights and education organizations to ensure that the needs of language minority students are met in every state."

    1030 15th St., NW, Suite 470, Washington, DC 20005; (202) 898-1829

National Head Start Association   (www.nhsa.org)

The National Head Start Association is a membership organization that represents the children, staff, and families of Head Start programs in the United States. "The Association provides support for the entire Head Start community by advocating for policies that strengthen services to Head Start children and their families; by providing extensive training and professional development to Head Start staff; and by developing and disseminating research, information, and resources that enrich Head Start program delivery."

    1651 Prince Street, Alexandria, VA 22314; (703) 739-0875

National Black Child Development Institute   (www.nbcdi.org)

The National Black Child Development Institute (NBCDI) focuses especially on the needs of African American children and of their families and communities. The NBCDI develops programs and resources related to early childhood education and health, parenting, elementary and secondary education, and child welfare. It also provides training and support for professionals, policy makers, and community leaders seeking to effectively serve African American children and support them to "take pride in their African American heritage and culture." NBCDI's Parent Empowerment Project (PEP) draws upon African and African American traditions as it seeks to "inspire parents to excellence as their child's first teacher." Originally designed "by and for lower income African Americans," PEP "has demonstrated effectiveness with a broad spectrum of parents."

    11-1 15th Street NW, Suite 300, Washington, DC 20005; (202) 833-8222

National Governors Association Center for Best Practices

(www.nga.org/center)

The Center's Web site provides policy makers with up-to-date resources and information on promising state policies and initiatives. The education division provides information on early childhood issues.

    Hall of States, 444 N. Capitol St., Washington, DC 20001-1512; (202) 624-5300

National Latino Children's Institute   (www.nlci.org)

The National Latino Children's Institute is "the only national Latino organization that focuses exclusively on children." Its *Words for the Future—Creando el futuro* kit "uses culturally appropriate materials and strategies to gently guide parents through the process of learning how to best provide their children with the experiences they need." "The underlying premise of *Words for the Future* is that during every moment a child is learning. Parents who talk, sing, read, explain and explore with their children, even during their first days of life, are giving their children a gift that will last a lifetime."

1325 N. Flores Street, Suite 114, San Antonio, TX 78212; (210) 228-9997

Ounce of Prevention   (www.ounceofprevention.org)

Informed by the latest research and theories, the Ounce develops model programs, tests them "in real-world circumstances," and shares effective approaches "as best practices with the entire early childhood field." Typically, the Ounce "uses private dollars as 'seed money' to launch innovative programs and to leverage public funding." The Ounce Web site provides information for policy makers, advocates, and professionals on effective prevention strategies and programs.

122 S. Michigan Ave., Suite 2050 Chicago, IL 60603-6198; (312) 922-3863

Parents Action for Children   (www.parentsaction.org)

Formerly known as the *I Am Your Child* Foundation, Parents Action for Children is a national organization that seeks to raise awareness about the importance of early childhood development. Its Web site provides a wide variety of resources for parents, early childhood professionals, child advocates, health care providers, policy makers, and the media. Its celebrity-hosted video series exploring critical issues in early childhood development is a valuable resource for parents, professionals, community organizers, and advocates. The Web site also makes it easy for parents and advocates to connect with each other and to add their voices to campaigns to improve child and family policies.

335 N. Maple Drive, Suite 135, Beverly Hills, CA 90210; (310) 285-2385

Parent Services Project   (www.parentservices.org)

The Parent Services Project (PSP) integrates family support into child-care, school, and early education settings. PSP's family support strategies, including family activities, parenting education, peer support, and information and referral services, are grounded in "warm, respectful relationships" that "nourish the personal connections that make change possible." PSP uses family support strategies to break down barriers among parents and program staff and "to create social support networks for all families."

79 Belvedere St. #101, San Rafael, CA 94901; (415) 454-1870

Parent–Child Home Program   (www.parent-child.org)

The Parent–Child Home Program (PCHP) "is a home-based literacy and parenting program for families challenged by poverty, low levels of education, language barriers and other obstacles to educational success." Participating families are visited twice a week for two years by trained and well-supported Home Visitors who speak their language, beginning when their child is approximately two years old. "In play sessions with the parent and the child together, the Home Visitor demonstrates parenting techniques. The Home Visitor emphasizes verbal interaction and learning through play, using carefully chosen books and toys. PCHP strengthens families and prepares children to succeed in school by increasing parent–child interaction."

800 Port Washington Boulevard, Port Washington, NY 11050; (516) 883-7480

Parents as Teachers   (www.patnc.org)

Parents as Teachers (PAT) is an international program serving families from pregnancy to their child's entry into kindergarten. Local PAT programs offer child development information, parenting education, and family support services and referrals to all parents in their communities. The Parents as Teachers National Center, Inc. (PATNC) develops curricula, trains early childhood professionals, and certifies parent educators.

2228 Ball Drive, St. Louis, MO 63146; (314) 432-4330

School of the 21st Century   (www.yale.edu/bushcenter/21C)

The School of the 21st Century (21C), an initiative of the Yale Center in Child Development and Social Policy at Yale University, is "a community school model that incorporates childcare and family support services into schools. Its overall goal is to promote the optimal growth and development of children beginning at birth." Using the public school as a base, the model provides high quality child care for all children in the community whose families choose to enroll them. The national 21C organization provides training, technical assistance, and evaluation services for schools and communities implementing the 21C model.

The Yale University Bush Center in Child Development and Social Policy, 310 Prospect Street, New Haven, CT 06511; (203) 432-9944

Stand for Children   (www.stand.org)

Stand for Children is a national membership organization that "enables everyday people to join together in a strong, effective voice to win concrete changes for children." Members of its grassroots chapters advocate for improved schools, early childhood education programs, after-school enrichment, and other services for children in their communities and states.

National Office: 516 SE Morrison Street, Suite 206, Portland, OR 97214; (503) 235-2305

United Way/Success By 6   (http://national.unitedway.org/sb6/)

"United Way Success By 6 is a national community-based movement of public and private partners that work together to deliver proven solutions that ensure all children ages zero to six are healthy, nurtured and ready to succeed. In more than 350 cities throughout the United States and Canada, United Way Success By 6 is creating effective community-based solutions that contribute to the positive quality of life for young children."

USA Childcare   (www.usachildcare.org)

USA Childcare is a professional organization of child-care providers committed to serving low- and moderate-income children. The national organization supports a network of local and state associations "with the goal of engaging providers in the policy dialogue and increasing their capacity to lead local communities in developing a system of high quality child care." The organization also supports national campaigns and legislation and provides expertise to legislators and policy makers.

703-875-8100

Voices for America's Children
(www.voicesforamericaschildren.org)

Voices for America's Children is a national child advocacy organization that supports organizations working at state and local levels to improve the well-being of children. "With member organizations in almost every state, Voices provides a voice for the voiceless—children—in city halls and statehouses across the country."

1522 K Street, NW, Suite 600, Washington, DC 20005-1202;(202) 289-0777

ZERO TO THREE: National Center for Infants, Toddlers, and Families   (www.zerotothree.org)

ZERO TO THREE's mission is "to promote the healthy development of our nation's infants and toddlers by supporting and strengthening families, communities, and those who work on their behalf." The organization is "dedicated to advancing current knowledge; promoting beneficial policies and practices; communicating research and best practices to a wide variety of audiences; and providing training, technical assistance and leadership development." Its Web site contains a wealth of resources for parents, professionals, and advocates.

2000 M Street, NW, Suite 200, Washington, DC 20036; (202) 638-1144

Notes

Preface

1. David Lawrence, Jr., President, The Early Childhood Initiative Foundation. Remarks at the Starting Points Leadership Meeting, University of South Florida, Tampa, FL, November 3, 1999. Sponsored by the A. L. Mailman Family Foundation.

2. This term was coined by journalist Daniel Goleman. See D. Goleman (1995) *Emotional Intelligence*, New York: Bantam Books.

3. In 2002, the National Assessment of Educational Progress (NAEP) results showed that 36% of a nationally representative sample of fourth graders were scoring "below basic" in reading. A large number of these children, who are still struggling to read in the fourth grade, entered school already behind. Indeed, a national study of the kindergarten class of 1998 (ECLAS-K) found that average cognitive scores of children in the highest income group were significantly higher than those of the middle-income group children and 60% above those of children in the lowest socioeconomic group. These findings echoed those of in-depth studies of language development. See V. Lee and D. Burkam (2002) *Inequality at the Starting Gate: Social Background Differences and Achievement as Children Begin School*, Washington, DC: Economic Policy Institute, for an analysis of inequalities at school entry and the ways in which these are exacerbated by instructional policies and by inequities among public schools.

4. See National Research Council and Institute of Medicine (2000) *From Neurons to Neighborhoods: The Science of Early Childhood Development*. Committee on Integrating the Science of Early Childhood Development. Jack P. Shonkoff and Deborah A. Phillips (eds.). Board on Children, Youth, and Families, Commission on Behavioral and Social Sciences and Education. Washington, DC: National Academy Press, p. 139.

5. National Research Council (1998) *Preventing Reading Difficulties in Young Children*. Committee on the Prevention of Reading Difficulties in Young Children. Catherine E. Snow, M. Susan Burns, and Peg Griffin (eds.). Washington, DC: National Academy Press.

6. S. Kamerman (2000) Early childhood education and care: An overview of developments in the OECD countries, *International Journal of Educational Research*, 33: 7–29.

Chapter One

1. Goals 2000: Educate America Act (P.L. 103–227), Enacted November 1994. "By the year 2000, all children in America shall start school ready to learn" was listed as the first of eight goals.

2. Jack and Jill are real children. The details of their lives and of their child-care experiences have been altered slightly to protect their privacy and that of their families and teachers.

3. National Research Council (1998) *Preventing Reading Difficulties in Young Children.* Committee on the Prevention of Reading Difficulties in Young Children. Catherine E. Snow, M. Susan Burns, and Peg Griffin (eds.). Washington, DC: National Academy Press.

4. B. Hart and T. Risley (1995) *Meaningful Differences in the Everyday Experience of Young American Children,* Baltimore, MD: Paul H. Brookes Publishing Company.

5. The class and family differences reported in the Hart and Risley research very likely have both genetic and experiential components. Temperamental characteristics such as shyness and flexibility are inherited, and most psychologists believe that genetic inheritance also contributes to differences in intelligence. However, differences in the child's experience are likely to play a greater role than inherited characteristics. Cultures (and early childhood programs) differ in the amount and kinds of talkativeness that are considered appropriate for young children in different settings. In addition, as will be explained throughout this book, children's early experiences with language have been shown in a wide range of studies to have a strong impact both on their language use as young children and on their later school performance. As Hart and Risley point out, children who use more and richer language are likely to elicit more and richer language from their conversation partners, creating a virtuous circle that facilitates rapid learning.

6. B. Hart and T. Risley (1999) *The Social World of Children Learning to Talk,* Baltimore, MD: Paul H. Brookes Publishing Company.

7. Hart and Risley, *Social World of Children Learning to Talk,* p. 3.

8. The family child-care center that Jack attends has been accredited by the National Association for Family Child Care (NAFCC).

9. For example, the *Early Childhood Environmental Rating Scale* authored by T. Harms, R. Clifford, and D. Cryer (1998), New York: Teachers College Press. The center that Jill attends has not been accredited by the National Association for Education of Young Children (NAEYC).

10. The *NICHD Study of Early Child Care,* prepared by Robin Peth-Pierce. Public Information and Communications Branch, NICHD (Washington, DC: National Institute of Child Health and Human Development, National Institutes of Health, U.S. Department of Health and Human Services, April 1998).

11. In fact, recent studies suggest that TV may be more harmful to toddlers than previously realized, either because of its highly stimulating, rapidly changing visual content or because it takes time away from play, hands-on learning, and conversation. A 2004 study by researchers at Children's Hospital in Seattle [D. A. Christakis, F. J. Zimmerman, D. L. DiGiuseppe, and C. A. McCarty (2004) Early television exposure and subsequent attentional problems in children, *Pediatrics,* 113: 708–713] found that toddlers' television exposure is associated with attentional problems at age seven, and that the risk increases with more viewing time. Unfortunately, American toddlers today are spending a lot of time in front of TV screens, more than enough to place many of them at risk. In November 2003, The Henry J. Kaiser Family Foundation released the report of a national study by Victoria Rideout, Elizabeth Vanderwater, and Ellen Martella: *Zero to Six: Electronic Media in the Lives of Infants, Toddlers, and Preschoolers.* Based on a telephone survey of a random sample of more than 1,000 households, the study found that "According to their parents, children six and under spend an average

of two hours a day with screen media," that "Two-thirds of zero- to six- year olds (65%) live in a home where the TV is on at least half the time, even if no one is watching," and that "In a typical day, 69% of all children under two use screen media (59% watch TV, 42% watch a video or DVD, 5% use a computer and 3% play video games) and these youngsters will spend an average of two hours and five minutes in front of a screen."

12. See www.nafcc.org for accreditation criteria, policies, and procedures.

13. The *Early Childhood Environmental Rating Scale* (ECERS; Harms, Clifford, and Cryer) is a widely used yardstick for assessing the quality of early childhood programs for three- to five-year-olds. The ECERS looks at both the physical and the social environment, for children and adults. Observers assess routines, policies, and program structures, interactions among children and between children and adults, furnishings, materials, activities, and opportunities for child-initiated exploration and learning. Using this measure, the four-state Cost, Quality, and Outcomes Study [Cost, Quality, and Outcomes Study Team (1995) *Cost, Quality, and Child Outcomes in Child Care Centers*, Public Report, Denver, CO: University of Colorado, Economics Department.] found that only 24% of classrooms for three- to five-year-olds provided "good" quality care that supported healthy development; a similar study in Massachusetts completed in 2001 [N. L. Marshall, C. L. Creps, N. R. Burstein, F. B. Glantz, W. W. Robeson, and S. Barnett (2001) *The Cost and Quality of Full Day, Year-Round Early Care and Education in Massachusetts: Preschool Classrooms. Executive Summary*, Wellesley, MA: Wellesley Centers for Women and Abt Associates, Inc.] found that "full-time early care and education for preschoolers in Massachusetts is comparable to, or better than, similar preschool care in other states. However, 65% of the classrooms did not meet the Good benchmark for language and cognitive stimulation." Not surprisingly, the classrooms rated "good" were more likely to serve upper-income children. "Only a quarter of classrooms serving low-to-moderate income families met the Good benchmark for language and cognitive stimulation." For toddlers, the Massachusetts results were somewhat better. Forty-three percent of all toddler classrooms met the Good benchmark in "listening/talking." Of toddler classrooms serving families in the low to moderate income range, however, only 36% met this benchmark [N. L. Marshall, C. L. Creps, N. R. Burstein, F. B. Glantz, and W. W. Robeson (2004) *The Cost and Quality of Full-Day, Year-Round Early Care and Education in Massachusetts: Infant and Toddler Classrooms*, Wellesley, MA: Wellesley Centers for Women and Abt Associates, Inc.] has not yet published a similar study of classrooms for children under age three; however, the study of such classrooms in four other states found that only one in twelve provided "developmentally appropriate care," and fully 40% provided care so poor that it "threatened health and safety."

14. For example, in polls conducted by *Education Week* in 2002 and 2004, voters ranked education second after jobs and the economy as the issue that concerned them most. Health care was third. *Learn. Vote. Act. The Public's Responsibility for Public Education,Public Education Network* (2004), Available at http://www.publiceducation.org/pdf/national_poll/2004_Learn_Vote_Act.pdf.

15. Peth-Pierce, *NICHD Study of Early Childhood Care.*

16. Peth-Pierce, *NICHD Study of Early Childhood Care*; Cost, Quality, and Outcomes Study Team, *Cost, Quality, and Child Outcomes in Child Care Centers*; E. Galinsky, C. Howes, S. Kontos, and M. Shinn (1994) *The Study of Children in Family Child Care and Relative Care: Highlights of Findings*, New York: Families and Work Institute; Marshall et al., *The Cost and Quality of Full Day, Year-Round Early Care and Education in Massachusetts.*

17. U.S. census, 2000.

18. The National Educational Goals Panel reported in 1993 (*National Education Goals Panel: Building a Nation of Learners: The National Education Goals Report, Executive Summary*. Washington, DC) that nearly half of the nation's infants and toddlers were "at risk" due to one or more of the following: inadequate prenatal care, isolated parents, or substandard child care. The Carnegie Corporation of New York's April 1994 publication, *Starting Points: Meeting the Needs of Our Youngest Children*, dubbed this problem "the quiet crisis" and proposed numerous solutions. Some of those solutions have been implemented, and there have been noticeable improvements in the past decade. Still, family support services remain spotty and studies of child-care programs, family child-care homes, and individual caregivers continue to find that fewer than half provide "positive caregiving" or "developmentally appropriate care" to children two and three years old.

Chapter Two

1. R. Shore (1997) *Rethinking the Brain: New Insights into Early Development*, New York: Families and Work Institute.

2. See *From Neurons to Neighborhoods: The Science of Early Childhood Development* (National Research Council and Institute of Medicine (2000) Committee on Integrating the Science of Early Childhood Development. Jack. P. Shonkoff and Deborah A. Phillips (eds.). Board on Children, Youth, and Families, Commission on Behavioral and Social Sciences and Education. Washington, DC: National Academy Press) for a discussion of the resilience of basic language learning, in the face of obstacles such as limited exposure to language models, sensory impairments, and brain injury, as well as for a full discussion of aspects of language learning that are not resilient and that depend upon experience, opportunities for practice, and interaction.

3. See "An Instinct to Acquire an Art," in S. Pinkner (1994) *The Language Instinct: How the Mind Creates Language*, New York: William Morrow and Company.

4. M. Segal, J. Leinfelder, B. Bardige, and M. J. Woika (forthcoming) *All About Child Care and Early Education*, New York: Allyn & Bacon.

5. A. Gopnik, A. Meltzoff, and P. Kuhl (1999) *The Scientist in the Crib*, New York: William Morrow and Company.

6. Pinkner, *The Language Instinct*.

7. Pinkner, *The Language Instinct*; Gopnik, Meltzoff, and Kuhl, *Scientist in the Crib*.

8. See *From Neurons to Neighborhoods* (National Research Council and Institute of Medicine), *The Scientist in the Crib* (Gopnik, Meltzoff, and Kuhl), and *What's Going on in There? How the Brain and Mind Develop in the First Five Years of Life* (L. Eliot (1999), New York: Bantam Books) for summaries of recent, fascinating research on what babies can learn and the role of language in supporting that learning.

9. Eliot, *What's Going on in There?*

10. M. Segal (1998) *Your Child at Play: One to Two Years: Exploring, Learning, Making Friends, and Pretending*, New York: Newmarket Press.

11. Pinkner, *The Language Instinct*, pp. 267–268.

12. R. E. Owens, Jr. (2000) *Language Development: An Introduction*, 5th edn., New York: Allyn & Bacon.

13. D. Barry (2002) Daughter, 2, Will be Allowed to Date in 2048, *The Miami Herald*, January 27, 2002.

14. S. Fraiberg (1977) *The Magic Years*, New York: MacMillan Publishing Company.

15. This statement is made frequently by early childhood professionals to argue that young children learn best through play. For example, in the cover story for the November 2003 issue of the *American School Board Journal*, Kathleen Vail quotes Ed Zigler, director of Yale's Center in Child Development and Social Policy: "We have known for 75 years that an important determiner of growth and development is play." "Play is the work of children."

16. Eliot, *What's Going on in There?*

17. B. Potter (2002) *The Tale of the Flopsy Bunnies*, London: Frederick Warne and Company.

18. P. Tabors (1997) *One Child, Two Languages: A Guide for Preschool Educators of Children Learning English as a Second Language*, Baltimore, MD: Paul H. Brookes Publishing.

19. S. Goldin-Meadow and C. Mylander (1998) Spontaneous sign systems created by deaf children in two cultures, *Nature*, 391: 279–281.

20. National Research Council and Institute of Medicine, *From Neurons to Neighborhoods*.

21. About half of the children who are late talkers at two (using fewer than fifty words and no word combinations) are likely to exhibit normal language development by age three; another 25% will be within the range of normal by the time they enter school. (Rescorla and Schwartz, 1990; Thal and Tobias, 1992; cited in *From Neurons to Neighborhoods* (National Research Council and Institute of Medicine), p. 144.)

22. National Research Council and Institute of Medicine, *From Neurons to Neighborhoods*, p. 139.

23. See C. Snow (2002) Ensuring reading success for African-American children, In B. Bowman (ed.), *Love to Read: Essays in Developing and Enhancing Early Literacy Skills of African-American children*, Washington, DC: National Black Child Development Institute, for a discussion of the ways in which vocabulary and reading influence each other.

24. See J. Helm and L. Katz (2001) *Young Investigators: The Project Approach in the Early Years*, New York: Teachers College Press.

25. When selecting prepared curricula, it is essential to take into account the ages, interests, developmental level, and linguistic and cultural backgrounds of the children. Programs that rely heavily on teacher presentations, worksheets, standardized art projects, and vocabulary drill tend to reduce the amount and richness of conversation in a preschool classroom. On the other hand, play-based approaches that include lots of book reading, pretending, problem-solving, and exploration along with interesting content and deliberate attention to literacy and math concepts tend to enhance young children's learning in all domains. See *Eager to Learn: Educating Our Preschoolers* (National Research Council (2001) Committee on Early Childhood Pedagogy. Barbara T. Bowman, M. Suzane Donovan, and M. Susan Burns (eds.). Commission on Behavioral Sciences and Education. Washington, DC: National Academy Press) for examples of exemplary practice and a discussion of effective approaches.

26. National Research Council, *Eager to Learn*.

27. The findings of this study are reported in detail in D. K. Dickinson and P. O. Tabors (2001) *Beginning Literacy with Language*, Baltimore, MD: Paul H. Brookes Publishing Company.

28. In her (unpublished) research, Catherine Snow has found that vocabulary at school entry predicts high school reading comprehension. Personal communication, May 16, 2004.

29. National Research Council and Institute of Medicine, *From Neurons to Neighborhoods*, p. 5.

Chapter Three

1. R. Fulghum (1993) *All I Ever Really Wanted to Know I Learned in Kindergarten*, Mass Market Paperback, pp. 6–7.

2. D. Goleman (1995) *Emotional Intelligence*, New York: Bantam Books.

3. M. Segal and D. Adcock (1983) *Making Friends*, New York: Prentice Hall.

4. R. Weissbourd (1997)*The Vulnerable Child: What Really Hurts America's Children and What We Can Do About It*, New York: Perseus Publishing.

5. E. E. Werner (1987) Vulnerability and resiliency in children at risk of delinquency: A longitudinal study from birth to adulthood, In J. D. Burchard and S. N. Burchard (eds.), *Primary Prevention of Psychopathology, Vol. 10: Prevention of Delinquent Behavior*, Newbury Park, CA: Sage, pp. 16–43.

6. See ZERO TO THREE's 1992 report, *Heart Start: The Emotional Foundations of School Readiness* (Washington, DC: ZERO TO THREE Press, www.zerotothree.org) for a discussion of how parenting and caregiving practices help children to develop "Confidence, Curiosity, Self-Control, Ability to Relate to Others, Capacity to Have an Impact and be Persistent, Capacity to Communicate (including Learning to Talk), and Cooperation," seven social–emotional "keys" to school readiness.

7. S. Wolin and S. Wolin (1993) *The Resilient Self: How Survivors of Troubled Families Rise Above Adversity*, New York: Villard Books.

8. L. Gilkerson (2001) Factors that place young children at risk, Plenary session presented at *Building Our Future Conference on the Emotional Roots of School Readiness*, Miami Beach, FL, October 17–19. The case described here comes from Dr. Dorothy Norton's research in Chicago. See D. G. Norton, (1996) Early linguistic interaction and school achievement: An ethnographical, ecological perspective, *ZERO TO THREE*, 16: 8–14; D. G. Norton (1994) My mommy didn't kill my daddy, In J. D. Osofsky and E. Fenichel (eds.), *Caring for Infants and Toddlers in Violent Environments: Hurt, Healing, and Hope*, Washington, DC: ZERO TO THREE Press; and D. G. Norton (1993) Diversity, early socialization and temporal development: The dual perspective revisited, *Social Work*, 38: 82–90.

9. Werner, *Primary Prevention of Psychopathology*, Vol. 10, pp. 16–43.

10. C. R. Cooper (2001) *Who Are these Writers?: An Exploration of the Connections Between Expressiveness in Children's Writing and Their Psychosocial Profiles*, Ed.D. Thesis, Harvard Graduate School of Education.

11. For a compelling case study, see V. Purcell-Gates (1995) *Other People's Words: The Cycle of Low Literacy*, Cambridge, MA: Harvard University Press.

12. National Research Council (1998) *Preventing Reading Difficulties in Young Children*. Committee on the Prevention of Reading Difficulties in Young Children. Catherine E. Snow, M. Susan Burns, and Peg Griffin (eds.). Washington, DC: National Academy Press, p. 21.

13. F. J. Morrison, E. M. Griffith, G. Williamson, and C. L. Hardaway (1995) The nature and sources of early literacy, Paper presented at the biennial meeting of the Society for Research in Child Development, Indiannapolis, IN; H. W. Stevenson, T.

Parker, A. Williamson, A. Hegion, and E. Fish (1976) Longitudinal study of individual differences in cognitive development and scholastic achievement, *Journal of Educational Psychology*, 68: 377–400, cited in *From Neurons to Neighborhoods*.

14. S. L. Kagan, E. Moore, and S. Bredekamp (eds.) (1995) *Reconsidering Children's Early Development and Learning: Toward Shared Beliefs and Vocabulary*, Washington, DC: National Goals Panel.

15. E. D. Hirsh, Jr. (2001) Overcoming the language gap, *Education Week*, May 2, 2001.

16. See U.S. Department of Health and Human Services (December 2003) *State Funded Pre-Kindergarten Programs: What the Evidence Shows* (http://aspe.hhs.gov/hsp/state-funded-pre-k/index.htm) for a summary of short and longer term effects of prekindergarten programs and a discussion of the fade-out phenomenon.

17. E. Zigler and S. Styfco (1993) *Head Start and Beyond: A National Plan for Extended Childhood Intervention*, New Haven, CT: Yale University Press. High quality programs that contain both early education and family support components are likely to have a stronger long-term impact than programs that provide only one or the other. H. Yoshikawa (1995) Long-term effects of early childhood programs on social outcomes and delinquency, *Future of Children*, 5: 51–75.

18. After Head Start's first summer, researchers reported dramatic gains in IQ scores. The designers were skeptical: How could a six-week intervention make such a difference? Had children become smarter or more knowledgeable, or had they just become more comfortable and motivated in the testing situation? The media frenzy led to inflated expectations, which turned to disappointment that nearly killed the program when the gains were not sustained. E. Zigler, M. Finn-Stevenson, and M. Hall (2002) *The First Three Years and Beyond: Brain Development and Social Policy*, New Haven, CT: Yale University Press.

19. C. T. Ramey and F. A. Campbell (1984) Preventive education for high-risk children: Cognitive consequences of the Carolina Abecedarian Project (Special Issue), *American Journal of Mental Deficiency*, 88: 515–523, Available at www.circ.uab.edu/craigramey/abceffect.htm.

20. C. T. Ramey and F. A. Campbell (1991) Poverty, early childhood education, and academic competence: The Abecedarian experiment, In A. C. Huston (ed.), *Children in Poverty*, New York: Cambridge University Press, pp. 190–221.

21. B. Hart and T. Risley (1995) *Meaningful Differences in the Everyday Experience of Young American Children*, Baltimore, MD: Paul H. Brookes Publishing Company.

22. S. Helburn and B. Bergmann (2002) *America's Childcare Problem: The Way Out*, New York: Palgrave, pp. 70–71 and 66–67.

23. S. W. Helburn (ed.) (1995) *Cost, Quality, and Child Outcomes in Child Care Centers*, Technical Report, Denver, CO: Department of Economics, Center for Research in Economic and Social Policy, University of Colorado at Denver.

24. S. Powers and E. Fenichel (1999) *Home Visiting: Reaching Babies and Families "Where They Live,"* Washington, DC: ZERO TO THREE Press.

25. P. Levenstein, S. Levenstein, J. A. Shiminski, and J. E. Stolzberg (1998) Long-term impact of a verbal interaction program for at-risk toddlers: An exploratory study of high school outcomes in a replication of the Mother–Child Home Program, *Journal of Applied Developmental Psychology*, 19: 267–285.

26. P. Levenstein, J. M. O'Hara, and J. Madden (1983) The Mother–Child Home Program of the Verbal Interaction Project, In Consortium for Longitudinal Studies (ed.), *As the Twig is Bent*, Hillsdale, NJ: Lawrence Erlbaum Associates.

27. C. T. Ramey, D. M. Bryant, B. H. Wasik, J. J. Sparling, K. H. Fendt, and L. M. LaVange (1992) Infant Health and Development Program for low birth weight, premature infants: Program components, family participation, and child intelligence, *Pediatrics*, 89(3): 454–465.

28. J. Brooks-Gunn, C. M. McCarron, P. H. Casey, M. C. McCormick, C. R. Bauer, J. C. Bernbaum, J. Tyson, M. Swanson, F. C. Bennett, D. T. Scott, J. Tonascia, and C. Meinert (1994) Early intervention in low-birth-weight premature infants: Results through age 5 years from the Infant Health and Development Program, *Journal of the American Medical Association*, 272(16): 1257–1262.

29. E. Zigler, M. Finn-Stevenson, and N. Hall (2002) *The First Three Years and Beyond*, New Haven, CT: Yale University Press, p. 211.

30. PL 107-110 The *No Child Left Behind Act* of 2001, signed January 2002 by President George W. Bush.

31. National Research Council and Institute of Medicine (2000) *From Neurons to Neighborhoods: The Science of Early Childhood Development.* Committee on Integrating the Science of Early Childhood Development. Jack P. Shonkoff and Deborah A. Phillips (eds.). Board on Children, Youth, and Families, Commission on Behavioral and Social Sciences and Education. Washington, DC: National Academy Press.

32. Rick Weissbourd used this argument to shape the Literacy Action Plan for the City of Cambridge's Agenda for Children. I am indebted to him for this strong position and perspective.

Chapter Four

1. Cambridge Family Literacy Collaborative (2001) Five Essential Messages (printed on bookmarks and other materials). TALK Campaign materials developed by Agenda for Children, Cambridge, MA: City of Cambridge Agenda for Children, Department of Human Services.

2. www.teachmorelovemore.org.

3. C. Lerner, A. Dombro, and K. Levine (2000) *The Magic of Everyday Moments: 12–15 Months*, Washington, DC: ZERO TO THREE Press.

4. http://www.zerotothree.org/magic/.

5. B. Bardige and M. Segal (2004) *Building Literacy with Love*, Washington, DC: ZERO TO THREE Press.

6. J. Ciborowski (2001) *Raising Readers* (video), Boston, MA: Children's Hospital.

7. G. J. Whitehurst, D. H. Arnold, J. N. Epstein, A. L. Amgell, M. Smith, and J. E. Fischel (1994) A picture book reading intervention in daycare and home for children from low income families, *Developmental Psychology*, 30: 679–689.

8. G. J. Whitehurst and C. J. Lonigan (1998) Child development and emergent literacy, *Child Development*, 68: 848–872.

9. Parent–Child Home Program training video, Port Washington, NY: Parent–Child Home Program, www.parentchildhomeprogram.org.

Chapter Five

1. These techniques were identified as particularly effective in the Home Study of Language and Literacy Development, described in D. Dickinson and P. O. Tabors (2001) *Beginning Literacy with Language*, Baltimore, MD: Paul H. Brookes Publishing

Company. *Starting Out Right* (M. Susan Burns, P. Griffin, and C. E. Snow (eds.). Committee on the Prevention of Reading Difficulties in Young Children, National Research Council, 1998), a resource designed to help parents and practitioners implement the recommendations of *Preventing Reading Difficulties in Young Children*, also recommends these approaches.

2. National Research Council (2001) *Eager to Learn: Educating Our Preschoolers*. Committee on Early Childhood Pedagogy. Barbara T. Bowman, M. Suzane Donovan, and M. Susan Burns (eds.). Commission on Behavioral Sciences and Education. Washington, DC: National Academy Press.

3. Dickinson and Tabors, *Beginning Literacy with Language*, p. 239.

4. L. Moats (2001) Overcoming the language gap: Invest generously in teacher professional education, *American Educator*, Summer 2001.

5. National Research Council, *Eager to Learn*, p. 232.

6. A. Burton, M. Whitebook, M. Young, D. Bellm, C. Wayne, R. Brandon, and E. Mahler (2002) *Estimating the Size and Components of U.S. Child Care Workforce and Caregiving Population: Key Findings from the Child Care Workforce Estimate (Preliminary Report)*, Washington, DC: Center for the Childcare Workforce, http://www.ccw.org/pubs/workforceestimatereport.pdf.

7. National Research Council, *Eager to Learn*, p. 13.

8. The Child Care Services Association provides national standards and implementation support for this program. See www.childcareservices.org.

Chapter Six

1. Jeudry's story was reported in *The Boston Globe* on the first day the English immersion law, or Unz Initiative, went into effect. A. Vaishnav (2003) School begins, immersed in English, *The Boston Globe*, August 27.

2. P. O. Tabors (1997) *One Child, Two Languages*, Baltimore, MD: Paul H. Brookes Publishing Company. See J. Cruzado-Guerrero (2003) Understanding literacy development in young bilingual children, in *Florida's Child*, Summer 2003 (Tallahassee, FL: Florida Children's Forum) for a discussion of pros and cons of different options for infants, toddlers, and preschoolers.

3. F. Genosee, W. E. Lambert, L. Mononen, M. Seitz, and D. Starch (1979) *Language Processing in Bilinguals*. Also see *From Neurons to Neighborhoods*, pp. 135–136, for a discussion of more recent research on the connections between the timing of second language acquisition and the areas of the brain involved in processing different aspects of the language. Function words and other grammatical information tend to be stored differently by those who learn a language later in life.

4. See C. Genishi (2002) Young English language learners: Resourceful in the classroom, In *Young Children*, July 2002, pp. 66–72.

5. B. Hart and T. Risley (1999) *The Social World of Children Leaning to Talk*, Baltimore, MD: Paul H. Brookes Publishing Company.

6. C. Snow (2002) Ensuring reading success for African American children, In B. Bowman (ed.), *Love to Read*, Washington, DC: National Black Child Development Institute.

7. Reading ability transfers across languages, even when different alphabets are used or when one language is written alphabetically and the other isn't. J. Cummins, M. Swain, K. Nakajima, J. Handscombe, D. Green, and C. Tran (1984) Linguistic

interdependence among Japanese and Vietnamese immigrant students, In C. Rivera (ed.), *Communicative Competence Approaches to Language Proficiency Assessment: Research and Application*, Clevedon, England: Multilingual Matters, pp. 60–81.

8. D. August and K. Hakuta (eds.) (1997) *Improving Schooling for Language-Minority Children: A Research Agenda*, Washington, DC: National Academy Press.

9. J. D. Ramírez, S. D. Yuen, and D. R. Ramey (1991) *Longitudinal Study of Structured English Immersion Strategy, Early-Exit and Late-Exit Transitional Bilingual Education Programs for Language-Minority Children*, San Mateo, CA: Aguirre, International. Prepared for the United States Department of Education under Contract No. 300-87-0156. For a discussion of the implications of these findings for educators of young children, see C. Eggers-Piérola (in press) *Connections and Commitments: Reflecting Latino Values in Early Childhood Programs*, Portsmouth, NH: Heinemann.

10. M. A. Zehr (2004) Study gives advantage to bilingual education over focus on English, *Education Week*, February 4.

11. Elizabeth Schaefer, Administrator, Early Learning Services, Massachusetts Department of Education, personal communication, January 14, 2004.

12. J. Cummins (2001) The academic and political discourse of minority language education: Claims and counter-claims about reading, academic language, pedagogy, and assessment as they relate to bilingual children's educational development. Paper presented at the *International Conference on Bilingualism*, Bristol, April 20, 2001. See http://www.iteachilearn.com/cummins/claims.html for a summary.

13. See *From Neurons to Neighborhoods: The Science of Early Childhood Development* (National Research Council and Institute of Medicine (2000) Committee on Integrating the Science of Early Childhood Development. Jack P. Shonkoff and Deborah A. Phillips (eds.). Board on Children, Youth, and Families, Commission on Behavioral and Social Sciences and Education. Washington, DC: National Academy Press), pp. 134–136, and B. Mclaughlin (1992) *Educational Practice Report #5: Myths and Misconceptions about Second Language Learning: What Every Teacher Needs to Unlearn* (Washington, DC: National Center For Research on Cultural Diversity and Second Language Learning).

14. V. Washington and J. D. Andrews (eds.) (1999) *Children of 2010*, Washington, DC: Children of 2010 and National Association for the Education of Young Children.

15. Washington and Andrews (eds.), *Children of 2010.*

16. Washington and Andrews (eds.), *Children of 2010.*

17. United States Census Bureau (2001) *Statistical Abstract of the United States: 2001*, Springfield, VA: National Technical Information Service.

18. See Tabors's *One Child, Two Languages* for a discussion of assessment challenges and techniques.

19. P. O. Tabors (2003) What early childhood educators need to know: Developing effective programs for linguistically and culturally diverse children and families, In D. Koralek (ed.), *Spotlight on Young Children and Language*, Washington, DC: National Association for the Education of Young Children.

20. L. W. Filmore (2000) Loss of family languages: Should educators be concerned? *Theory Into Practice*, 39(4): 203–210.

21. L. Tse (2001) *"Why Don't They Learn English?": Separating Fact from Fallacy in the U.S. Language Debate*, New York: Teachers College Press.

22. L. Rodriguez (1993) *Always Running*, New York: Simon and Schuster, p. 219.

23. See S. B. Heath (1983) *Ways with Words: Language, Life and Work in Communities and Classrooms*, Cambridge, UK: Cambridge University Press, for a classic study of

the ways in which children in two different working-class communities, one African American and one white, learn to use language and how differences between their ways of speaking and the language of schooling and power lead to unequal opportunity for academic advancement. Unfortunately, a large body of research shows that children who speak English differently continue to be misunderstood, disadvantaged, and discriminated against in schools that do not validate their home language. See L. Delpitt and J. K. Dowdy (eds.) (2003) *The Skin That We Speak: Thoughts on Language and Culture in the Classroom*, New York: New Press.

24. The above vision is part of the mission statement of the Early Childhood Equity Alliance. See www.rootsforchange.net.

25. J. Cummins and M. Swain (1986) Bilingualism in Education: Aspects of Theory, Research and Practice, London: Longman.

26. K. Hakuta and R. M. Diaz (1984) The relationship between degree of bilingualism and cognitive ability: A critical discussion and some new longitudinal data, In K. Nelson (ed.), *Children's Language*, Vol. 5, Hillsdale, NJ: Lawrence Erlbaum Associates.

27. H. C. Barik and M. Swain (1976) A longitudinal study of bilingual and cognitive development, *International Journal of Psychology*, 11: 251–263; B. Harley and S. Lapkin (1984) The effects of early bilingual schooling on first language development, OISE. Mimeo.

28. S. Bochner (1996) The learning strategies of bilingual vs. monolingual students, *British Journal of Educational Psychology*, 66: 83–93.

Chapter Seven

1. See S. Kamerman (2000) Early childhood education and care: An overview of developments in the OECD countries, *International Journal of Education Research*, 33: 7–29.

2. C. J. Cooper (1999) *A Welcome for Every Child III: Ready to Learn: The French System of Early Education and Care Offers Lessons for the United States*, New York: French-American Foundation.

3. F. Sonenstein, G. Gates, S. R. Schmidt, and N. Bolshun (2002) *Primary Child Care Arrangements of Employed Parents: Findings from the 1999 National Survey of America's Families*, Washington, DC: Urban Institute.

4. Cost, Quality & Outcomes Study Team (1995) Cost, quality, and child outcomes in child care centers, Public Report, Denver, CO: Economics Department, University of Colorado.

5. S. Helburn and B. Bergmann (2002) *America's Childcare Problem: The Way Out*, New York: Palgrave, p. 89.

6. E. Galinsky, C. Howes, S. Kontos, and M. Shinn (1994)*The Study of Children in Family Child Care and Relative Care: Highlights of Findings*, New York: Families and Work Institute.

7. NICHD Early Child Care Research Network (2000) Characteristics and quality of child care for toddlers and preschoolers, *Journal of Applied Developmental Science*, 4(3): 116–135.

8. U.S. Bureau of Labor Statistics (2000) Occupational Employment Statistics, Table 1, National Employment and Wage Data from the Occupational Employment Statistics Survey by Occupation, 1999.

9. Center for the Childcare Workforce (2004) *Current Data on Salaries and Benefits for the U.S. Early Childhood Education Workforce*, Washington, DC: American Federation of Teachers Foundation.

10. See M. Whitebook (2001) *Working for Worthy Wages: The Child Care Compensation Movement 1970–2001*, New York: Foundation for Child Development, for a history of this campaign.

11. See M. Whitebook, L. Sakai, E. Gerber, and C. Howes (2001) *Then and Now: Changes in Child Care Staffing, 1994–2000 Technical Report*, Washington, DC: Center for the Child Care Workforce (a project of the American Federation of Teachers Educational Foundation, http://www.aft.org/). This report documented an annual turnover rate of 30% in teaching staff in a sample of higher-than-typical quality centers, all of which had received or were seeking NAEYC accreditation. Only 24% of 1996 teaching staff in these centers were still present four years later. Among centers with fewer resources, the turnover rate is often considerably higher. For example, researchers in Kansas City documented an annual turnover rate of 100% among a group of centers that were not able to participate in the city's Smart Start initiative. *Kansas City Star*, March 26, 2004.

12. For example, a study by Jeffrey Capizzano and Gina Adams at the Urban Institute found that only 36.4% of low-income three- and four-year-olds with employed mothers were in center-based care, as compared to 45.5% of higher-income age mates whose mothers were employed. The authors expressed concern that this discrepancy "may represent a missed opportunity to assist low-income children in becoming school-ready." J. Capizzano and G. Adams (2004) *Children in Low-Income Families Are Less Likely to Be in Center-Based Child Care*, Washington, DC: Urban Institute, www.urban.org.

13. A. Crittenden (2001) *The Price of Motherhood: Why the Most Important Job in the World Is Still the Least Valued*, New York: Metropolitan Books.

14. NICHD Early Child Care Research Network (2002) Early child care and children's development prior to school entry: Results from the NICHD Study of Early Child Care, *American Educational Research Journal*, 39: 133–164.

15. U.S. Department of Education. National Center for Education Statistics (2001) *Entering Kindergarten: A Portrait of American Children When They Begin School: Findings from The Condition of Education 2000*, Nicholas Zill and Jerry West. NCES 201-035, Washington, DC: U.S. Government Printing Office.

16. National Research Council (2001) *Eager to Learn: Educating Our Preschoolers*. Committee on Early Childhood Pedagogy. Barbara T. Bowman, M. Suzanne Donovan, and M. Susan Burns (eds.). Commission on Behavioral and Social Sciences and Education. Washington, DC: National Academy Press.

17. National Research Council and Institute of Medicine (2000) *From Neurons to Neighborhoods: The Science of Early Childhood Development*. Committee on Integrating the Science of Early Childhood Development. Jack P. Shonkoff and Deborah A. Phillips (eds.). Board on Children, Youth, and Families, Commission on Behavioral and Social Sciences and Education. Washington, DC: National Academy Press.

18. B. Fuller, S. L. Kagan, and S. Loeb (2000) *Executive Summary. Wave 1 Findings, Growing Up in Poverty Project, February 2000*, Berkeley, CA: Policy Analysis for California Education, http://pace.berkeley.edu/pace_index.html.

19. K. A. Frankel and R. J. Harmon (1996) Depressed mothers: They don't always look as bad as they feel, *Journal of the American Academy of Child and Adolescent Psychiatry*, 35(3): 289–298.

20. E. Z. Tronick and M. K. Weinberg (1997) Depressed mothers and infants: Failure to form dyadic states of consciousness, In L. Murray and P. J. Cooper (eds.), *Postpartum Depression and Child Development*, New York: Guilford Press; C. H. Zeanah, N. W. Boris, and J. A. Larrieu (1997) Infant development and developmental risk: A review of the past 10 years, *Journal of the American Academy of Child and Adolescent Psychiatry*, 36(2): 165–178.

21. M. Segal (1985) A study of maternal beliefs and values within the context of an intervention program, In I. E. Sigel (ed.), *Parental Belief Systems: The Psychological Consequences for Children*, Hillsdale, NJ: Lawrence Erlbaum Associates, pp. 271–286.

22. For example, the Parent Services Project works with child-care programs to build parent networks, active parent participation, parent-run support and education programs, and other hallmarks of "family-centered care." A study conducted by Alan Stein and Associates (1985–1988) found that child-care programs that had incorporated PSP were "...effective in reducing parents' (psychological) symptom levels in the short term and preventing symptom development on a longer-term basis. This symptom reduction promotes parent empowerment and healthy family function." The NICHD Study found that high quality care contributed to improvements in problematic mother/child relationships.

23. M. Whitebook and Cost, Quality & Outcomes Study Team (1995) Cost, quality, and child outcomes in child care centers, Public Report, Denver, CO: Economics Department, University of Colorado; E. Galinsky, C. Howes, and S. Kontos (1995) *The Family Child Care Training Study: Highlights of Findings*, New York: Families and Work Institute; C. Howes, E. Galinsky, M. Shinn, A. Sibley, M. Abbott-Shim, and J. McCarthy (1998) *The Florida Child Care Quality Improvement Study: 1996 Report*, New York: Families and Work Institute.

24. National professional organizations include The National Association for the Education of Young Children (NAEYC), the National Family Child Care Association (NAFCC), The Ecumenical Child Care Network (ECCN), The National Head Start Association, ZERO TO THREE: National Center for Infants, Toddlers, and Families, National Association of Resource and Referral Agencies (NACCRA), Family Support America, and USA Childcare. Many of these groups also have state and local affiliates.

25. N. D. Campbell, J. C. Appelbaum, K. Martinson, and E. Martin (2000) *Be All That We Can Be: Lessons from the Military for Improving Our Nation's Childcare System*, Washington, DC: National Women's Law Center.

26. S. Powers and E. Fenichel (1999) *Home Visiting: Reaching Babies & Families*, Washington, DC: ZERO TO THREE Press.

Chapter Eight

1. Bureau of Labor Statistics, *Employment and Earnings*, January 2002.

2. Bureau of Labor Statistics, *Employment and Earnings*, January 1995.

3. J. Mezey, M. Greenberg, and R. Schumacher (2002) *The Vast Majority of Federally-Eligible Children Did Not Receive Child Care Assistance in FY 2000—Increased Child Care Funding Needed to Help More Families*, Washington, DC: Center for Law and Social Policy.

4. In Boston, for example, the self-sufficiency standard (income needed for basic necessities, without public subsidy) for a family with two parents, a preschooler, and a school-aged child was $42,564 in 1998 and $54,612 in 2003. D. Pierce and J. Brooks

(2003) *The Self-Sufficiency Standard for Massachusetts*, Boston, MA: Women's Educational and Industrial Union.

5. F. Sonenstein, G. Gates, S. R. Schmidt, and N. Bolshun (2002) Primary child care arrangements of employed parents: Findings from the 1999 National Survey of America's Families, Occasional Paper No. 59, Washington, DC: The Urban Institute.

6. For full-time workers in dual-earner couples, the average was 48.9 hours. For couples with children under eighteen, the average was 50.5 hours for men and 40.6 hours for women, reflecting the fact that more women were working part-time. J. Bond, E. Galinsky, and J. Swanberg (1997) *The 1997 National Study of the Changing Workforce*, New York: Families and Work Institute.

7. J. T. Bond, E. Galinsky, C. Thompson, and D. Prottas(2002) *The 2002 National Study of the Changing Workforce*, New York: Families and Work Institute.

8. A. Crittenden (2001) *The Price of Motherhood: Why the Most Important Job in the World Is Still the Least Valued*, New York: Metropolitan Books.

9. The NICHD Study of Early Child Care, prepared by Robin Peth-Pierce. Public Information and Communications Branch, NICHD (Washington, DC: National Institute of Child Health and Human Development, National Institutes of Health, U.S. Department of Health and Human Services, April 1998).

10. *The Right Start for America's Newborns: City and State Trends, 1990–2001*, Baltimore, MD: Annie E. Casey Foundation.

11. Children's Defense Fund (2001) *The State of America's Children Yearbook, 2001*, Washington, DC: Children's Defense Fund.

12. M. Carlson, I. Garfinkel, S. McLanahan, R. Mincy, and W. Primus (2003) The effects of welfare and child support policies on union formation, Center for Research on Child Well-Being, Working Paper #02-10-FF. Fragile Families Study, Princeton, NJ: Princeton University Press; B. Fuller, S. L. Kagan, and S. Loeb (2000) *Executive Summary. Wave 1 Findings, Growing Up in Poverty Project, February 2000*, Berkeley, CA: Policy Analysis for California Education, http://pace.berkeley.edu/pace_index.html.

13. Child Trends (2001) *Facts at a Glance, 2001*, Washington, DC: Alan Guttmacher Institute.

14. U.S. Census Bureau, Current Population Survey, 1960–2003, Annual Social and Economic Supplements.

15. National Research Council and Institute of Medicine (2000) *From Neurons to Neighborhoods: The Science of Early Childhood Development*. Committee on Integrating the Science of Early Childhood Development. Jack P. Shonkoff and Deborah A. Phillips (eds.). Board on Children, Youth, and Families, Commission on Behavioral and Social Sciences and Education. Washington, DC: National Academy Press.

16. S. B. Neuman (1999) Books make a difference: A study of access to literacy, *Reading Research Quarterly*, 34.

17. H. Lu (2003) *Low-Income Children in the United States (2003): Fact Sheet*, New York: National Center for Children in Poverty.

18. H. Hodgkinson (2003) *Leaving Too Many Children Behind: A Demographer's View on the Neglect of America's Youngest Children*, Washington, DC: Institute for Educational Leadership.

19. T. Piketty and E. Saez (2001) Income Inequality in the United States, 1918—1998, NBER Working Paper 8467, September 2001, Tables A1 and A3, Washington, DC: Center on Budget and Policy Priorities.

20. M. Miringoff (2003) *2003 Index of Social Health: Monitoring the Nation's Well-Being*, New York: Fordham University Institute for Innovation in Social Policy.

21. D. Cohen (2003) *Chasing the Red, White, and Blue—A Journey in Tocqueville's Footsteps Through Contemporary America*, New York: Picador.

22. D. Cohen (Winter 2002) What would Tocqueville say? *National Center for Children in Poverty News & Issues*, p. 3.

23. Harvard Immigration Project (2001) *The Transnationalization of Families: Immigrant Separations and Reunifications*, Cambridge, MA: Harvard Immigration Project.

24. R. J. Sampson, S. W. Raudenbush, and F. Earls (1997) Neighborhoods and violent crime: A multilevel study of collective efficacy, *Science*, 277: 918–924.

25. Voices for America's Children and the Child and Family Policy Center (2004) *Early Learning Left Out: An Examination of Public Investments in Education and Development by Child Age*, Washington, DC: Voices for America's Children.

26. K. Schulman (2000) *The High Cost of Child Care Puts Quality Care Out of Reach for Many Families*, Washington, DC: Children's Defense Fund.

27. G. Ames, L. Thames, A. O'Leary, and E. Bisson ("The LEAP Players") (2001) "The Itsy-Bitsy Paycheck," Cambridge, MA: Child Care Resource Center.

28. W. Hussar (1999) *Predicting the Need for Newly Hired Teachers in the United States to 2008—09*, Washington, DC: National Center for Education Statistics.

29. J. Lombardi (2003) *Time to Care: Redesigning Child Care to Promote Education, Support Families, and Build Communities*, Philadelphia, PA: Temple University Press.

Chapter Nine

1. White House Conference on Children, *Report to the President*, 1970.

2. *Goals 2000: A Progress Report* (Fall 1996), U.S. Department of Education.

3. Carnegie Task Force on Meeting the Needs of Young Children (1994) *Starting Points: Meeting the Needs of Our Youngest Children*, New York: Carnegie Corporation.

4. *Ready to Read, Ready to Learn: The White House Summit on Early Childhood Cognitive Development*, held at Georgetown University, Washington, DC, July 26, 2001.

5. B. Hart and T. Risley (1995) *Meaningful Differences in the Everyday Experience of Young American Children*, Baltimore, MD: Paul H. Brookes Publishing Company.

6. M. J. Neuman and S. Peer (2002) *Equal from the Start: Promoting Educational Opportunity for All Preschool Children—Learning from the French Experience*, Washington, DC: French-American Foundation.

7. E. Zigler, S. L. Kagan, and N. Hall (eds.) (1996) *Children, Families, and Government: Preparing for the Twenty-first Century*, Cambridge, UK: Cambridge University Press.

8. Zigler, Kagan, and Hall, *Children, Families, and Government*.

9. S. S. Svestka (December 1995) Financing preschool for all children, *Eric/EECE Digests*.

10. Svestka, *Eric/EECE Digests*.

11. H. R. Clinton (1996) *It Takes a Village*, New York: Simon and Schuster.

12. See, for example, G. C. Griffen (1999) *It Takes a Parent to Raise a Child*, New York: Golden Books Adult Publishing.

13. N. Folbre (2001) *The Invisible Heart: Economics and Family Values*, New York: New Press.

14. Despite its popularity and evidence of success, the Minnesota program was canceled in 2003, owing to a state fiscal crunch. It was reinstated in 2004.

15. T. B. Brazelton and S. Greenspan (2001) *The Irreducible Needs of Children: What Every Child Must Have to Grow, Learn, and Flourish*, New York: Perseus Publishing.

16. B. Holcomb (2002) *Why Americans Need Family Leave Benefits—And How They Can Get Them*, Washington, DC: National Partnership for Women and Families.

17. Brazelton and Greenspan, *The Irreducible Needs of Children*.

18. NAEYC Position Statement (1998) *Code of Ethical Conduct*, Washington, DC: National Association for the Education of Young Children.

19. J. Lombardi (2002) *Time to Care*, Philadelphia, PA: Temple University Press.

20. D. A. Phillips and N. J. Cabrera (eds.) (1996) *Beyond the Blueprint: Directions for Research on Head Start's Families*, Washington, DC: National Academy Press.

21. W. S. Barnett (1996) *Lives in the Balance: Age-27 Benefit–Cost Analysis of the High/Scope Perry Preschool Program* (Monographs of the High/Scope Educational Research Foundation, 11), Ypsilanti, MI: High/Scope Press.

22. L. J. Schweinhart (2004) *The High/Scope Perry Preschool Study Through Age 40: Summary, Conclusions, and Frequently Asked Questions*, Ypsilanti, MI: High/Scope Press.

23. See R. Shore (1997) *Rethinking the Brain: New Insights into Early Development* New York: Families and Work Institute, for an explanation of key insights from neuroscience and their implications for child development.

24. U. Bronfenbrenner (1979) *Ecology of Human Development: Experiments by Nature and Design*, Cambridge, MA: Harvard University Press.

25. www.fightcrime.org.

Chapter Ten

1. National Research Council (1998) *Preventing Reading Difficulties in Young Children*. Committee on the Prevention of Reading Difficulties in Young Children. Catherine E. Snow, M. Susan Burns, and Peg Griffin (eds.). Washington, DC: National Academy Press.

2. National Research Council and Institute of Medicine (2000) *From Neurons to Neighborhoods: The Science of Early Childhood Development*. Committee on Integrating the Science of Early Childhood Development. Jack P. Shonkoff and Deborah A. Phillips (eds.). Board on Children, Youth, and Families, Commission on Behavioral and Social Sciences and Education. Washington, DC: National Academy Press.

3. National Research Council (2001) *Eager to Learn: Educating Our Preschoolers*, Committee on Early Childhood Pedagogy. Barbara T. Bowman, M. Suzanne Donovan, and M. Susan Burns (eds.). Commission on Behavioral and Social Sciences and Education. Washington, DC: National Academy Press.

4. National Research Council, *Eager to Learn*, pp. 17–18.

5. Communications Consortium Media Center Early Care and Education Collaborative (2002) Polling Report to National Governor's Association, http://www.earlycare.org/pollingtonga.htm.

6. The Policy Matters Project estimated the cost of full-day care of sufficiently high quality to promote school readiness at $10,000 to $15,000 for infants and toddlers and $8,000 to $12,000 for three- and four-year-olds. Yet, a survey conducted by the Children's Defense Fund found that parents, though often stretching to the limits of their resources, were paying an average of only $6,651 for a one-year-old and $5,219

for a four-year-old in center-based care, and paying considerably less for family child care. S. L. Kagan and E. Rigby (2003) *Policy Matters: Setting and Measuring Benchmarks for State Policies*, Washington, DC: Center for the Study of Social Policy; K. Schulman (2000) *The High Cost of Child Care Puts Quality Out of Reach of Many Families*, Washington, DC: Children's Defense Fund.

7. O. Golden (2000) Sustaining change: Lessons of leadership in the policy arena, Address delivered at *Inspiring Leaders for 2000 and Beyond: Leading the Ways to Quality Care and Education for Our Youngest Children*, a symposium sponsored by the A. L. Mailman Family Foundation, Yale Club, New York City, June 26, 2000.

8. Head Start Bureau (2000) *Head Start Family and Child Experiences Study (FACES)*, FACES Findings: New Research on Head Start Program Quality and Outcomes, Washington, DC: U.S. Department of Health and Human Services, http://www.acf .dhhs.gov/programs/core/ongoing_research/faces/pamphlet/sld001.htm.

9. Cost, Quality & Outcomes Study Team (1995) Cost, quality, and child outcomes in child care centers, Public Report, Denver, CO: Economics Department, University of Colorado.

10. Children's Defense Fund (2003) *Head Start Basic Fact Sheet*, Washington, DC: Children's Defense Fund.

11. Commissioner's Office of Research and Evaluation and the Head Start Bureau (2001) *Building Their Futures: How Early Head Start Programs Are Enhancing the Lives of Infants and Toddlers in Low-Income Families: Summary Report*, Washington, DC: Administration on Children, Youth and Families, Department of Health and Human Services.

12. Children's Defense Fund, *Head Start Basic Fact Sheet*.

13. E. Zigler and S. J. Styfco (1993) *Head Start and Beyond*, New Haven, CT: Yale University Press.

14. This recommendation of *From Neurons to Neighborhoods* is being implemented on a pilot basis in Florida and Massachusetts. See C. S. Lederman and S. Adams (2001) Innovations in assessing and helping maltreated infants and toddlers in a Florida court, *Zero to Three* 21(6): 16–20; C. S. Lederman, J. D. Osofsky, and L. Katz (Fall 2001) When the bough breaks the cradle will fall: Promoting the health and well being of infants and toddlers in Juvenile Court, *Juvenile and Family Court Journal*, and S. Rosenberg and C. Robinson (2003) Is Part C ready for substantiated child abuse and neglect? *Zero to Three*, 24(2): 45–46.

15. D. J. Ackerman (2003) States' Efforts in Improving the Qualifications of Early Care and Education Teachers, New Brunswick, NJ: National Institute for Early Education Research; http://nieer.org/resources/research/Ackerman.pdf.

16. Child Care Services Association administers the national T.E.A.C.H. Early Childhood® Project and provides technical assistance to states in implementing this system; www.childcareservices.org.

17. J. P. Jadotte, S. C. Stacie Carolyn Golin, and B. Gault (2002) *Building a Stronger Child Care Workforce: A Review of Studies of the Effectiveness of Public Compensation Initiatives*, Washington, DC: Institute for Women's Policy Research.

18. See www.naccrra.org for information on this nationwide network.

19. www.patnc.org.

20. www.parentchildhomeprogram.org.

21. www.hippyusa.org.

22. www.avance.org.

23. http://www.smartstart-nc.org/overview/main.htm.

24. Quality Early Education through Salaries and Training (QUEST) (2002) *Virtual Strike: Parent Letter to Employer*, Philadelphia, PA: QUEST, www.paquest.org.

25. Carnegie Task Force on Meeting the Needs of Young Children (1994) *Starting Points: Meeting the Needs of Our Youngest Children*, New York: Carnegie Corporation.

26. See *The Statement of the Advisory Committee on Services for Families with Infants and Toddlers* (1994), Washington, DC: U.S. Department of Health and Human Services.

27. A. Radin (1999) *Universal Prekindergarten in Georgia: A Case Study of Georgia's Lottery-Funded Pre-K Program*, New York: Foundation for Child Development.

28. Governor's Task Force on Early Childhood Care and Education (2002) *Early Care and Education: The Keystone of Pennsylvania's Future*, State of Pennsylvania; http://www.state.pa.us/papower/lib/papower/earlychildhoodpart2.pdf.

29. www.iamyourchild.org. In 2004, the *I Am Your Child* Foundation became Parents Action for Children.

30. States spend more than $1 billion on preschool programs for three- and four-year-olds (the majority are for four-year-olds only), but less than one quarter of that to support the well-being of infants and toddlers. See *Education Week* (2000) "Building Blocks for Success: State Efforts in Early Childhood Education, Quality Counts," 17.

Chapter Eleven

1. M. Segal (1971) *You Are Your Baby's First Teacher*, Fort Lauderdale, FL: Nova University. The title has become a widely used catch phrase in the early childhood profession.

2. "The AAP Highlight"—October 22, 2002, Elk Grove Village, IL: American Academy of Pediatrics.

3. J. Flower (November/December 1992) Growing the business of caring: T. Berry Brazelton on Healthcare, *Healthcare Forum Journal*, 35(6).

4. T. B. Brazelton (1992) *Touchpoints: Your Child's Emotional and Behavioral Development: Birth-3: The Essential Reference for the Early Years*, New York: Perseus Publishing.

5. Brazelton Touchpoints Center, www.touchpoints.org.

6. See Parents as Teachers National Center, www.patnc.org.

7. The following summaries are taken from the Parents as Teachers National Center Web site:

- In 1985, an independent evaluation of the Parents as Teachers (PAT) pilot project was conducted. Evaluators randomly selected 75 project families from a group of 380 first-time parents representing Missouri's urban, rural and suburban communities, and, from the same communities, 75 comparison families who had not received PAT services. Posttest assessments of children's abilities and parents' knowledge and perceptions showed PAT children at age three were significantly more advanced in language, problem-solving and other intellectual abilities, and social development than comparison children. PAT parents were more knowledgeable about child rearing practices and child development.

  J. Pfannenstiel and D. Seltzer (1985) *Evaluation Report: New Parents as Teachers Project*, Overland Park, KS: Research & Training Associates.
- A follow-up study of the pilot project showed PAT children scored significantly higher on standardized measures of reading and math at the end of

first grade than did comparison children. In all behavioral areas assessed by their teachers, the PAT participant children received higher ratings than the comparison group children. A significantly higher proportion of PAT parents initiated contacts with teachers and took an active role in their child's schooling.

      J. Pfannenstiel (1989) *New Parents as Teachers Project Follow-Up Study*, Overland Park, KS: Research & Training Associates..

- Results of the 1991 Second Wave evaluation of the PAT program's impact on 400 randomly selected families enrolled in 37 diverse school districts across Missouri indicated both children and parents benefited. At age three, PAT children performed significantly higher than national norms on measures of language and intellectual abilities, despite the fact the Second Wave sample was over-represented on all traditional characteristics of risk. More than one-half of the children with observed developmental delays overcame them by age three. Parent knowledge of child development and parenting practices significantly increased for all types of families. There were only two documented cases of abuse and neglect among the 400 families over a three-year period.

      J. Pfannenstiel T. Lambson, and V. Yarnell (1991) *Second Wave Study of the Parents as Teachers Program*, Overland Park, KS: Research & Training Associates.

- A follow-up study of the Second Wave sample was initiated in 1993 to assess the longer-term impacts of program participation. This study focused on early school experiences and performance of the PAT children, and their parents' involvement in their children's school and in activities to support learning in the home. PAT children scored high on measures of complex and challenging tasks. Overall, the relative level of achievement children demonstrated at age three on completion of the PAT program was maintained in the first (or in some cases second) grade. This held true despite broad diversity in children's experiences with preschool, child care, kindergarten and primary grades. PAT parents demonstrated high levels of school involvement, which they frequently initiated.

      J. Pfannenstiel (1995) *Follow-Up to the Second Wave Study of the Parents as Teachers Program*, Overland Park, KS: Research & Training Associates.

- A series of studies of PAT program participation and school readiness has been carried out in the Binghamton, New York, School District. Children enrolled in kindergarten in Binghamton in 1992 were tested in pre-kindergarten and again in kindergarten. PAT children had significantly higher cognitive, language, motor, and social skills than non-participants. These advanced skills led to higher grades in kindergarten and lower remedial and special education costs in Grade 1. PAT families also had substantially reduced welfare dependence and half the number of suspected child abuse and neglect cases compared to comparison groups. When assessed again in second grade, PAT children continued to perform better on standardized tests and require fewer remedial and special education placements.

      S. Drazen and M. Haust (1994) *Increasing Children's Readiness for School by a Parental Education Program*, Binghamton, NY: Community Resource Center; S. Drazen and M. Haust (1995) *The Effects of the Parents and Children*

Together (PACT) Program on School Achievement, Binghamton, NY: Community Resource Center; S. Drazen and M. Haust(1996) *Lasting Academic Gains from and Home Visitations Program*, Binghamton, NY: Community Resource Center.

- Significant findings were reported in December 1992 by SRI International from a study launched in 1990 to determine whether PAT helps parents in at-risk situations offset the threats to their children by teaching effective parenting approaches that support healthy child development. The study looked at 113 predominantly Hispanic families in Salinas, California—67 of whom were randomly assigned to PAT and 46 to a control group. Assessments of parent and child outcomes at the children's first birthday showed PAT parents consistently scored higher on measures of parenting behavior. The report states PAT has the potential to demonstrate significant benefits for families who participate in the program.

  M. Wagner(1992) *Home the First Classroom: A Pilot Evaluation of the Northern California Parents as Teachers Project*, Menlo Park, CA: SRI International.

- A study demonstrating the effectiveness of PAT was released in July 1994 by the Parkway School District, a large suburban district in St. Louis County. Third graders who had received PAT with screening services from birth to age three scored significantly higher on standardized measures of achievement than non-participating counterparts. PAT children had a national percentile rank of 81, while non-participating students had a rank of 63 on the Stanford Achievement Test . . . The study also reported PAT "graduates" were less likely to receive remedial reading assistance or to be held back a grade in school. PAT "graduates" continued to significantly outperform non-PAT children on the Stanford Achievement test in fourth grade.

  D. Coates (1994) Early Childhood Evaluation, Missouri: A report to the Parkway Board of Education; D. Coates (1996) Memo on One-Year Update on Stanford Scores of Students-Early Childhood Evaluation Study Group, St. Louis County, MO: Parkway School District. * Researchers in North Carolina have followed 97 families who were involved in the Rutherford County PAT program beginning in 1991. The PAT children were compared to 61 children whose families did not receive PAT services, and another 61 whose families received a quarterly educational newsletter from PAT, but no direct services. Children were assessed upon entry into kindergarten. The PAT children outperformed children from both comparison groups on measures of cognitive, language, motor, and self-help skills, with significant differences on the language and self-help measures. Also, PAT parents talked to their children significantly more often about their daily activities. M. Coleman, B. Rowland, and B. Hutchins (1997) Parents as Teachers: Policy implications for early school intervention, Paper presented at the 1997 annual meeting of the National Council on Family Relations, Crystal City, VA, November, 1997.

8. See Missouri Department of Education (2000) *Parents as Teachers in Missouri: 1999–2000*, http://www.dese.state.mo.us/divimprove/fedprog/earlychild/ECDA/ patfact.htm.

9. *Born to Learn Curriculum* (1999) St. Louis, MO: Parents as Teachers National Center.

10. P. J. DeVito and J. P. Karon (1984) *Pittsfield Parent–Child Home Program, Chap. 1. Longitudinal Evaluation Pittsfield Public Schools*, Final Report.

11. DeVito and Karon, *Pittsfield Parent–Child Home Program, Chap. 1*, Final Report.

12. I. Lazar and R. Darlington (1982) Lasting Effects of Early Education: A Report from the Consortium of Longitudinal Studies, *Monographs of the Society for Research in Child Development*, 47 (serial #195).

13. L. McLaren (1988) Fostering mother–child relationships, *Child Welfare*, 67: 353-365.

14. L. T. Williams and D. P. Fromberg (eds.) (1992) *Encyclopedia of Early Childhood Education*, New York: Garland.

15. Williams and Fromberg (eds.), *Encyclopedia of Early Childhood Education*.

16. P. Levenstein, S. Levenstein, J. A. Shiminski, and J. E. Stolzberg (1998) Long-term impact of a verbal interaction program for at-risk toddlers: An exploratory study of high school outcomes in a replication of the Mother–Child Home Program, *Journal of Applied Developmental Psychology*, 19: 267-285.

17. P. Levenstein, S. Levenstein, and D. Oliver (2002) First grade school readiness of former child participants in a South Carolina replication of the Parent–Child Home Program, *Journal of Applied Developmental Psychology*, 23(3): 331–353.

18. U.S. Department of Education (1998) *National Evaluation of The Even Start Family Literacy Program–1998: What Difference has Even Start Made to Families?* http://www.ed.gov/pubs/EvenStart/ch3families.html.

19. F. Tao, B. Gamse, and H. Tarr (1998) *National Evaluation of The Even Start Family Literacy Program: 1994–1997 Final Report*, Arlington, VA: Fu Associates, Ltd., pp. 140–146.

20. J. Pfannenstiel (1999) *School Entry Assessment Project: Report of Findings*, Missouri Department of Education.

21. E. Zinzeleta and N. K. Little (1997) How do parents really choose childcare programs? *Early Childhood Education*, 52(7): 8–11.

22. See www.naeyc.org for accreditation criteria and procedures and to search for accredited centers.

23. See www.nafcc.org for accreditation criteria and procedures and to search for accredited family child-care homes.

24. According to 2000 Bureau of Labor Statistics data, the average hourly wage of a "child-care worker" is $7.86, while that of a parking lot attendant is $7.69. Early childhood workers who are classified as "teachers" earn slightly more: an average hourly wage of $9.66. "Child-care workers" are defined as those who care for children in child-care centers, homes, or other settings; they may be aides or teachers in center-based programs or family child-care homes or may work as nannies. "Teachers" are defined as those who "provide instruction," generally in preschools or other center-based settings. *Current Data on Child Care Salaries and Benefits in the United States: March, 2002*, Washington, DC: Center for the Childcare Workforce, http://www.ccw.org/pubs/2002Compendium.pdf.

25. www.parentservices.org.

26. PSP was one of seven programs in the nation to receive a Families Count Award from the Annie E. Casey Foundation in 1999, the first year these awards were given. A longitudinal study of program sites in Delaware found that PSP decreased parents' isolation, fostered family adaptability and cohesion and use of community resources, and improved parents' leadership and decision-making skills, while also improving teachers' skills and contributing to their retention.

27. M. Segal (1965) *Run Away Little Girl*, New York: Random House.

28. M. Blood and S. Lakis (1995) *State Legislative Leaders: Keys to Effective Legislation for Children and Families, Centreville*, MA: State Legislative Leaders Foundation.

29. http://www.ctprevention.com/act/plti.html.

30. *All Kids Need to Start Smart*. Booklet for participants at Mayor's Children's Summit '99. Convened by Miami-Dade Mayor Alex Pinellas, Natacha Seijas Millan, Dave Lawrence, and Dorothy Wallace, September 30, 1999.

31. See C. Snow (2002) Enduring reading success for African American children, In B. Bowman (ed.), *Love to Read: Essays in Developing and Enhancing Early Literacy Skills of African American Children*, Washington, DC: National Black Child Development Institute, for a discussion of challenges faced by children learning to read in their second language.

32. www.teachmorelovemore.org.

33. J. Hampton (2003) *How Florida's Voters Enacted UPK When Their Legislature Wouldn't*, New York: Foundation for Child Development, www.ffcd.org.

34. For a summary of this theory, see U. Bronfenbrenner (1979) *Ecology of Human Development: Experiments by Nature and Design, Cambridge*, MA: Harvard University Press.

35. See www.avance.org.

36. G. Rodriguez (2003) Connecting with parents: The AVANCE experience, In J. Mendoza, L. G. Katz, A. S. Robertson, and D. Rothenberg (eds.), *Connecting with Patents in the Early Years*, Urbana-Champaign, IL: Early Childhood and Parenting Collaborative, College of Education, University of Illinois at Urbana-Champaign.

37. D. L. Johnson and T. B. Walker (1996) *Final Report of an Evaluation of the AVANCE Parent Education and Family Support Program*, San Antonio, TX: AVANCE.

38. M. Belenky, L. Bond, and J. Weinstock (1999) *A Tradition That Has No Name: Nurturing the Development of People, Families, and Communities*, New York: Harper-Collins.

Chapter Twelve

1. S. J. Bagnato (2002) *Quality Early Learning—Key to School Success: A First-Phase Program Evaluation Research Report for Pittsburgh's Early Childhood Initiative (ECI)*, Pittsburgh, PA: Children's Hospital of Pittsburgh, SPECS Evaluation Research Team.

2. B. P. Gill, J. W. Dembosky, and J. P. Caulkins (2002) *A "Noble Bet" in Early Care and Education: Lessons from One Community's Experience*, Pittsburgh, PA: RAND.

3. Bagnato, *Quality Early Learning*.

4. G. Oliphant and D. Root (Spring 2002) "Pittsburgh's "Noble Bet," In *h: The Magazine of The Heinz Endowments*, pp. 14–32.

5. http://www.frenchamerican.org.

6. Perhaps the most controversial aspect of the ecoles maternelles is their large class size—which can be as high as twenty-five children with one teacher. The trade-off is that the teachers are highly educated and supported by a national curriculum and a strong infrastructure of training and supervision. U.S. experts who visit these preschools are impressed with the French children's learning and behavior, but note that U.S. preschoolers tend not to get enough language practice in such large classrooms, even when their teachers are well prepared. M. J. Neuman and S. Peer (2002) *Equal*

from the Start: Promoting Educational Opportunity for All Preschool Children—Learning from the French Experience, Washington, DC: French-American Foundation.

7. For discussions of French models and their relevance for U.S. policy, see *A Welcome for Every Child* and *Equal from the Start: Promoting Educational Opportunity for All Preschool Children—Learning from the French Experience* by Michelle J. Neuman and Shanny Peer, French-American Foundation, 2002. A French-American Foundation sponsored tour of French preschoolers inspired Florida advocates to work for universal, state-funded prekindergarten, which was adopted three years later by initiative petition. (J. Hampton (2003) *How Florida Voters Enacted UPK When Their Legislature Wouldn't*, New York: Foundation for Child Development, www.ffcd.org.

8. For a detailed description of the implementation of Head Start in one state and the benefits perceived by parents and communities, see P. Greenberg (1969, 1990) *The Devil has Slippery Shoes*, Washington, DC: Youth Policy Institute.

9. E. Ziegler and S. Muenchow (1992) *Head Start: The Inside Story of America's Most Successful Educational Experiment*, New York: Basic Books.

10. E. Zigler, S. J. Styfco, and E. Gilman (1993) The national Head Start program for disadvantaged preschoolers, In E. Zigler and S. J. Styfco (eds.), *Head Start and Beyond*, New Haven, CT: Yale University Press; J. Currie and D. Thomas (1995) Does Head Start make a difference? *American Economic Review*, 85(3): 341–364; E. Garces, D. Thomas, and J. Currie (2002) Longer term effects of Head Start, *The American Economic Review*, 92(4): 999–1012. For the more recent results, see Head Start Bureau (2004) *Head Start Family and Child Experiences Study (FACES)*, Washington, DC: U.S. Department of Health and Human Services.

11. M. Segal, personal conversation.

12. Even though Head Start programs are far more likely to be of good quality than preschool programs in general (see Head Start Bureau (2000) *Head Start Family and Child Experiences Study (FACES)*, FACES Findings: New Research on Head Start Program Quality and Outcomes, Washington, DC: U.S. Department of Health and Human Services), the strength of Head Start's language and literacy component has been controversial. The Bush administration, the Abell Foundation (The Untapped Potential of Baltimore City Public Preschools, Baltimore, MD: The Abell Foundation, 2000), and others have argued that there needs to be a greater focus on early literacy, vocabulary development, and beginning phonics, as Head Start graduates still tend to score behind peers from higher income backgrounds in these areas. However, both the FACES study (Head Start Bureau, *Head Start Family and Child Experiences Study*) and a comparative study of Head Start children with those attending other private and public kindergarten programs in Tulsa, OK (described in detail in Chapter 13), show that Head Start narrows the gap in vocabulary and emergent literacy between Head Start children and the general population during the Head Start year(s) and that Head Start children continue to gain ground after completing the program.

13. C. T. Ramey and F. A. Campbell (1991) Poverty, early childhood education, and academic competence: The Abecedarian experiment, In A. C. Huston (ed.), *Children in Poverty*, New York: Cambridge University Press, pp. 190–221.

14. www.zerotothree.org.

15. See WestEd's Program for Infant/Toddler Caregivers, www.pitc.org.

16. www.brighthorizons.com.

17. Fortune 100 Best Companies to Work For, *Fortune Magazine*, January 2004. (Bright Horizons Family Solutions has been named to this list five times.)

18. Roger Brown, Executive Chairman and Founder, Bright Horizons Family Solutions, personal communication, May 19, 2004.

19. www.montessori.org.

20. www.highscope.org.

21. W. S. Barnett (1996) *Lives in the Balance: Age-27 Benefit–Cost Analysis of the High/Scope Perry Preschool Program* (Monographs of the High/Scope Educational Research Foundation, 11), Ypsilanti, MI: High/Scope Press; L. J. Schweinhart, J. Montie, Z. Xiang, W. S. Barnett, C. R Belfield, and M. Nores (2005) *Lifetime Effects: The High/Scope Perry Preschool Study Through Age 40* (Monographs of the High/Scope Educational Research Foundation, 14), Ypsilanti, MI: High/Scope Press.

22. http://www.highscope.org/Research/TotEvaluation/totevaluation.htm.

23. N. D. Campbell, J. C. Appelbaum, K. Martinson, and E. Martin (2000) *Be All That We Can Be: Lessons from the Military for Improving Our Nation's Childcare System*, Washington, DC: National Women's Law Center.

24. G. Zellman and A. S. Johansen (1998) *Examining the Implementation and Outcomes of the Military Child Care Act of 1989*, Santa Monica, CA: RAND Child Policy Project.

25. See www.naeyc.org and www.nafcc.org for accreditation guidelines, policies, and procedures, as well as to search for accredited providers.

26. W. Masi (1999) Training, mentoring and technical assistance: Making connections—Enhancing the quality of infant toddler care through training of center directors, *Zero To Three*, (19)6: 49–50.

27. Student Achievement and Accountability Programs Office of Elementary and Secondary Education (2002) A synopsis of the 2002 Early Childhood Educator Professional Development (ECEPD) Grantees, Washington, DC: U.S. Department of Education.

28. HeadsUp! Reading: The Early Childhood Distance Education Resources, http://www.huronline.org/.

29. R. Shore (2003) *Formative Evaluation of the HeadsUp! Reading Program*, Washington, DC: National Head Start Association.

30. For example, Janet Currie and Matthew Neidell found that graduates of Head Start programs with relatively high levels of spending had higher reading scores and were less likely to be retained in grade than graduates of programs that were funded at relatively low levels. (*Getting Inside the Black Box of Head Start Quality: What Matters and What Doesn't*, Washington, DC: Administration for Children, Youth, and Families, 2003).

31. D. M. Bryant, K. L. Maxwell, and M. Burchinal (1999) Effects of a community initiative on the quality of child care, *Early Childhood Research Quarterly*, 14: 449–464.

32. Head Start Bureau (2000) *Head Start Family and Child Experiences Study (FACES)*, FACES Findings: New Research on Head Start Program Quality and Outcomes, Washington, DC: U.S. Department of Health and Human Services.

33. Campbell, Appelbaum, Martinson, and Martin (2000) *Be All That We Can Be*.

34. C. Howes, E. Galinsky, M. Shinn, A. Sibley, M. Abbott-Shim, and J. McCarthy (1998) *The Florida Child Care Quality Improvement Study: 1996 Report*, New York: Families and Work Institute.

35. Helburn and Bergmann (*America's Childcare Problem: The Way Out*, New York: Palgrave, 2002) estimate that it would cost about $2,000 per child per year to bring a "mediocre" center up to "good" quality. They base this figure on the increases that would be necessary in order to bring employees' wages up to the market rate for people with comparable levels of education and experience.

Chapter Thirteen

1. Carnegie Task Force on Meeting the Needs of Young Children (1994) *Starting Points: Meeting the Needs of Our Youngest Children*, New York: Carnegie Corporation.

2. S. L. Kagan and N. E. Cohen (1997) *Not By Chance: Creating and Early Care and Education System for America's Children*, New Haven, CT: The Bush Center in Child Development and Social Policy at Yale University.

3. S. J. Meisels, J. R. Jablon, D. B. Marsden, M. L. Dichtelmiller, A. B. Dorfman, and D. M. Steele (1995) *The Work Sampling System: An Overview*, Ann Arbor, MI: Rebus Planning Associates, Inc.

4. Smart Start Georgia Grants Nearly $1 Million to Georgia Educators, Peachtree Corners, GA: *The Weekly*, December 8, 2003, http://www.theweekly.com/news/2003/December/08/SmartStart.html.

5. For example, the percentage of lead teachers with BA degrees in Boston Head Start and child-care programs dropped from 55% in 1995 to only 29% in 1999. Massachusetts Department of Education (2001) *Securing Our Future: Planning What We Want for Our Youngest Children. Future Trends*, Vol. VI.

6. Build Ohio Alliance (2002) *State Plan Synopsis*, Columbus, OH: Ohio Child Care Resource and Referral Association, http://www.buildinitiative.org/synopsis_oh.htm. http://www.buildinitiative.org/synopsis_oh.htm.

7. L. Miller, A. Melaville, and H. Blank (2002) *Bringing It Together: State-Driven Community Early Childhood Initiatives*, Washington, DC: Children's Defense Fund, p. 19.

8. J. P. Jadotte, S. C. Golin, and B. Gault (2002) *Building a Stronger Child Care Workforce: A Review of Studies of the Effectiveness of Public Compensation Initiatives*, Washington, DC: Institute for Women's Policy Research.

9. C. Howes, E. Galinsky, M. Shinn, A. Sibley, M. Abbott-Shim, and J. McCarthy (1998) *The Florida Child Care Quality Improvement Study: 1996 Report*, New York: Families and Work Institute.

10. C. S. FitzPatrick and N. D. Campbell (2002) *The Little Engine that Hasn't: The Poor Performance of Employer Tax Credits for Child Care*, Washington, DC: National Women's Law Center.

11. In Florida, some of the state's largest employers formed a Child Care Executive Partnership to meet the child-care needs of low-wage workers who were being hired as a consequence of Welfare Reform. Working with the Florida Children's Forum, they established a network of child-care offerings, filled in "gaps," supported quality improvements, and donated their lobbyists to help pass legislation that would provide incentives and supports for quality improvement. J. Knitzer and F. Adely (2001) *Learning from Starting Points: Findings from the Starting Points Assessment Project*, New York: National Center for Children in Poverty. Nationally, the American Business Collaboration for Dependent Care (www.abcdependentcare.com) invested $125 million over a ten-year period to support early education, child care, and elder care in more than sixty-five communities. The collaboration supported training, accreditation, and capacity building projects, in addition to direct services.

12. See, for example, B. Wolfe and S. Scrivner (2003) Providing universal preschool for four-year-olds, In I. Sawhill (ed.), *One Percent for the Kids*, Washington, DC: Brookings Institution Press, pp. 113–135.

13. S. W. Barnett, K. Brown, and R. Shore (2004) *Policy Brief—The Universal vs. Targeted Debate: Should the United States Have Preschool for All?* NIEER Policy Brief (Issue 6, April 2004).

14. G. Henry, C. Gordon, A. Mashburn, and B. Ponder (2001) *PreK Longitudinal Study: Findings from 1999–2000*, Atlanta, GA: Georgia State Applied Research Center.

15. Henry, Gordon, Mashburn, and Ponder, *PreK Longitudinal Study.*

16. W. T. Gormley and D. Phillips (2003) *CROCUS Working Paper #2: The Effects of Universal Pre-K in Oklahoma: Research Highlights and Policy Implications*, Washington, DC: Center for Research on Children in the US, Georgetown, University.

17. A. Burton, M. Whitebook, M. Young, D. Bellm, C. Wayne, R. Brandon, and E. Mahler (2002) *Estimating the Size and Components of U.S. Child Care Workforce and Caregiving Population: Key Findings from the Child Care Workforce Estimate (Preliminary Report)*, Washington, DC: Center for the Childcare Workforce, http://www.ccw.org/pubs/workforceestimatereport.pdf.

18. K. Lekies, E. Heitsman, and M. Cochran (2001) *Early Care for Infants and Toddlers: Examining the Broader Impacts of Universal Prekindergarten*, Ithaca, NY: Cornell Early Childhood Program.

19. David and Lucille Packard Foundation (2003) Children, families, and communities program guidelines, http://www.packard.org/index.cgi?page=cfc-upe.

20. D. Stahl, N. S. O'Donnell, P. Sprague, and M. Lopez (2003) *Sparking Connections: Community Based Strategies for Helping Family, Friend and Neighbor Caregivers Meet the Needs of Employees, Their Children and Employers*, New York: Families and Work Institute.

21. See K. Lekies and M. Cochran (2002) *Early Care and Education Workforce Recruitment and Preparation in New York*, Ithaca, NY: Cornell Early Childhood Program.

22. www.betterbabycare.org.

23. www.voicesforamericaschildren.org.

24. B. Welsh (2004) *The Better Baby Care State Advocacy Project: Investing in Our Nation's Infants and Toddlers*, Washington, DC: Voices for America's Children.

25. www.stand.org.

26. The CARES model provides stipends to child-care program staff whose prior education and training makes them eligible to join a "Child Development Corps" and who agree to obtain additional professional development. It also provides resources to programs, including financial incentives to maintain higher levels of quality and Quality Improvement Rewards to help programs achieve accreditation and improve staff retention. See A. Burton, J. Mihaly, J. Kagiwada, and M. Whitebook (2000) *The CARES Initiative in California: Pursuing Public Policy to Build a Skilled and Stable Child Care Workforce, 1997–2000*, Washington, DC: Center for the Child Care Workforce.

Chapter Fourteen

1. Goals 2000: Educate America Act, signed by President Clinton in 1994.

2. L. Schorr (1988) *Within Our Reach: Breaking the Cycle of Disadvantage*, New York: Anchor.

3. B. Hart and T. Risley (1995) *Meaningful Differences in the Everyday Experience of Young American Children*, Baltimore, MD: Paul H. Brookes Publishing Company.

4. Hart and Risley, *Meaningful Differences in the Everyday Experience of Young American Children*; B. Hart and T. Risley (1999) *The Social World of Children Learning to Talk*, Baltimore, MD: Paul H. Brookes Publishing Company.

5. D. Dickinson and P. Tabors (2001) *Beginning Literacy with Language*, Baltimore, MD: Paul H. Brookes Publishing Company.

6. Dickinson and Tabors, *Beginning Literacy with Language*.

7. D. G. Norton (1996) Early linguistic interaction and school achievement: An ethnographical, ecological perspective, *Zero to Three*, 16: 8–14.

8. J. M. DeTemple and D. E. Beals (1991) Family talk: Sources of support for the development of decontextualized language skills, *Journal of Research in Childhood Education*, 6(1): 11–19.

9. Dickinson and Tabors, *Beginning Literacy with Language*.

10. M. Susan Burns, P. Griffin, and C. E. Snow (eds.) (1998) *Starting Out Right: A Guide to Promoting Children's Reading Success*, Committee on the Prevention of Reading Difficulties in Young Children, National Research Council. Also see W. Teale (1984) Reading to young children: Its significance for literacy development, In H. Goelman, A. Oberg, and F. Smith (eds.) *Awakening to Literacy*, Portsmouth, NH: Heinemann.

11. G. Whitehurst, D. Arnold, J. Epstein, A. Angell, M. Smith, and J. Fischel (1994) A picture book reading intervention in day care and home for children from low-income families, *Developmental Psychology*, 30(6): 79–89.

12. Burns, Griffin, and Snow, *Starting Out Right*.

13. National Research Council (1998) *Preventing Reading Difficulties in Young Children*. Committee on the Prevention of Reading Difficulties in Young Children. Catherine E. Snow, M. Susan Burns, and Peg Griffin (eds.). Washington, DC: National Academy Press.

14. Burns, Griffin, and Snow, *Starting Out Right*.

15. National Research Council and Institute of Medicine (2000) *From Neurons to Neighborhoods: The Science of Early Childhood Development*. Committee on Integrating the Science of Early Childhood Development. Jack P. Shonkoff and Deborah A. Phillips (eds.). Board on Children, Youth, and Families, Commission on Behavioral and Social Sciences and Education. Washington, DC: National Academy Press; National Research Council, *Preventing Reading Difficulties*.

16. See Chapter 4 of A. Gopnik, A. N. Meltzoff, and P. K. Kuhl (1999) *The Scientist in the Crib: Minds, Brains, and How Children Learn*, New York: William Morrow and Company, for research on how much children learn about language before they begin to talk.

17. Hart and Risley, *Meaningful Differences in the Everyday Experience of Young American Children*.

18. Hart and Risley, *Meaningful Differences in the Everyday Experience of Young American Children*.

19. National Research Council (2001) *Eager to Learn: Educating Our Preschoolers*. Committee on Early Childhood Pedagogy. Barbara T. Bowman, M. Suzanne Donovan, and M. Susan Burns (eds.). Commission on Behavioral and Social Sciences and Education. Washington, DC: National Academy Press.

20. National Research Council (2001), *Eager to Learn*. Also see C. Copple and S. Bredekamp (2003) *Developmentally Appropriate Practice for Early Childhood Programs* (Revised Edition), Washington, DC: National Association for the Education of Young Children (www.naeyc.org), for expert and practitioner consensus on how young children learn.

21. Handling books themselves facilitates children's knowledge of "concepts of print," such as where to begin reading, which provide a foundation for learning to read. See *Starting Out Right* (Snow, Burns, and Griffin).

22. For scientific evidence and expert consensus on the importance of play-based learning as a foundation for literacy, see E. Zigler, D. Singer, and S. Bishop-Josef (2003) *Children's Play: The Roots of Reading*, Washington, DC: ZERO TO THREE Press. For National Academy of Sciences-recommended activities to provide broad-based support for language and literacy, see *Starting Out Right* (Snow, Burns, and Griffin).

23. Based on their review of a large body of research, the authors of *Preventing Reading Difficulties in Young Children* emphasize the importance of a strong preschool foundation in these areas as well as in oral language. Reports of misinterpretation of "play-based learning" and "developmentally appropriate practice" as discouraging rather than facilitating the teaching of ABCs spurred the National Association for the Education of Young Children to clarify these issues in position statements. *See Developmentally Appropriate Practice in Early Childhood Programs Serving Children from Birth Through Age 8* (1997) and *Learning to Read and Write* (1998), Washington, DC: The National Association for the Education of Young Children, www.naeyc.org.

24. National Research Council, *Preventing Reading Difficulties.*

25. See Chapter 11 of this volume for evidence from the Parent–Child Home Program, Even Start, and AVANCE.

26. This finding has been documented repeatedly in classic studies such as the Abecedarian Project and the Perry Preschool Project. Recent strong evidence comes from J. Pfannenstiel (1999) *School Entry Assessment Project: Report of Findings*, Missouri Department of Education.

27. *Early Head Start Research: Making a Difference in the Lives of Infants and Toddlers and Their Families: The Impacts of Early Head Start*, U.S. Department of Health and Human Services.

28. J. Lombardi (2003) *Time to Care: Redesigning Child Care to Promote Education, Support Families, and Build Communities*, Philadelphia, PA: Temple University Press.

29. Cost, Quality & Outcomes Study Team (1995) Cost, quality, and child outcomes in child care centers, Public Report, Denver, CO: Economics Department, University of Colorado; C. Howes, E. Galinsky, M. Shinn, A. Sibley, M. Abbott-Shim, and J. McCarthy (1998) *The Florida Child Care Quality Improvement Study: 1996 Report*, New York: Families and Work Institute, www.familiesandwork.org.

30. Programs accredited by NAEYC or NAFCC must exceed state licensing standards and meet professional standards for staff qualifications, staff/child ratio and group size, relationships and interactions, and learning activities, among others.

31. Evidence for the effectiveness of training and of the CDA and BA credentials comes from a number of studies, including *The Florida Child Care Quality Improvement Study* (New York: Families and Work Institute, 1996) and the *Cost, Quality & Outcomes Study* (Cost, Quality & Outcomes Study Team, Denver, CO: Economics Department, University of Colorado, 1995). Based on their review of evidence, the authors of *Eager to Learn* (National Research Council, 2001) recommend that teachers of two- to five-year-olds hold BA degrees in early childhood and receive ongoing professional training.

32. H. N. Chang, A. Muckelroy, and D. Pulido-Tobiassen (1996) *Looking In, Looking Out: Redefining Child Care and Education in a Diverse Society*, San Francisco: California Tomorrow, www.californiatomorrow.org.

33. J. Park-Jadotte, S. C. Golin, and B. Gault (2002) *Building a Stronger Child Care Workforce: A Review of Studies of the Effectiveness of Public Compensation Initiatives*, Washington, DC: Institute for Women's Policy Research, www.iwpr.org.

34. U.S. Department of Education (1998) *National Evaluation of The Even Start Family Literacy Program—1998: What Difference Has Even Start Made to Families?*

35. For example, evaluations of both Even Start and Early Head Start showed stronger results for children and families who had been involved for a longer period.

36. The Hart and Risley (1995) and Abecedarian studies (e.g., C. T. Ramey and F. A. Campbell (1984) Preventive education for high-risk children: Cognitive consequences of the Carolina Abecedarian Project (Special Issue), *American Journal of Mental Deficiency*, 88: 515–523) show the power of early support and the difficulty of catching up later.

37. D. T. Slaughter-Defoe (1993) Home Visiting with Families in Poverty: Introducing the Concept of Culture, *The Future of Children*, 3(3): 172–183.

38. For example, New Chance, an early intervention program for teen parents on welfare and their children, showed positive results for most participants, but negative results for children whose mothers were depressed. Apparently, those mothers were overwhelmed by the program's demands, to the detriment of their children. J. C. Quint, J. M. Bos, and D. F. Polit (1997) *New Chance Demonstration Project: Final Report on a Program for Young Mothers in Poverty and Their Children*, New York: Manpower Demonstration Research Corporation.

39. U.S. Department of Health and Human Services (January 2001) *Head Start FACES: Longitudinal Findings on Program Performance*, Third Progress Report; Cost, Quality & Outcomes Study Team, *Cost, quality, and child outcomes*.

40. R. Schumacher, K. Irish, and J. Lombardi (2003) *Meeting Great Expectations: Integrating Early Education Program Standards in Child Care*, New York: Foundation for Child Development Washington, DC: Center for Law and Social Policy.

41. This strategy was a particularly effective element in raising the quality of care in the U.S. Military Child Development Program (See N. D. Campbell, J. C. Appelbaum, K. Martinson, and E. Martin (2000) *Be All That We Can Be: Lessons from the Military for Improving Our Nation's Childcare System*, Washington, DC: National Women's Law Center) and has proven effective in selected sites where private funding was available (American Business Collaborative, 2003). Several states, including California, Oklahoma, Pennsylvania, Maine, and Arkansas are using various kinds of incentives and supports for accreditation.

42. L. Miller, A. Maelaville, and H. Blank (2002)*Bringing It Together: State-Driven Community Early Childhood Initiatives*, Washington, DC: Children's Defense Fund.

43. See www.childcareservices.org for information on the impact of the T.E.A.C.H. Early Childhood® Project.

44. J. Park-Jadotte, S. C. Golin, and B. Gault (2002) *Building a Stronger Child Care Workforce: A Review of Studies of the Effectiveness of Public Compensation Initiatives*, Washington, DC: Institute for Women's Policy Research, www.iwpr.org.

45. J. Knitzer and F. Adely (2001) *Learning from Starting Points: Findings from the Starting Points Assessment Project*.

46. A. Raden (1999) *Universal Prekindergarten in Georgia: A Case Study of Georgia's Lottery-Funded Pre-K Program*, New York: Foundation for Child Development, www.ffcd.org.

47. Cost, Quality & Outcomes Study Team, *Cost, quality, and child outcomes*.

48. Providers who can't afford the cost of stringent standards may be forced to close, "go underground", or raise parent fees. Parents who can't afford the higher fees required to maintain quality may be forced to use unlicensed care. Thus, in the absense

of mimimally adequate resources, higher quality for some can lead to lower quality for others—and often for those most in need of the higher quality.

49. Yale University Professor Edward Zigler, an architect of Head Start and a leading authority on early childhood policy, told a Senate Committee in 1990, "Below a certain threshold of quality the program is useless, a waste of money no matter how many children are served." The same can be said for other early education and family support programs. E. Zigler, S. L. Kagan, and N. W. Hall (1996) *Children, Families, and Government: Preparing for the Twenty-First Century*, Cambridge, United Kingdom: Press Syndicate of the University of Cambridge.

50. C. S. FitzPatrick and N. D. Campbell (2002)*The Little Engine That Hasn't: The Poor Performance of Employer Tax Credits for Child Care*, Washington, DC: National Women's Law Center.

51. D. L. Vandell and B. Wolfe (2000) *Child Care Quality: Does It Matter and Does It Need to be Improved?* Institute for Research on Poverty, University of Wisconsin-Madison for the Office of the Assistant Secretary for Planning and Evaluation, U.S. Department of Health and Human Services. Also see J. Lombardi (2003) *Time to Care: Redesigning Child Care to Promote Education, Support Families, and Build Communities*, Philadelphia, PA: Temple University Press.

52. For a collection of successful strategies, see *Sparking Connections: Community-Based Strategies for Helping Family, Friend and Neighbor Caregivers Meet the Needs of Employees, Their Children and Employers* by Deborah Stahl, Nina Sazer O'Donnell, Peg Sprague, and Marta López, Families and Work Institute, 2003.

53. Bureau of Economic Analysis, U.S. Department of Commerce.

54. U.S. Office of Management and Budget.

55. National Education Association (2003) Rankings and Estimates: Ranking of the States 2002 and Estimates of School Statistics 2003, www.nea.org.

56. Administration on Children, Youth, and Families (1998) Head Start Program Performance Measures: Second Progress Report, Washington, DC: U.S. Department of Health and Human Services; G. Resnick and N. Zill (1999) Is Head Start providing high quality education services?: Unpacking classroom processes, Paper presented at the biennial meeting of the Society for Research in Child Development, Albuquerque, New Mexico.

57. Head Start Bureau (2003) *Head Start FACES 2000: A Whole Child Perspective on Program Performance*, Presented at the biennial meeting of the Society for Research in Child Development, Tampa, FL.

58. *Early Head Start Research: Making a Difference in the Lives of Infants and Toddlers and Their Families: The Impacts of Early Head Start*, U.S. Department of Health and Human Services, http://www.mathematica-mpr.com/PDFs/ehsfinalvol1.pdf.

59. See the Georgia Office of School Readiness (www.osr.state.ga.us/), for most recent data.

60. Cost, Quality, and Outcomes Study Team, *Cost, quality, and child outcomes.*

61. A. Radin (1999) *Universal Prekindergarten in Georgia: A Case Study of Georgia's Lottery-Funded Pre-K Program*, New York: Foundation for Child Development, www.ffcd.org; W. T. Gormley, Jr. and D. Phillips (2003)*The Effects of Universal Pre-K in Oklahoma: Research Highlights and Policy Implications*, New York: Foundation for Child Development, www.ffcd.org; M. Cochran, *Collaborating for Kids: New York State Universal Prekindergarten 1999–2000*, Ithaca, NY: Cornell Early Childhood Program, http://www.human.cornell.edu/units/hd/cecp/index.html.

62. See E. Zigler and S. J. Syfco (1993) Strength in unity: Consolidating federal education programs for young children, In E. Zigler and S. J. Syfco (eds.), *Head Start and Beyond: A National Plan for Extended Childhood Intervention*, New Haven, CT: Yale University Press, for a review of evidence from the Abecedarian Project and other studies. See Study: preschool children better prepared for kindergarten than peers without preschool, *Boston Globe*, March 28, 2004, for results of a recent Connecticut study showing that preschool experience makes a substantial difference in whether or not entering kindergartners in poor districts have the literacy and math skills needed to be "ready for kindergarten." This study found that two years of preschool provided a distinct advantage over one, especially for predominately Spanish-speaking children.

63. These arguments were made cogently by Georgia governor Zell Miller when faced with a choice to serve all four-year-olds or all low-income three- and four-year-olds in pre-K programs funded by a state lottery. See A. Raden (1999) *Universal Prekindergarten in Georgia: A Case Study of Georgia's Lottery-Funded Pre-K Program*. Similar concerns shaped the campaign for UPK in Florida. In Massachusetts, however, advocates of Early Education for All are campaigning for a universal system for three- and four-year-olds.

64. L. Miller, A. Maelaville, and H. Blank (2002) *Bringing It Together: State-Driven Community Early Childhood Initiatives*, Washington, DC: Children's Defense Fund.

65. M. Finn-Stevenson (2000) *Schools of the 21st Century: Linking Child Care and Education (Renewing American Schools)*, Boulder, CO: Westview Press.

66. S. Helburn and B. Bergmann (2002) *America's Childcare Problem: The Way Out*, New York: Palgrave.

67. Children's Defense Fund (2003) *Head Start Reauthorization: Questions and Answers*, Washington, DC: Children's Defense Fund.

68. S. L. Kagan and E. Rigby(2003) *State Policies That Work: Improving the Readiness of Children for School*, Policy Matters Project Brief No. 2, New York: Center for the Study of Social Policy, www.cssp.org.

69. Pell grants could be extended to part-time students, or to part-time students in early childhood. Another possibility would be a national T.E.A.C.H. program, or a program of full loan forgiveness modeled on various state efforts. For example, Pennsylvania has instituted a modest loan forgiveness program for early childhood teachers ("Gordner promotes loan-forgiveness program for Pennsylvania's early childhood educators," *The News-Item*, December 11, 2003).

70. HeadsUp! Reading: The Early Childhood Distance Education Resources, http://www.huronline.org/.

71. Focus Act: $5 Billion for Child Care (Focus on Committed and Underpaid Staff for Children's Sake Act), http://www.ccw.org/policy_FOCUS.html.

72. J. P. Jadotte, S. C. Stacie Carolyn Golin, and B. Gault (2002) *Building a Stronger Child Care Workforce: A Review of Studies of the Effectiveness of Public Compensation Initiatives*, Washington, DC: Institute for Women's Policy Research.

73. This strategy is being used in Kansas City, as part of a comprehensive, community-wide campaign to improve school readiness. See the Metropolitan Council on Early Learning, http://www.marc.org/mccc/.

74. See M. Harrington (1999) *Care and Equality: Inventing a New Family Politics*, New York: Random House, for an economic analysis of care as a public good and a discussion of public investment in industries and infrastructure that benefit the community as a whole.

75. National League of Cities (2003) *Action Kit: Supporting Early Childhood Success*, Washington, DC: Institute for Youth, Education, and Families. National League of Cities, http://www.nlc.org/nlc_org/site/files/reports/EarlyChildcare.pdf.

76. L. Schweinhart, H. B. Barnes, and D. P. Weikert (1993) *Significant Benefits: The High/Scope Perry Preschool Study Through Age 27*, Ypsilanti, MI: High Scope Press.

77. A. Rolnick and R. Grunewald (2003) Early childhood development: Economic development with a high public return, Minneapolis, MN: Federal Reserve Bank of Minneapolis, *Fedgazette*, March 2003.

Index